Chinese Private Manufacturing Firms

Since the beginning of China's economic reform in 1978, private manufacturing firms have played an indispensable role in, and have made a remarkable contribution to, the country's economic development. This book, based on extensive original research, explores the current development challenges for Chinese private manufacturing firms as China's integration with the global economy deepens. At the heart of the book are rich, nuanced empirical case studies of private manufacturing firms in the footwear and electrical equipment industries based in the city of Wenzhou, which was where private enterprise in China was pioneered in the 1980s. Particular subjects considered include the competition situation, the interaction of foreign and indigenous firms in both domestic and international markets, and the facilitating role of industrial development areas.

Xiao Chen achieved her PhD degree in Development Studies from the University of Cambridge. She currently works as a researcher in the China Center for International Knowledge on Development. Her research interests include globalisation and firm competition, industrial policy and Chinese economy.

Routledge Studies on the Chinese Economy

Series Editor:

Peter Nolan

Director, Centre of Development Studies

Chong Hua

Professor in Chinese Development; and Director of the Chinese Executive Leadership Programme (CELP), University of Cambridge

Founding Series Editors:

Peter Nolan

University of Cambridge

Dong Fureng

Beijing University

The aim of this series is to publish original, high-quality, research-level work by both new and established scholars in the West and the East, on all aspects of the Chinese economy, including studies of business and economic history.

59 **US-China Relations in the Twenty-First Century**
A Question of Trust
Michael Tai

60 **Understanding China**
The Silk Road and the Communist Manifesto
Peter Nolan

61 **Being Middle Class in China**
Identity, Attitudes and Behaviour
Ying Miao

62 **Governing the Commons in China**
Yan Zhang

63 **The Economic Cycle and the Growth of the Chinese Economy**
Li Jianwei

64 **China's Rural Areas**
Building a Moderately Prosperous Society
China Development Research Foundation

65 **The Political Economy of Banking Governance in China**
Xuming Yang

66 **Reforming China's Healthcare System**
China Development Research Foundation

67 **Chinese Private Manufacturing Firms**
The Challenges of Global Competition
Xiao Chen

Chinese Private Manufacturing Firms

The Challenges of Global Competition

Xiao Chen

Routledge
Taylor & Francis Group
LONDON AND NEW YORK

First published 2018
by Routledge
2 Park Square, Milton Park, Abingdon, Oxon OX14 4RN

and by Routledge
605 Third Avenue, New York, NY 10017

First issued in paperback 2021

Routledge is an imprint of the Taylor & Francis Group, an informa business

British Library Cataloguing-in-Publication Data
A catalogue record for this book is available from the British Library

Library of Congress Cataloging-in-Publication Data
Names: Chen, Xiao, 1989– author.
Title: Chinese private manufacturing firms : the challenges of global competition / Xiao Chen.
Description: Abingdon, Oxon ; New York, NY : Routledge, 2018. | Series: Routledge studies on the Chinese economy ; 67
Identifiers: LCCN 2017056410 | ISBN 9780815353911 (hardback) | ISBN 9781351134712 (ebook) | ISBN 9781351134682 (mobipocket)
Subjects: LCSH: Manufacturing industries—China. | Private companies—China. | China—Commerce.
Classification: LCC HD9736.C62 C445 2018 | DDC 338.4/7670951—dc23
LC record available at https://lccn.loc.gov/2017056410

Typeset in Times New Roman
by Apex CoVantage, LLC

ISBN 13: 978-0-8153-5391-1 (hbk)
ISBN 13: 978-0-367-43855-5 (pbk)

Book DOI: 10.4324/9781351134712

For My Parents

Contents

Figures and maps

Figures

Maps

Tables

Acknowledgements

The book would not be possible without the support and help from many people and institutions. I am extremely grateful to my PhD supervisor, Professor Peter Nolan, for his intellectual guidance and comprehensive support during the research. His extensive knowledge, professional advice and hardworking spirit always enlighten my thoughts, sharpen my insights and encourage my work. I also thank Dr Ha-Joon Chang, Dr Shailaja Fennell, Dr Jin Zhang, Dr Maha Abdelrahman and Michael Kuczynski at the University of Cambridge for their advice on my research.

I highly appreciate my funding bodies for their generous financial support to my study at Cambridge and my fieldwork within and outside China. They include China Scholarship Council, Cambridge Overseas Trust, King's College, the Centre of Development Studies and the Department of Politics and International Studies at the University of Cambridge.

I wish to give my gratitude to all the people and organisations involved in my fieldwork. Special thanks to Qi Yinong, Wang Zhibin, Zheng Guohong and Zhu Xinmin, for their knowledge and kindness to support my fieldwork. Many thanks to Juyi Group, Zhejiang Aokang Shoes Limited Company, Menglani Shoes Limited Company and Chint Group for their willingness to be the study cases of my research.

I am greatly indebted to Peter Sowden, Becky McPhee and Leela Vathenen at Taylor & Francis and Lisa Salonen at Apex CoVantage for their help and patience for the delivery of the book.

I want to express my appreciation to my friends for their company and help during my study and research at the University of Cambridge. Particularly, I am grateful to my good friends in the Centre of Development Studies, Sidney Sussex College, King's College and Peking University Alumni Association.

I would like to give my deepest acknowledgements to my parents for their selfless love and unstinting support to me.

Abbreviations

AC	alternating current
ACB	air circuit breakers
APICCAPS	Portuguese Footwear Components and Leather Goods Manufacturers' Association
CBP	cold bounding production
CPPCC	Chinese People's Political Consultative Conference
DIP	direct injection production
DIY	do-it-yourself
EE	electrical equipment
EPC	engineering, procurement and construction
FDI	foreign direct investment
FIEs	foreign invested enterprises
GDP	gross domestic product
GNI	gross national income
GVCs	global value chains
GW	gigawatt
HV	high voltage
IDs	industrial districts
IPRs	intellectual property rights
IEA	International Energy Agency
IEC	International Electrotechnical Commission
ILO	International Labour Organization
Intl$	Geary–Khamis dollars
ISO	International Organization for Standardization
IT	information technology
ITC	International Trade Centre
JPY	Japanese yen
LV	low voltage
LVEE	low-voltage electrical equipment
M&A	mergers and acquisitions
MCB	miniature circuit breakers
MCCB	moulded case circuit breakers
MV	medium voltage

MW	megawatt
OBM	original brand manufacturing
ODM	original design manufacturing
ODI	outward direct investment
OEM	original equipment manufacturing
PECVD	plasma enhanced chemical vapour deposition
PU	polyurethane
R&D	research and design
RMB	renminbi
SEARI	Shanghai Electrical Apparatus Research Institute
SMEs	small and medium-sized enterprises
SOEs	state-owned enterprises
TVEs	township and village enterprises
UNCTAD	United Nations Conference on Trade and Development
UNESCO	United Nations Educational Scientific and Cultural Organization
UNIDO	United Nations Industrial Development Organization
WTO	World Trade Organization

1 Introduction

In 1978, China adopted the twin policy of economic reform and opening-up and started to transform from a closed planned system towards a more open and market-led system. In 1992, China set up the goal of establishing a socialist market economy for the transformation. At the end of 2001, China joined the World Trade Organization (WTO) and aimed for further progress of its reform through deep integration with the global economy. The double forces of marketization and globalisation have tremendously driven China's development in a wide range of fields. Among all the sectors, the manufacturing industry has been the one that took the lead in system reform, greatly boosted national growth and forged the strongest global competitiveness (Jin, 2009). Thanks to the prosperous manufacturing industry, China became the world's largest merchandise exporter in 2009, with 9.5% of global export value and the global biggest manufacturer in 2010 with 18.6% of the world's manufacturing value added (The World Bank, 2017).

During the past four decades, the competitive landscape in the Chinese manufacturing industry has changed remarkably. State-owned enterprises (SOEs) retreated nationwide to a few strategic fields, while private firms and foreign invested enterprises (FIEs) developed rapidly in the remaining and new industries. The definition of private firms in China is vague. They are usually called people-run firms (民营企业), private-run firms (私营企业), private-owned firms (私有企业) or non-public owned firms (非公有制企业). They can be understood as the firms within a wide spectrum between SOEs and individual operations. The scale of private firms differs based on different definitions. The broad definition includes all the firms that are not owned or operated by the state. The narrow view accounts for only private firms that are totally owned and operated privately. This study mainly uses the narrow definition to discuss private firms.

Nowadays, private manufacturing firms have become indispensable indigenous players in both domestic and international territories. From 1978 to 2011, the proportion of the industrial output value of SOEs decreased from 77.6% to 26.2%, while the percentages of private firms and FIEs increased to 34.8% and 22.1% respectively (Industry Statistics Division of National Bureau of Statistics, 2012). From 1978 to 2015, the percentage of industrial employment of SOEs declined from 76.2% to 18.2%, while the ratios of private firms and FIEs grew to 35.4% to 24.1% individually (Industry and Transportation Division of National Bureau of

Statistics, 2000; Department of Industry Statistics National Bureau of Statistics of China, 2016). In 2013, SOEs contributed to 11% of Chinese export value, while private firms and FIEs accounted for 39% and 47% respectively (Lardy, 2014: 87). In 2015, as Table 1.1 shows, private firms accounted for 34.8% of the total revenues of 41 main industries in China, while SOEs and FIEs had 21.8% and 18.8% correspondingly (National Bureau of Statistics of China, 2016). In 2016, Huawei, a Chinese private manufacturing company specialising in telecommunication equipment and service, ranked 129th among the global top Fortune 500 firms, making the best record for mainland Chinese private firms in the list (Fortune, 2017).

Table 1.1 Revenue proportions of private firms, SOEs and FIEs in China's main industrial sectors, (%), year 2015

Industrial Sectors	*Private Firms*	*SOEs*	*FIEs*
National total	34.8	21.8	18.8
Mining of other ores	81.4	0.0	0.0
Processing of timber, manufacture of wood, bamboo, rattan, palm and straw products	69.2	1.6	6.4
Mining and processing of non-metal ores	59.3	10.3	1.7
Manufacturing of metal products	55.4	6.0	14.4
Manufacturing of furniture	53.5	1.2	19.4
Manufacturing of textile	53.4	2.2	12.3
Manufacturing of non-metallic mineral products	53.3	7.7	7.5
Mining and processing of ferrous mental ores	52.0	14.9	8.1
Manufacturing of rubber and plastics products	50.6	3.0	17.5
Printing and reproduction of recording media	50.4	7.0	13.6
Processing of food from agricultural products	49.3	5.3	13.8
Manufacturing of textile, wearing apparel and accessories	47.8	0.9	23.9
Utilization of waste resources	47.7	4.5	9.2
Manufacturing of special purpose machinery	46.8	12.3	14.3
Manufacture of articles for culture, education, arts and crafts, sport and entertainment activities	46.7	3.5	26.3
Other manufacture	44.9	15.5	17.9
Manufacturing of general purpose machinery	44.8	9.8	18.9
Manufacturing of leather, fur, and related products and footwear	44.7	0.7	28.5
Manufacturing of chemical fibres	43.7	8.5	24.1
Manufacture of paper and paper products	39.9	5.2	21.3
Manufacturing of measuring instruments and machinery	39.7	9.5	22.5
Manufacture of raw chemical materials and chemical products	38.5	15.0	17.8
Smelting and pressing of ferrous metals	36.8	28.2	8.5
Manufacturing of electrical machinery and apparatus	36.1	7.9	20.6
Manufacturing of foods	35.3	5.2	18.9
Mining and processing of non-ferrous metal ores	32.7	33.4	1.2

Industrial Sectors	*Private Firms*	*SOEs*	*FIEs*
Smelting and pressing of non-ferrous metals	32.0	32.4	9.3
Manufacturing of liquor, beverages and refined tea	32.0	14.5	17.3
Manufacturing of railway, ship, aerospace and other transport equipment	29.9	40.0	14.6
Manufacturing of medicines	29.5	9.1	12.7
Mining and washing of coal	20.1	58.4	4.2
Manufacturing of automobiles	17.9	41.3	37.3
Repair service of metal products, machinery and equipment	17.2	42.6	32.5
Processing of petroleum, coking and processing of nuclear fuel	15.8	59.4	8.2
Manufacturing of computers, communication and other electronic equipment	13.9	8.8	57.0
Production and supply of gas	8.7	46.0	29.1
Production and supply of water	6.8	68.5	10.2
Support activities for mining	3.0	82.9	5.5
Production and supply of electric power and heat power	1.5	92.9	3.5
Extraction of petroleum and natural gas	0.4	83.7	4.0
Manufacturing of tobacco	0.1	99.3	0.0

Data source: National Bureau of Statistics of China, 2016.

Note: Private Firms refers to profit-making economic units invested and established by natural persons or controlled by natural persons using employed labour. Included in this category are private limited liability corporations, private share-holding limited corporations, private partnership enterprises and private-funded enterprises. SOEs refers to non-corporation economic units where the entire assets are owned by the state. Not included in this category are solely state-funded corporations in the limited liability corporations. FIEs refers to enterprises established in mainland China with investment from foreign, Hong Kong, Macao and Taiwan investors.

Given its global reputation and dramatic changes, China's manufacturing industry is facing severe challenges in global competition. According to *Global Value Chains and China's Trade Value Added Accounting Report* published by the Ministry of Commerce of the People's Republic of China in 2014, although China had advantages over trading partners in export volume, it created comparatively low value added because most Chinese export merchandise was labour intensive and a large part of the export was processing trade. In 2012, for instance, China's trade surplus to the United States of America was USD 218.9 billion, but the figure was reduced by 53.6% to USD 101.7 billion considering value added (The Research Group of China's Global Value Chains, 2014: 27). According to *China's Top 500 Manufacturing Firms Report* released by China Enterprise Federation in 2016, the net profit of the Chinese Top 500 Manufacturing Firms was reduced by renminbi (RMB) 8.9 billion[1] (USD 1.3 billion) and their profit per capita was reduced by 10.7% compared with the previous year (Sina News, 2016). *Made in China 2025* (The State Council, 2015), China's national guideline for building a strong manufacturing country, pointed out that the manufacturing sector is the key to the new impetus of China's economy and the new advantage of China's global competitiveness. However, the Chinese manufacturing industry is currently large but not strong. There are clear gaps between China and advanced countries in the manufacturing sector. It is an urgent and tough mission for China to accomplish transformation and upgrade and realise a leapfrog development.

China 2030: Building a Modern, Harmonious, and Creative Society (2013), a collaborative report by the World Bank and the Development Research Centre of the State Council, the People's Republic of China, put forward that China's rapid growth benefited from the restructuring of SOEs and the expansion of private firms. A vibrant corporate sector will be critical for China to sustain relatively fast growth in the future. The report recommended that more domestic and international competition will be key to improving the efficiency and the innovation capability of Chinese enterprises. Increasing competition can provide opportunities and stimulate initiatives for the firms in China to enhance innovation and efficiency, but it will also bring indigenous firms more challenges. Chinese private firms, in particular, will encounter huge pressure. Due to their importance in economic growth, employment, export, global competition and system reform, it is of significance to examine the current challenges of private firms and explore feasible ways to their further development.

This book focuses on Chinese private manufacturing firms and analyses their development challenges. The book consists of six chapters. Chapter 1 is the introduction. Chapter 2 puts forward the research question: What are the current development challenges for Chinese private manufacturing firms in global competition? Fitting the study into a broader theoretical discussion, the chapter reviews related literature and points out the contribution of the research to existing knowledge. It also describes the methodology that the study used to organise, collect and analyse information and data during the research.

Chapter 3 provides a contour of Wenzhou's economic development with a close association of China's economic history. Wenzhou is an outstanding pioneer in developing private economy. It can reflect China's development in globalisation to a large extent. The chapter traces Wenzhou's long-standing tradition in developing private economy, reveals its pioneer role in advancing China's economic reform after 1978 and discusses its current predicaments after China's full integration with the global economy.

Chapter 4 observes the first case study on the footwear industry. It discusses global competition and China's competitiveness in the industry, traces the history of Wenzhou's footwear industry and analyses its current situation. It then displays three case studies of leading firms and discusses in detail about their practices and development challenges.

Chapter 5 shows the second case study on the electrical equipment (EE) industry. Observing the industry from a global perspective, it discusses the history and current situation of Chinese and Wenzhou's EE industry. It concentrates on one leading firm to analyse its diverse approaches towards industrial upgrade and reveal its development challenges.

Chapter 6 is the conclusion. Based on the comparison and contrast of the footwear industry and the EE industry, the chapter summarises the competition situation of Chinese private manufacturing firms in the global era. Then, it concludes with a series of development challenges that these firms are facing currently. Finally, it tries to put forward theoretical implications for global competition and policy implications for China's industrial upgrade.

Note

1 The book converted the figures of RMB into USD based on their yearly average currency exchange rates in corresponding years. See Table 1 in Appendix for more details. Data source: The World Bank (2017).

2 Study design

This chapter describes the study design. It will firstly construct the research question and discuss its relevance to the broader study of development studies. Secondly, it will review related literature and point out the contribution of the study to existing knowledge. Thirdly, it will deliberate the methodology used to organise, collect and analyse information and data during the research.

Research question

Given China's rising global competitiveness in the manufacturing industries in the twenty-first century, Chinese private manufacturing firms have encountered various problems and been stuck in development predicaments. Nowadays, exploring the development challenges and seeking feasible solutions for China's manufacturing sector have been prominent agendas in many discussions. Academics and policymakers came to a consensus that China needs further reforms to address development challenges, but they still have disputes on the specific roles of the government and the market in the reforms. Although market force has greatly expanded in China in the past four decades, the answer is far from clear to the question of where the boundary of the government and the market should be. Before jumping into the debate over the roles of the government and the market, it is a more fundamental task to consider what development challenges China's manufacturing sector is facing now. Without a comprehensive understanding on the challenges, any hasty move for reform will hardly solve complex problems and achieve desirable results.

The study aims to analyse the question: What are the current development challenges for Chinese private manufacturing firms in global competition? In this research, Chinese private manufacturing firms are the core actors and the units of analysis. They are owned and operated by Chinese natural persons using employed labour. They mainly undertake manufacturing, which is a full-cycle business process including product design, production, distribution and after-sales service. The current time refers to the period from the early twenty-first century to the present. The development challenge is an inclusive concept, consisting of economic, political, social, cultural and environmental aspects. All these aspects will be discussed from a view of firm development and competition. The globalisation refers to the action and process of global integration that contains bilateral procedures of China's going out and the world's entry into China.

The research question appears to be a practical issue on the development of Chinese private manufacturing firms, but it is relevant to a wide range of theoretical and policy research. Broadly speaking, the research question is about firm competition in the global economy. More specifically, it contains a few interconnected sub-questions: What is the current situation of global competition? What pressure are firms facing from global competition? How do firms respond to the pressure? What are the difficulties preventing firms from success under the pressure? Given the context of China's development, the research involves the discussions of competition among Chinese private firms, SOEs and FIEs in the global field as well as domestic territory, the challenges for private firms to survive and develop under the global pressure, the opportunities for them to catch up with opponents from developed countries and possible promoters and barriers from national and international institutions for firm competitiveness. The exploration of the research question can not only benefit the understanding of firm competition in the global economy, but also provide implications for industrial policy of developing countries in the global era.

Literature review

There is rich literature related to firm competition in the global economy. It provides useful insights and lays a solid foundation to discuss the research question. The study will critically review the literature from the following aspects: firm competition in global value chains (GVCs), industrial districts (IDs) in the global economy, large business in global competition and global battles within China. It then will point out the contribution of this study to existing knowledge.

Firm competition in global value chains

Since the 1970s, the global economy has become spectacularly integrated by international trade, but the production processes of manufactured goods have been increasingly fragmented and the production activities widely dispersed to an expanding global network (Feenstra, 1998). The analytical framework of GVCs thereby emerged to track the global spread of industries and study the implications for firms and countries (Gereffi and Korzeniewicz, 1994). "The value chain describes the full range of activities which are required to bring a product or service from conception, through the different phases of production (involving a combination of physical transformation and the input of various producer services), delivery to final consumers, and final disposal after use" (Kaplinsky and Morris, 2002: 4).

The GVCs' approach observes the global economy from two contrasting vantage points: top-down and bottom-up. From the view of top-down, governance is the central concept, which focuses on lead firms (Humphrey and Schmitz, 2002). Governance refers to the coordination of economic activities through non-market relationships. Lead firms are the actors who have power over other firms (as their followers) in the chain. Lead firms seek for chain governance due to product definition and risk of supplier failure. They make and shape strategic decisions which affect the configuration and direction of the chain and influence and control other firms within the chain. Profit distribution within GVCs is uneven. The greatest profitability exists in relatively concentrated segments characterised by high barriers to the entry of new firms. Lead firms are distinguished from their followers because they control access to major resources – like new technologies, product design, brand names and consumer demand – that generate the most profitable returns in the industry.

From the perspective of bottom-up, upgrading is the key to understanding GVCs (Schmitz, 2004). Upgrading refers to the process whereby firms use strategies to maintain and improve their positions by moving from low-value activities to more profitable, technologically sophisticated and capital- and skill-intensive economic niches. There are four types of upgrading: process upgrading (transforming inputs into outputs more efficiently), product upgrading (moving into more sophisticated product lines), functional upgrading (acquiring new and superior functions in the chain), and chain upgrading (moving into a new value chain).

The GVCs' framework emphasises the importance of inter-firm relations for upgrading. If follower firms want to gain upgrading opportunities, they must understand who the lead firms are and how they govern the chain. Based on different production systems in various industries, GVCs can be classified into producer-driven and buyer-driven chains (Gereffi, 1994, 1999a). Producer-driven chains exist in capital- and technology-intensive industries, where large transnational manufacturers as lead firms play the central roles in coordinating production networks, including their backward and forward linkages. Buyer-driven chains are common in labour-intensive and consumer goods industries, where large retailers, marketers and branded manufacturers as leader firms set up decentralised production networks in the developing world to source finished goods.

In terms of the connection between lead firms and followers, GVCs can be divided into five types (Gereffi et al., 2005). One extreme comprises market chains where the buyers and the suppliers do not have close relationships and their interaction mechanism is price. Another extreme comprises hierarchical chains where the lead firms take direct ownership of production processes. Between these two extremes are three network forms of chains: modular, relational and captive. Network-style governance represents a situation where the lead firms exercise power through coordination of production to varying degrees without direct ownership of their suppliers. Captive chains are most common in developing countries, where the suppliers are dependent on a few powerful buyers and the lead firms have a high degree of monitoring and control.

Although GVCs have created a new platform for the firms from developing countries to participate in the world economy, many producers are locked into a race to the bottom and finally achieve very limited gains due to dynamic rents, governorship and systemic efficiency (Kaplinsky, 2000). The upgrading situations and results differ across regions and chains. Gereffi (1999b) revealed that the firms from East Asian economies like Taiwan, South Korea, Hong Kong and Singapore transited from assembly to original equipment manufacturing (OEM), to original design manufacturing (ODM) and to original brand manufacturing (OBM) in the buyer-driven chain of the global apparel industry. He believed that upgrading in East Asia was produced by the information flows and learning potential associated with the buyer-seller links and by a distinctive pattern of organisational succession among the lead firms. Lead firms with primary sources of material inputs, technology transfer and knowledge in organisational networks can promote the process, product, and functional upgrading of their suppliers.

However, other scholars are less optimistic. Schmitz (2006a, 2006b) thought that latecomers face technological and market gaps in global competition. Their upgrading effect is not automatic, because upgrading requires continuous investment from local firms, and global buyers do not always provide support. Giuliani, Pietrobelli and Rabellotti (Pietrobelli and Rabellotti, 2005; Giuliani et al., 2005), based on their research in Latin America, argued that sectoral specificities influence the mode and the extent of upgrading in GVCs. For instance, in traditional industries, technology has tacit and idiosyncratic elements, and upgrading strongly depends on the intensity of technological externalities and cooperation among local actors. Global buyers may be more involved in their providers' upgrading if the technology required is mainly tacit and requires intensive interaction. On the contrary, in natural resource-based industries, technology is more codified and access to external sources of knowledge is more critical for upgrading. The global buyers are less keen to get directly involved in the upgrading process and often impose strict quality standards. Zhuo and Zhang (2008) found that the relationships between Chinese firms and their lead firms are captive in China's textile industry. Lead firms helped local firms in process and product upgrading, but they did not support local firms for functional and chain upgrade, which contributed to the lock-in of Chinese firms at the bottom of the GVC. Liu and Zhang (2007) further suggested that cultivating national value chains might be a possible solution for developing countries to get rid of the captive relationships controlled by global buyers. Qin (2011) argued that modularity in production systems of GVCs resulted in information encapsulation and patent packages, which established barriers for Chinese firms to achieve knowledge learning, technological innovation and industrial upgrade.

The GVCs' framework focuses on the dynamics of inter-firm relationship in the entire process of value creation and provides a holistic view of how competitive advantages are constructed for firms in global competition. It points out that GVCs give the firms from developing countries opportunities to participate in and gain from the global economy, although they have limited initial resources of capital and technology. It also reveals the uneven distribution of power and gains between lead firms usually from developed nations and followers often in developing countries. It suggests possible ways for firms to upgrade in the chain by learning and getting information from lead firms and making progress through different types of upgrading.

However, much research based on the GVCs' approach assumes that firms from the Third World must link up with their lead firms to achieve development. The possibility for local firms to upgrade is largely decided by lead firms from outside. It is true that in many export-oriented economies, global buyers are influential in the local economy, but the efforts of local firms and the importance of the domestic market should not be overlooked. Firstly, local firms matter. The impacts of lead firms will not automatically bring in upgrading, so it is important to analyse how local firms respond to the power from lead firms and transfer the external pressure to internal force for development. In addition, some indigenous firms in developing countries have power and play leading roles to some extent within their local territories and industries. It is relevant to further discuss the role of indigenous firms and their interaction with external lead firms in the GVC. Secondly, the domestic market and demand are also relevant. In recent decades, the market demand in the developing world has increased rapidly. Countries like China have forged a large domestic market that can feed many firms. The influence of global buyers in these countries thereby have been reduced relatively. Although few researchers noticed the importance of national value chains, more studies should be conducted to observe how the domestic market shapes the upgrading opportunities and trajectories of firms in developing countries

Industrial districts in the global economy

The research on IDs attaches great importance to locality. The notion of IDs can be tracked back to Alfred Marshall (1920). He set out that a population of small-sized firms concentrated in particular localities and specialising in different stages of production can achieve economies of scale. After Marshall's death, IDs were pushed to the periphery of academic discourse because mainstream research focused on the roles of large firms for economic development in the golden age of mass production from the late 1940s to the 1960s. The research on IDs revived in the late 1970s, when Giacomo Becattini resurrected the concept to explain the unusual industrial take-off of some Italian regions. In central and northeastern Italy, clustered small firms relying on flexible production created remarkable economic performance. Since then, a multidisciplinary group of scholars have conducted research on IDs firstly in Italy and then all over the world (Piore and Sable, 1984; Best, 1990; Pyke and Sengenberger, 1992; Krugman, 1991; Markusen, 1996; Porter, 1990, 1998; Nadvi and Schmitz, 1994; Cawthorne, 1995; Knorringa, 1999; Schmitz, 1999; Rabellotti, 1999).

Becattini (1992: 38) defined an ID as "a socio-territorial entity which is characterised by the active presence of both a community of people and a population of firms in one natural and historically bounded area". He pointed out that communities and firms tend to merge in IDs and a comprehensive understanding of IDs should consider not only economic activities, but also local networks, conditions and interactions. Another influential scholar, Michael Porter (1998), used the term "clusters" to explain the importance of IDs for national competitive advantages. He defined clusters as geographic agglomerations of companies, suppliers, service providers and associated institutions in particular fields that compete as well as cooperate. He argued that clusters can increase the productivity and innovation of firms and stimulate new business formation. He also emphasised the crucial roles of local rivalry and government policies for regional competitiveness. Given disputes on the definition of IDs, most scholars agreed on two fundamental factors: Many small firms frequently cluster in small zones where they collaborate on finance, technology, information and specialisation in making products at a low degree of vertical integration; social relationships and local institutions are deeply embedded in the economic tissues and play indispensable roles.

As globalisation evolved more widely and deeply after the 1990s, the boundaries between local and global areas of production blurred and the pressure of the global economy challenged the resources of local systems. A large volume of literature researched the interaction of IDs and the global economy and showed that regions across the world responded differently (Becattini et al., 2009). Among all the studies of IDs, Brazil and Italy are the two most frequently discussed cases. Brazil is one of the largest developing countries in the world and Italy is the developed nation taking the lead in developing IDs. Their experience thus sheds the most light on the understanding of Chinese manufacturing firms in IDs to deal with global competition.

In terms of Brazilian IDs, Schmitz (1999) noticed that Brazilian firms in the Sinos Valley changed from spontaneous economies of clustering to bilateral vertical cooperation in order to achieve better product quality, response and flexibility. However, they failed to raise exports and profits in the tough phase of globalisation since the late 1980s. Upgrading in sale and design was not successful because some local leading enterprises put their alliances with major global buyers above the cooperation with local manufacturers, and the local government failed to mediate at important moments. Bazan and Navas-Alemán (2004) examined the governance and upgrading of the American, European, national and Latin American chains in Brazil's footwear industry. They revealed that a series of initiatives for collective upgrading emerged within local IDs, which suggested that loosening vertical ties within the GVC offered opportunity to reposition IDs in the world's markets. Giuliani and Rabellotti (2005: 291) commented that "external linkages may indeed play a crucial role in increasing clusters' and firms' competitiveness, but they are not a panacea. There is a great deal of heterogeneity in terms of patterns of governance of value chains, of sectoral specificity of the upgrading and learning processes, of firms' absorptive capacity and the role played by policy." Navas-Alemán (2011), based on comparative research in Brazilian furniture and footwear IDs, argued that domestic and regional value chains offered greater upgrading opportunities and provided space for design, sale, marketing and branding. Many firms simultaneously served multiple value chains, and these firms had better upgrade prospects than those primarily for export in GVCs.

As to Italian IDs, Dei Ottati (1996a), based on Prato's textile industry, found that firms were vertically or horizontally integrated into formal or informal groups in globalisation. It was because they needed organisational structures to deal with the spread of risky transactions in local systems and the increased uncertainty of the final markets. In another study (Dei Ottati, 1996b), focusing on Tuscany, he discovered that IDs' restructuring for globalisation tended to be a more conscious and planned form of governance. A closer coordination was needed to meet new competitive requirements and support new risky investments. Cainelli et al. (2012) argued that the intertwining of inter-firm production and credit relationships in IDs became extremely important after the international crisis hit Italy, when local firms were exposed to demand declines and credit restrictions from formal banking institutions. They concluded that although IDs enabled firms to share the risk of a moderate shock and to be more resilient in normal conditions, they did not help and were actually disadvantageous in the face of the recent heavy financial crisis.

Corò and Grandinetti (1999, 2001) revealed that many Italian IDs transformed their relatively closed systems of exchange and integrated into a network economy, where they opened up local systems of value and moved beyond pre-existent links. Amighini and Rabellotti (2006) focused on Italian footwear IDs and showed that some IDs specialising in low-end market sectors decentralised low-value-added activities to foreign sub-contractors and achieved functional upgrading. However, other IDs specialising in the high-end market accepted a functional downgrading by focusing on production and losing some of their key competencies in favour of their lead firms.

More importantly, as Whitford (2001) pointed out, although analyses in the past focused mainly on the system of IDs, propositions based on a firm-centred view gained increasing credibility and lead firms attracted more and more attention in recent years. Crestanello (1996) found that between the 1980s and 1990s, the presence of large leader firms and production concentration were significant in some IDs of Veneto. Although most of the leading firms were owned by local entrepreneurs, some were occupied by external industrial groups via mergers and acquisitions (M&A), which served to maintain a continuity of important direction, image projecting, advertising and research and design (R&D) within IDs. Lazerson and Lorenzoni (1999) argued that it was a mistake to assume that firms in districts were organisationally symmetrical. Larger firms frequently organised production among groups of smaller firms, introduced technological innovations and expanded existing markets. Carbonara's (2002) empirical research on four Italian IDs suggested that the strategies of growth adopted by the leader firms dominated the formation of structured inter-firm networks. Rinaldi (2007) found that Emilian IDs appeared as business groups led by the most dynamic local lead firms tended to play paramount roles in orchestrating activities. Rabellotti et al.'s (2009) studies based on wider regions and diverse industries also supported the emergence and functions of business groups. Chiarvesio et al. (2013) found that the autonomy and independence of leading firms opened up new issues of governance in IDs and transformed the internal coherence of IDs as known in the past. Chiarvesio and Micelli (Ramazzotti, 2010) argued that leader firms act as interfaces between ID and the global economy. They can take advantage of local competences and knowledge within the global productive and commercial network.

Ingstrup (2014) summarised that due to their experience, number of relationships, size, resources and ability to collect and transfer information, lead firms can play a series of roles to facilitate economic activities in IDs, which give them a central position and dominating role.

When it comes to the studies on Chinese IDs, Zeng (2010) pointed out that numerous IDs and a few special economic zones are the two most important engines for driving China's growth since the 1970s. The scale and volume of Chinese IDs are large, especially in the coastal provinces, and they play indispensable roles in labour-intensive manufacturing sectors. Wang and Mei (2009) revealed that China's development of massive labour-intensive IDs was driven by global-local tension and supported by strong local forces. They pointed out that Chinese IDs are more open to globalised production systems than those in Italy due to China's export-oriented strategies, but global power of multinational companies might impede the local production system from innovation and functional upgrading. Chinese IDs need to transform from production ability to innovation capacity for the local small firms to compete and win in global markets. Zhao and Peng (2011) argued that Chinese IDs are vulnerable to global risks, weak in innovation, stuck in price battles and lacking in good local environments for upgrading. Chinese IDs should find their best location in GVCs, enhance internal innovation systems, improve inter-firm coordination and get more government support. Lu (2014) revealed that Chinese IDs face external barriers from lead firms in GVCs (unbalanced bargain power, increasing procurement requirements, peer competition and technological monopoly) and internal difficulties (lack of entrepreneurship, low-end locked-in and weak technological capability). He claimed that Chinese IDs should more actively participate in the governance of GVCs and take opportunities to upgrade, and government agencies should adopt more effective public policies to facilitate the development of IDs.

The research on IDs reveals the fundamental roles of local actors in the global economy. It values the importance of local relations, institutions and cultures and reflects the local complexity and diversity in economic development. Much research associated IDs with GVCs and displayed more details about the interaction between local and international actors. It pointed out the contradictory interests of local firms and global firms and showed the efforts and experience of local firms for upgrading and development. Since a large proportion of Chinese private manufacturing firms were nurtured from IDs and develop their business based on IDs, the studies on IDs are highly relevant to examine the social, local and historical foundations for the development of Chinese private firms. These studies provide not only theoretical statements but also empirical evidence to further discuss the situation of Chinese firms in global competition.

However, the existing literature is not sufficient to explain the research question. Firstly, most studies still analysed IDs as a system of SMEs, so they failed to observe the challenges and responses of firms as individuals. The roles of firms are differentiated and inter-firm relationship has greatly changed in IDs recently due to globalisation. The local leading firms increasingly become key actors to coordinate other firms in IDs to respond to global pressure. Thus, more research on leading firms is necessary and beneficial for understanding the current situation of IDs in globalisation. Secondly, some researchers based on Italian IDs noticed the importance of leader firms recently, but literature focusing on leading firms from developing countries is still rare. The leading firms from developed and developing world have different capabilities of production, technological, branding and coordination and contrary positions in global competition. It is important to conduct more research on leading firms from developing countries like China to enrich the existing knowledge. Finally, at present, most Chinese research mainly discussed the development predicaments of IDs and put forward some countermeasures that should be done. It pinned the hope either on government agencies or the collective actions of small and medium-sized enterprises (SMEs) as a whole for development. Yet, very few studies have examined in detail the comprehensive challenges and possible solutions for firms (especially leading firms) as different individual cases. As firms are the core units of economic activities, careful research on the development reality of firms is relevant to find realistic and feasible ways to increase China's global competitiveness.

Large business in global competition

The influence and roles of large business have been widely recognised in both development theories and realities all over the world. From the perspective of the development of capitalist firms, Marx (1976: 777) argued that there is a law of the centralisation of capital: "The battle of competition is fought by the cheapening of commodities. The cheapness of commodities depends, all other circumstances remaining the same, on the productivity of labour, and this depends in turn on the scale of production. Therefore, the larger capitals beat the smaller." Penrose (2009) stated that large multi-plant firms have managerial economies. Larger firms can take advantage of an increased division of managerial labour, closely allied mechanisation of certain administrative processes, fully using existing managerial resources, buying and selling on a large scale, reserving more economically, requiring capital on cheaper terms and supporting large-scale research. She further pointed out that large firms can adapt their management structures to growth and there are no theoretical limits to the size of firms. Chandler and his colleagues (Chandler, 1990; Chandler et al., 1997) studied the national experiences of big business in America, Europe and East Asia. They demonstrated the central role of large and oligopolistic firms in technical progress, which is central to the growth of modern capitalism. Large firms can contribute to improved productivity in a wide range of other industries and spill over a rich spring of managerial and organisational information into wider spheres. They pointed out that the core of the dynamic is organisational capabilities, which refers to collective physical facilities and human skills within enterprises. Only if these facilities and skills were carefully coordinated and integrated could the enterprises achieve the economies of scale and scope to compete in national and international markets.

As to the roles of large firms in national development, Gerschenkron (1962), based on the development of European countries, such as Germany, France, Italy and Russia, put forward the theory of late development. He argued that the later a country develops, the more it will have strong institutional involvement in economic development and larger firms driving industrialisation. This is because late developers can follow earlier industrialisers as examples and take shortcuts by using the organising power of institutions. Due to their lack of capital, late developers also must deliberately concentrate and invest limited capital into vital areas. Gerschenkron's view was further proved by the development experience of Northeast Asian economies. Johnson (1982), Amsden (1989) and Wade (1990) agreed that developmental states created the economic success of Northeast Asia after the Second World War. Developmental states boosted economic development by using selective industrial policies of promoting specific industries, nurturing large national champion firms and using a mix of import substitution and export promotion.

Taking GVCs into consideration, Nolan et al. (2007) showed that large capable firms are mainly distributed in developed regions. Dicken (2015) revealed that the world economy is a qualitatively different place from that of 70 years ago. The geographies of production, trade and FDI are highly uneven, strongly concentrated and shaped by large transnational companies. Whittaker et al. (2010) put forward that the path of economic development for developers has changed to be compressed development since the 1980s. Compressed development is different from late development due to the extent and consequences of compression, the primary mode of engagement with the world economy and the interaction of these. They thought that GVCs foreclose the late development path and create powerful challenges to most recent developers.

Peter Nolan (2001) uncovered profound changes at the heart of the global business structure since the 1990s. He named the phenomenon the "global business revolution", which can be explained from three major aspects (Nolan et al., 2007: 3–4): "First, the explosion of M&A activities at the end of the twentieth century has produced unprecedented levels of concentration in almost all of the high value-added, high technology parts of the world economy. Global competition has forced firms in related industries to consolidate in order to achieve greater economies of scale and scope in critical business activities that constitute core competitive advantages of firms. These activities include branding, technology acquisition, human resources, financing, R&D, information technology (IT) and logistics. Second, competitive pressures and increasing complexity involved in organizing economic production have strengthened the planning and coordination function of leading firms, that is, 'systems integrators' or core firms, in global value chains. . . . [T]he planning and coordination function of systems integrators has extended beyond the legal boundaries of the firm to reach segments deep in the value chain. Third, these systems integrators persistently pass on the pressure for consolidation to their first-tier suppliers, through increased requirements in product quality, costs and technological progress. As first-tier suppliers consolidate, they pass along the same pressure to their suppliers through the same mechanisms. The pressure for consolidation therefore 'cascades' down the supply chain so that economies of scale and scope are maximized in key business activities of the value chain."

Hobday et al. (2005) believed that system integration is the core capability of the world's lead firms to achieve competitive advantage. They traced the military- and engineering-based origins of systems integration in various sectors back to the 1940s. They (2005: 1136) argued that system integration capabilities enable "high-technology firms to shape their boundaries and position in an industry value stream, enabling them to decide who to compete with, who to collaborate with, what to make in-house and what to outsource". It also enabled lead firms to move selectively up- and downstream through vertical integration and disintegration. More specifically, systems integrators of low-volume, high-cost capital goods exploit downstream relationships with system users by integrating service-intensive offerings such as maintenance, finance, consultancy and operations. By contrast, systems integrators of high-volume, consumer goods exploit upstream relationship with input suppliers based on different phases of each product life cycle.

Within China, the significance of large firms in development has been well recognised. When it comes to the national strategy, policymakers (Commission for the Reform of the Economic System, 2003) believed that large business groups have profound and long-term importance to improve production capabilities, deepen the reform of the economic system and develop China's competitiveness in the global economy. Vice-Premier Wu Bangguo stated (Sutherland, 2001: 71): "International economic confrontations show that if a country has several large companies or groups it will be assured of maintaining a certain market share and a position in the international economic order. . . . [O]ur nation's position in the international economic order will be to a large extent determined by the position of our nation's large enterprises and groups."

As to academic research, Bai (2002) thought that China's entry into the WTO brought domestic firms to an important stage from which to transform their strategies. The core of their strategies was to develop global competitive firms with core competitiveness. The success of both the nation and its firms was highly decided by the strengths of large firms and their core businesses. He and Li (2010) pointed out that the development of Chinese firms made impressive progress. Chinese firms grew faster and had more potential than foreign companies. In the list of the Fortune Global 500 enterprises, Chinese firms increased their numbers, improved their ranks and enhanced their profit performance. However, Chinese large firms still fell behind global large firms in many aspects. They have big gaps in scale, productivity, technological innovation, governance, branding, development history and the capabilities of participating in GVCs, coordinating resources, competing in the market and globalisation.

Moreover, since the 1990s, Nolan and his colleagues (Nolan, 1999, 2001, 2007, 2014; Nolan et al., 2007) have conducted in-depth investigations on Chinese large firms in a wide range of industries, including aerospace, pharmaceuticals, power equipment, oil and petrochemicals, automobile, steel, coal, brew, beverage, retailing and bank industries. They concluded that China's objective of nurturing a group of globally competitive SOEs succeeded beyond most expectations, but China's SOEs are still not catching up with the world's leading firms. These SOEs are mainly supported by the Chinese government with exclusive resources and preferential policies and their sales are still mainly in the domestic market. These researchers demonstrated that the global business revolution has fundamentally changed the nature of the capitalist firm and the pattern of global competition. Firms from the Third World like China face immense difficulties in not only catching up with leading systems integrators, but also catching up with the powerful firms (mainly from developed nations) that dominate almost every segment of the supply chain in GVCs. Nolan (2001) identified some key issues preventing China from constructing large and globally competitive firms. The issues include autonomy, the drive to diversify, the attraction of financial and property speculation, and other special difficulties, such as battles with domestic SMEs, more difficulty in downsizing and restructuring, weak supplier networks and spatial distribution of industrial assets.

The literature on large business traced the dynamics of capitalist firms and uncovered the nature of capitalist production systems. It proved the importance of large enterprises for advanced economics in history and for developing countries to catch up with the developed nations at present. The studies examining large firms within GVCs revealed the brutal reality that firms from developed countries have controlled the commanding heights of almost every segment in global production systems, while firms from developing countries have tremendous barriers to move up and change their unpleasant status quo. More importantly, the studies highlighted the importance of system integration capabilities to global competition. The arguments and empirical evidence put forward by Peter Nolan and his colleagues vividly displayed the diverse challenges for Chinese firms in global competition. They provide a fertile foundation to further explore the challenges for Chinese private manufacturing firms in globalisation.

Given much merit, the existing studies cannot fully explain the research question. Firstly, Chinese private manufacturing firms are the core analysis units of this research, but most literature mainly focused on large SOEs. In China, private firms and SOEs have very different development histories, governance mechanisms, organisation structures and positions in national strategies, so their development challenges are not all the same. Research on private manufacturing firms is beneficial to comprehensively understand the differential challenges for Chinese firms with different ownerships.

Secondly, the conclusions of current literature are mostly based on investigations conducted between the late 1990s and the early 2000s, but the research aims to observe the competition landscape after the early 2000s. Admitting some similarities, the research believes that the development environment and competitive state of firms have changed. Private firms have developed very quickly and their competitive strengths are much larger now than one decade ago. Huawei's rise to be a global competitor has demonstrated the increasing importance of Chinese private firms in globalisation. Therefore, it is highly necessary to present the latest investigation on Chinese private firms and trace the changes of their development challenges.

Thirdly, the research notices that despite the growing number of large firms, most Chinese private firms are still SMEs. Current literature either analyses SMEs as a whole or focuses on large firms, but there is little research on individual cases of SMEs. Since the development challenges for Chinese private SMEs and large firms are also different, case studies on outstanding SMEs are relevant to enrich the existing knowledge.

Global battles within China

As one of the largest growing economies, China has been an important battlefield for both indigenous and foreign firms in their global competition. Elms and Low (2013) pointed out that China offered a large pool of low-wage workers, increasingly capable manufacturing and trade infrastructures, abundant raw materials and huge underserved domestic markets with incipient middle classes. Therefore, large lead firms from developed countries have rushed to set up operations and grab market shares in China and to cut costs on goods produced for export back to home markets. Nolan (2014) revealed that the producers of global high-technology and branded goods have rapidly expanded their investment within China in many sectors. Global oligopolies have dominated large parts of the Chinese market. The subsidiaries of global firms within China have contributed most of China's exports of high-technology goods. Many Chinese scholars (Zhong, 2003; Li, 2003; Bai, 2004; Shang, 2006; Qing, 2009; Wan, 2011) also reported the massive entry of global firms into China, which brought large challenges in a wide range of industries, such as food, energy, EE, automobile, construction materials, machine tools and IT industries.

Zeng and Williamson (2007) recognised that Chinese companies have to learn to survive in the domestic market under global competition at the early stage of their development. Chinese firms use the strategy of cost innovation to hold their positions. They offer customers high technology at low cost, an unmatched choice of products in mass-market segments and specialty products at dramatically low price. Zeng and Williamson hold that differentiators separating competitors from low-cost countries and frothier counterparts in high-cost locations are further flattened, pushing global competition to an even higher value-for-money frontier. Chinese companies have developed large advantages at home which enable them to have great impacts on global competition.

Ghemawat and Hout (2008) revealed that in China multinational companies dominate knowledge- and brand-intensive industries, whereas Chinese companies hold advantages in sectors where production and logistics matter most. Multinational firms try out new management structures and ways of being more responsive to local customers without losing the advantage of global knowledge, but their vulnerabilities are slower movement and higher costs than for local players. Chinese firms have lower costs, simpler management structures, more adaptation to the emerging market and more ability to manage very large workforces with low overhead costs, but their large vulnerabilities are inexperience in coordination, conflict management across borders and lack of deep knowledge of global customers and channels.

Gadiesh et al. (2007) pointed out that China has recently developed an expanding good-enough segment in the domestic market. To grasp the good-enough space, leading multinationals in the premium segment attack from above by lowering their manufacturing costs, introducing simplified products or services and broadening their distribution networks while maintaining reasonable quality. Chinese challengers in the low-end segment try to burrow up by providing new offerings that ratchet up quality but cost much less than the premium products. Foreign players have shortcomings, such as high costs, limited distribution capabilities and the possibility of cannibalising their own products. In contrast, local companies have the limitations of managerial talents and inability to compete through innovation or branding.

Brandt and Thun (2015) put forward that the technology gap confronting Chinese firms is smaller and the marketing gap will largely disappear in the home market. Due to the intensive competition at the bottom and the increasing demand in the middle, Chinese firms and FIEs are fighting for the middle: Domestic firms strive to upgrade their products by improving design and manufacturing, while FIEs try to decrease costs to capture the market. Brandt and Thun's case studies on automotive, construction equipment and machine tools showed that the interaction of these two dynamics fostered capability building in Chinese industries. They suggested that the Chinese government should worry less about who (SOEs, private firms or FIEs) exactly have the competitive capabilities and should put more emphasis on fostering an environment where these capabilities are nurtured and allowed to grow.

The literature on global battles within China displays the relevance of the Chinese market to Chinese indigenous firms as well as global giants for their global competition. The entry of foreign firms has exposed Chinese firms to opportunities for learning and at the same time highly increased their competition. It revealed that the middle market is an important field for the competition of Chinese firms and FIEs. It also pointed out the efforts, potential, advantages and disadvantages of domestic firms and FIEs to increase their competitiveness in the Chinese market. Such literature provides much enlightenment on the research question, but more careful investigations can be done on the following aspects.

Firstly, it is important to see how Chinese firms (especially leading firms) respond to the pressure from global competitors in the domestic market. Firms in diverse industries and various sections of the value chain might have differential strategies. Research on the development strategies from diverse firms can not only reveal the different competition situations of Chinese firms, but also facilitate the sharing of successful experience and useful lessons among firms. Secondly, more detailed study can be conducted on how the large domestic market impacts the will and chances for Chinese firms to compete in the global field. Although the large domestic market can provide indigenous firms with the place to expand their competitive advantages and make up their disadvantages, it is also possible that the domestic market will reduce firms' will to compete in the global market. The analyses on the double effects of the large domestic market will not only further display the development challenges for Chinese firms, but also provide important insights for the Chinese government to adopt more supportive and inspiring policies for firms' development.

Methodology

The research mainly conducted an in-depth qualitative inquiry. Qualitative research is "often used to explore, describe, or explain [a] social phenomenon; . . . build a depth of understanding about some aspect of social life; explore new or under researched areas" (Leavy, 2014: 2). A qualitative approach is suitable for the research question because it can offer thick descriptions of China's industrialisation and firms' development, decode their diverse challenges and form a more detailed and deeper understanding of global competition. Given the qualitative methodology in general, when necessary, the research also utilises relevant quantitative figures and data to display accurate landscapes of global competition and firms' competitiveness.

In terms of research method, I conducted case studies. "The case study offers a means of investigating complex social units consisting of multiple variables of potential importance in understanding the phenomenon" (Merriam, 2009: 50). A case study can help the research to achieve rich and holistic accounts of certain instances and then draw a broad understanding of China's economy. Despite these advantages, a case study might seek to grasp the issue of generalisability by focusing on only a single unit. Social phenomena are always complicated with diverse aspects, so that a single example can hardly describe a complete picture. However, since the general lies in the particular, what we learn from a particular case can be transferred to similar situations to some extent. In addition, if research can include more cases and have great variation across cases, its interpretation is also possibly compelling (Yin, 2009). Given limited time and funding, conducting several case studies is a reasonable and feasible way to explain the research question.

My research case studied Wenzhou's regional economy to observe China's development of the private manufacturing sector. Within the scope of China, Wenzhou is just a small place geographically. However, it has stood out in the development course of China's private economy because of its long-standing tradition and pioneer role of advancing economic reform. Whether Wenzhou rises or falls has always been closely related to the fortune of the nation. The study notices that Wenzhou, as a regional case, cannot totally explain the complicated situation of China's economy, but it believes that Wenzhou, as one of the most outstanding pioneers, plays a significant part in China's economic development. Wenzhou's story will provide relevant cases to trace China's development in the past, reflect China's challenges at present to a considerable extent and give potential warning for China's reform in the future.

This study regards industrial firms as the core units of Wenzhou's economy and examines Wenzhou's development through its leading firms in different industries. The standards for the selections of specific industries and firms were mainly twofold: Cases should mostly reflect the common situation of Wenzhou's development; cases should also be different from each other so that they can display as much diversity and complexity as possible. As to industry selection, my research chose the footwear and EE industries – because they are the largest and most influential industries in Wenzhou. These two industries are also representative among Wenzhou's industries in terms of their development history, industrial characteristics and social relations. Secondly, the two industries have some difference. Footwear is a consumer product existing in China since ancient times, while EE is a capital good invented in Western countries after the nineteenth century. According to the *Trade and Development Report* (UNCTAD, 2002), the footwear industry is labour intensive and resource based, while the EE industry is medium skill intensive and technology intensive. With the comparison and contrast of these two industries, my research not only provides the diverse profiles of industrial development in China, but also tries to summarise the common challenges of these different industries and seek for possible solutions correspondingly.

As to company selection, the research focused on local Chinese leading firms. These leading firms are usually large firms that have either large production scales, or advanced technology, or strong brands, or can have these merits at the same time. In some cases, outstanding SMEs can also have leadership roles by their highly developed technology. Therefore, the research mainly focused on large firms, but also looked at outstanding SMEs based on their importance and influence in the local economy. The research finally chose Aokang, Juyi and Menglani in the footwear industry and Chint in the EE industry as study cases. Aokang and Juyi are the largest firms in terms of their assets and output capability separately. However, Aokang is mainly based on the domestic market and Juyi is export oriented. Menglani is a typical SME, but it takes the lead in R&D and stands out among its peers. Chint is the national champion in its field. It has the strongest capabilities of production, R&D, marketing and branding among Chinese firms. When necessary, the research also investigated the opponents of these leading firms and companies in their forward and backward linkages.

To fully understand these industries and companies, the research used several methodological tools to collect data. The author utilised the following sources to access data: yearbooks, books, reports, newspapers, archives, journals, firms' annual reports and documents from industry associations and government agencies. The author also conducted eight months of fieldwork between 2015 and 2016 to get first-hand data and the latest information. The methodological tool of fieldwork consisted mainly of observation and interviews. The author visited the firms' factories and observed their daily operation and management. The interviews were semi-structured, so that the author not only got information of existing interest, but also gained more deep and diverse knowledge about the fields. The interviewees included the responsible persons from the firms, the government and social organisations. In the firms, the author interviewed chief executive officers (CEOs) and managers of R&D, marketing, finance, production, procurement and public relationship sectors. Besides, the author also talked to some workers. In the government, the author interviewed current and previous officers from the Wenzhou Municipal Commission of Development and Reform and the Wenzhou Economic and Information Commission. In the social organisations, the author interviewed the chairmen of the Wenzhou Shoes and Leather Industry Association and the Wenzhou Electrical Equipment Industry Association.

3 Wenzhou's economic development

This chapter displays a contour of Wenzhou's economic development with the association of China's economic history. It will firstly discuss Wenzhou's long-standing tradition in developing a private economy, which reveals the origin and internal forces of Wenzhou's modern economy. Secondly, it will show Wenzhou's pioneer role in advancing China's economic reform after 1978, to verify the importance of Wenzhou in China's economic development course. Thirdly, it will reveal Wenzhou's current economic predicaments and show its relevance to China's economy.

Wenzhou (温州) is a prefecture-level city located at the southeastern coast of Zhejiang Province in China. As Map 3.1 shows, its borders connect to Lishui City on the west, Taizhou City on the north, and Fujian Province on the south. It is surrounded by mountains on land and the East China Sea as well as islands on the east. It has a land area of 12,083 km^2 with 76% of the surface mountainous and 17% plains. Originally known as Yongjia, Wenzhou got its current name, literally translated as "a mild land", due to its climate. It is neither extremely hot in summer nor extremely cold in winter, which is often regarded as a pleasant condition for living. In 2015, Wenzhou administered four districts, two county-level cities and five counties with a total residential population of 9.1 million. Blocked by mountains in the north, west and south, Wenzhou was isolated overland and remote from the control of the central government in many periods of its history. The local dialects are very distinct from not only other parts of China, but also neighbouring areas. However, Wenzhou has a fine natural deep-water port, which provides advantageous conditions for trade and communication with the outside world.

Wenzhou's long-standing tradition

In pre-modern times, China, based on its advanced agricultural civilisation, was one of the most prosperous countries in the world. For a long time, it took the lead in scientific discovery, technical progress, productivity, trade and wealth creation. Imperial China deeply influenced the economy and culture of neighbouring countries and attracted people from these countries and the West to visit, learn and trade. In China's history, a commodity economy emerged during the Tang (618–907) and the Song (960–1279)[1] dynasties. This period witnessed the flourishing of cities,

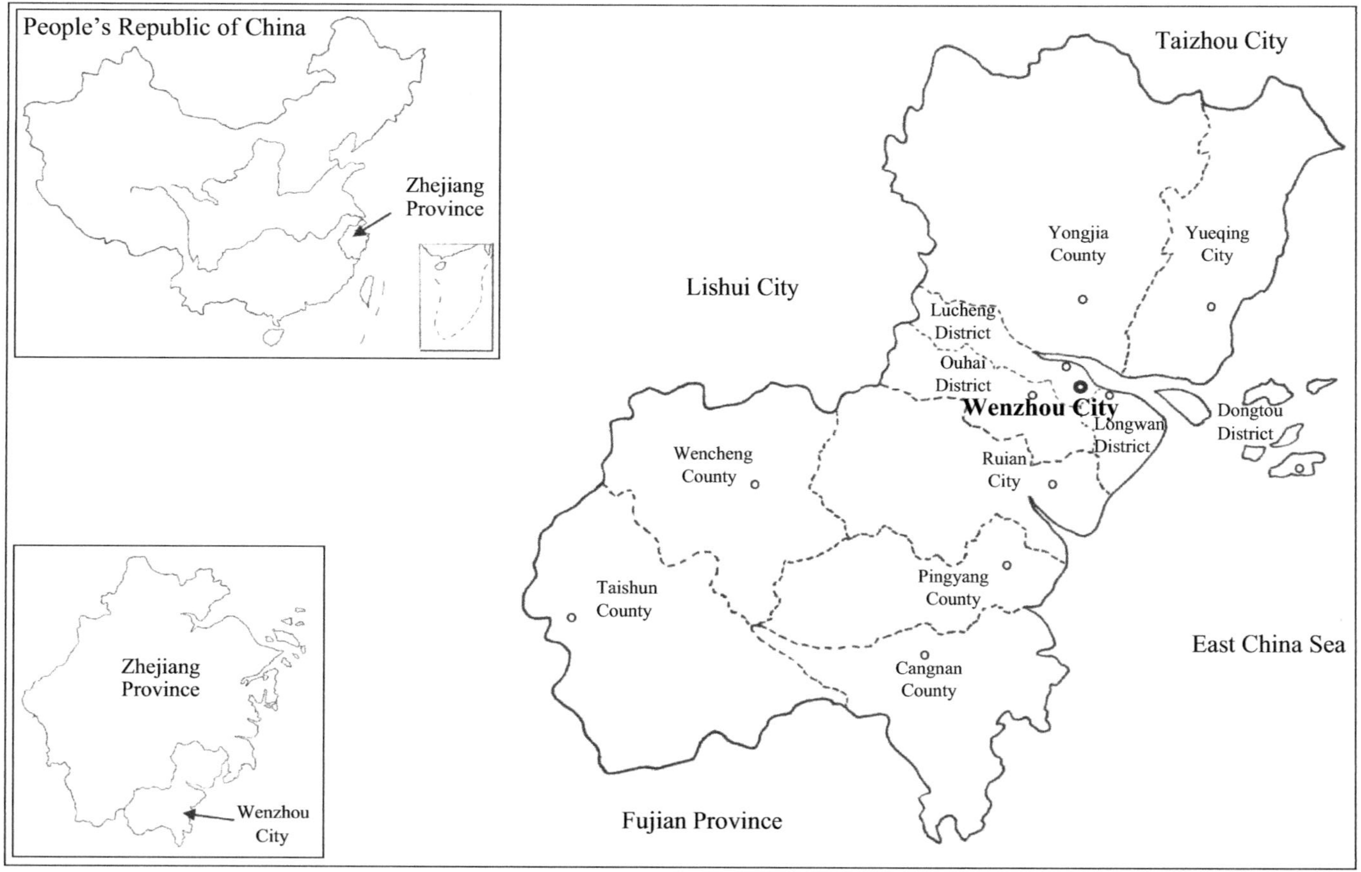

Map 3.1 The map of Wenzhou City

Note: The author drew the map.

the development of township and rural markets, the appearance of credit relationships and guilds and the prosperity of foreign trade (Wang, 2012). The commodity economy further developed in the Yuan dynasty (1279–1368). Needham (2004) documented a wide range of China's technical advances between the tenth and the thirteenth centuries. Maddison (1998) estimated that China's gross domestic product (GDP) per capita increased from 450 international dollars (Intl$) in 960 C.E. to Intl$ 600 in 1300, which were above the European levels of Intl$ 422 and Intl$ 576, respectively.[2]

Although Wenzhou was blocked by high mountains and was situated far from the emperor ("山高皇帝远") in early times, it achieved great progress of development after the Tang and Song dynasties. In the Tang dynasty, Wenzhou's citrus, sugar cane, seafood and textile products became tributes to the imperial court. Its paper products ranked among the top 5 most famous papers, and its porcelain and brewery industries were well known within China. The Wenzhou port started to be a trading hub and launched its own non-governmental connections with Japan. In the Northern Song, Wenzhou became an important production base for citrus, tea and salt. It made technical advances in making paper, silk and lacquerware. It developed into the domestic centre of celadon manufacturing, and its celadon products from Longquan County were famous around the world. Its shipmaking industry was advanced, with an annual output of 600 vessels, ranking at the top in the country (Xu, 1957: 5658). The trade in the Wenzhou port was very vibrant, transporting grains, citrus, tea, paper, silk, porcelain, lacquerware and timber to other regions in China and to foreign countries by transferring in Quanzhou[3] and Mingzhou.[4] A senior government official of Wenzhou named Yang Pan wrote about the prosperity of Wenzhou, that the local economy on the sea was extremely flourishing, and Wenzhou was therefore called a "Little Hangzhou" ("一片繁华海上头, 从来唤作小杭州"[5]).

In the Southern Song, China moved its capital to Hangzhou and Jiangnan[6] achieving unprecedentedly great importance in national development. Thereby, the conditions of Wenzhou's location greatly changed and its commodity economy developed remarkably. During the twelfth century, Wenzhou's population increased more than 2.5 times.[7] Wenzhou's output of citrus doubled compared with the figure in the Tang dynasty. One local official even wrote the first monograph on citrus in the world. Wenzhou's industries of making lacquerware, porcelain, ships, salt, paper and silk developed into their prime. Take the shipmaking industry, for example. In the Southern Song, private factories boomed to build ships for daily business, which were also allocated by the government for coastal defence if needed. In 1257, the number of private ships reached 5,083, among which 1,099 ships had the width of 3.07 meters.[8] During the Yuan dynasty, besides making large ships for grain transportation, Wenzhou also constructed many big warships that could travel long distances and on stormy seas. In 1292, Yuan's army took the warships made in Wenzhou to conduct punitive expeditions for Java in Indonesia.

In 1131, the central government established a customs administration ("市舶司") in Wenzhou, and the Wenzhou port was officially opened for foreign trade.[9] Many of Wenzhou's products were transported easily and cheaply to international markets. Take Wenzhou's main export product, Longquan celadons, for instance. They were transported from Wenzhou to Japan, Korea, Southeast Asia, India, East and middle Africa and then to Europe, which played a very important role in enhancing foreign trade and cultural exchange on China's maritime porcelain route. In addition, foreign products, such as gold dust, mercury, sulphur, cloth and all kinds of handcrafts, were imported into Wenzhou. The prosperity of Wenzhou's commodity economy was widely recognised. An official in the Southern Song, Cheng Ju, commented that Wenzhou's products were exquisite and that many local people undertook business ("其货纤靡, 其人多贾"[10]). Huang Jin in the Yuan dynasty wrote that Wenzhou gathered a wide range of goods and attracted all ordinary people as well as businessmen to visit ("百货所萃, 廛氓贾竖, 咸附趋之"[11]).

The vigorous development of the commodity economy made it possible for Wenzhou to feed a larger population than its local resources could support. It also resulted in further labour division, social cooperation and a thriving culture within the region. As regards the textile industry, in Wenzhou appeared the earliest individual industrial and commercial households in China, called Jihu ("机户"), meaning machine-weaving households. In the rural area, employed labour emerged and many people got out of farming to sell commodities. The social stratum of rich workers, businessmen and landlords who operated industry and commerce rose and cultivated a mature school of thought called the Yongjia School ("永嘉学派").[12] This School along with the Rationalism School and the Idealism School became the three most influential schools of Confucianism in China in the Southern Song. The Yongjia School emphasised utility, pragmatism and profits and advocated to reduce taxes and levies, facilitate industry and commerce, respect free trade and businessmen and value wealth as well as virtue.

Given its legend, China struggled with a series of foreign intrusions, domestic rebellions, imperial colonisation and civil wars from the Ming dynasty (1368–1644) until 1949. After the Opium War in 1840, the Chinese devoted themselves to fighting for national independence and self-strengthening for more than one century. In these chaotic times, foreign-capitalist enterprises penetrated into treaty ports, and Chinese bureaucratic-capitalist operations and national-capitalist firms developed with difficulties and setbacks.[13] In contrast, the Western countries, rising after the Industrial Revolution, gained their power rapidly. Maddison (2007b) estimated that from 1820 to 1950, China's share of the world's GDP dropped from 32.9% to 4.6%. On the contrary, Western Europe and the USA raised their shares of global GDP to 26.2% and 27.3% individually. In 1890, the USA took over China to be the world's largest economy, although China had been in the position for nearly two millennia (Maddison, 2007a: 43). Bairoch (1982) believed that China's share of world manufacturing output reduced from 32.8% in 1750 to 6.2% in 1900 and further declined to 2.3% in 1953. In contrast, the US enhanced its share from 0.1% to 23.6% in 1990 and further to 44.7% in 1953.[14]

During the Ming and Qing (1644–1912) period, Wenzhou's agriculture and handcraft industries continuously developed and there appeared capitalist sprouts ("资本主义萌芽") in its economy. The capitalist sprouts created conditions of thought awareness, skilled labour, production relations, long-distance trade and physical and capital bases for the growth of local modern economy. In the silk weaving industry, business capital widely involved in the production and circulation processes and merchant employers and putting-out systems were common phenomena.[15] The production was highly oriented to market demands and the local people were full of commercial awareness. In addition, the operation division of business further developed. A wide range of properly licensed businesses ("行") specialised in the fields of pawn, copper, wine, paper, cloth, rice, fruit, fish and fowl. Wenzhou's business networks were widely developed in the whole country to sell Chinese medicine, silk goods, sauces and pickles and delicacies from South China. What's more, Wenzhou attracted a great number of businessmen from all over the country, especially from Ningbo, Anhui and Fujian, to invest in Wenzhou and specialised in transit trade. Several shopping streets also took shape in some local regions. A provincial inspector of the Qing dynasty named Fang Dingrui praised the prosperity of Wenzhou's business streets, that the windows of shops were still bright until midnight and the evening market was unexpectedly as prosperous as the day market ("三更灯火映窗栊, 宵市居然晓市同"[16]).

In certain periods of this era, the central government adopted a few rounds of sea bans to the Wenzhou port. Their implementation negatively affected the daily operation of the Wenzhou port. Smuggling emerged to continue illegal business, and foreign trade always revived quickly when the sea ban policies were relaxed. Since 1526, many of Wenzhou's officials, gentries and businessmen conspired with Chinese pirates, Portuguese colonialists and Japanese smuggling rings to exchange local silk products, cotton cloth and grains for foreign products of various spices, gold and silver. It was in 1757 that all Chinese ports including the Wenzhou port except the Guangzhou port were closed for foreign trade. In 1876, Wenzhou was reopened as a trading port due to the Chefoo Convention[17] and the British government built a consulate to control local customs. Afterwards, many foreign goods flooded into the market, shook the local economic structure and resulted in many bankruptcies of local traditional agricultural and handcraft production. In the late Qing, Wenzhou could hardly support its large population with its internal resources and thereby many local people were forced to leave Wenzhou to make a living.

In the early twentieth century, Wenzhou stepped into the stage of modern production and emerged on a tide of national-capitalist development. Many modern factories were established to produce textile machinery, milk products, footwear, textile, knitting, porcelain, paper and brew. At the same time, related vocational schools were set up to teach knowledge and technology and train workers. Many outstanding local entrepreneurs established industrial corporations. For example, Li Yumeng introduced the first gin into China in 1916 and built an iron factory in Wenzhou in 1925. Wu Baiheng launched the first Chinese condensed milk factory in 1926 and its condensed milk was evaluated as a first-rate product in 1929. In 1939, he continued to set up a porcelain factory, a canned food factory and a paper mill in Wenzhou. The development of Wenzhou's modern industry triggered huge enthusiasm among the local people and accumulated valuable experience for further development of modern firms.

However, the scale of Wenzhou's modern industry at that time could not compete with the conditions in other regions of the Yangtze River Delta, like Shanghai and South Jiangsu, where foreign- and bureaucratic-capitalist operations were highly developed. In that chaotic century, Wenzhou's national-capitalist firms grew slowly and struggled to survive under the great competition from foreign- and bureaucratic-capitalist enterprises. The business of the Wenzhou port experienced unbalanced ups and downs. A great number of Wenzhou people had to leave their homes, travel outside and migrate to foreign countries for survival. Wenzhou once witnessed a few upsurges of outward migration, especially between the 1920s and the 1930s. For example, an investigation conducted by the local office of overseas Chinese affairs showed that between 1920 and 1923, Japan, as only one of many foreign destinations, attracted more than 5,000 people from the juncture region of Qingtian, Ruian and the Yongjia Country of Wenzhou to sell carved stones.[18]

In 1949, the Communist Party of China (CPC) established the People's Republic of China and finally ended the martial chaos in the mainland. China started to seek for a way of reconstructing itself to be a thriving nation again in the unfavourable conditions of hostility, isolation and embargoes from the West and poverty and backwardness within the country. Aiming to build a strong and independent socialist country quickly, the new regime under the leadership of Mao Zedong referred to the development practices of the Soviet Union and adopted a centralised planned system to develop a heavy-industry-oriented economy. SOEs in urban areas dominated in the industrial structure, agricultural collectivisation took shape in rural areas, foreign- and national-capitalist enterprises were nationalised and foreign trade became a state monopoly whose goal was self-sufficiency. Government administration replaced market forces to allocate resources, guide production, circulate products and distribute consumption.

The planned system enhanced China's economic structure and performance to some extent. From 1952 to 1978, the percentage of China's primary sector in GDP decreased from 50.5% to 28.1% and the figure of the secondary sector grew from 20.9% to 48.2% (National Bureau of Statistics of China, 2001). According to the estimate of the World Bank (2017), China's GDP increased from USD 59.7 billion in 1960 to USD 149.54 billion. However, the system was extremely inefficient, lacked incentives and restricted the labour force within the agricultural sector. From 1952 to 1978, China's labour force employed in agriculture decreased slowly from 83.5% to 70.5% (National Bureau of Statistics of China, 2001). Despite Chinese people's great efforts, the planned economy failed to bring the desired result of a prosperous nation. In 1978, one-third of the Chinese rural population (roughly 260 million people) lived in absolute poverty.[19] In 1981, 88.3% of the Chinese population was in poverty.[20] People's living standards were hardly improved due to the lack of light industrial products and daily necessities. China fell behind nearby East Asian economies that had achieved tremendous growth after the 1960s.[21] For example, based on the estimate of the World Bank (2017), although Japan's GDP was only 74.2% of China's level in 1960, it improved its number to USD 966.74 billion in 1978 that was 6.5 times of China's figure. Japan increased its share of world's GDP from 3.3% to 11.5% when China reduced its ratio from 4.4% to 1.8%.[22] From 1953 to 1980, although China's share of world manufacturing output increased by 2.7 percentage points to 5.0%, Japan improved its share by 6.2 percentage points to 9.1% (Bairoch, 1982).

Under China's centralised planned system, Wenzhou's economy was lethargic. Local capitalist firms were nationalised and private elements in agriculture, industry and commerce were eliminated to the greatest possible extent due to the radical pursuit of a communist ideology. The state invested only one-third of the national average funds in Wenzhou because at that time it was the front line against military attacks from the Nationalist Party of China in Taiwan.[23] The trade in the Wenzhou port was negatively affected by military conflicts and political movements. In 1978, Wenzhou's GDP was RMB 1.3 billion (USD 764.7 million) ranking 9th out of 11 cities in Zhejiang. Most people lived in the rural areas, where 44% to 49% (792,000 to 882,000) of working-age people were unemployed or underemployed (Tsai, 2002: 123), and residents' annual income of RMB 113 (USD 66.5) was 15% lower than the national average (Statistics Bureau of Wenzhou Municipality, 2016; Statistics Bureau of Zhejiang Province, 2016; National Bureau of Statistics of China, 2016).

In such poverty, Wenzhou's people were highly motivated to take any opportunity for change. Due to the border closure, a lot of Wenzhou's people travelled within China to conduct small business or sell their labour and craftsmanship. Many local people secretly operated household responsibility systems, underground factories and private businesses for extra income to improve living conditions. During the movements of the People's Communes and the Cultural Revolution, Wenzhou's private economy was regarded as the tail of capitalism ("资本主义尾巴") that should be cut off. Despite stern and frequent suppression from the government at that time, the local private economy was very resilient. The private economic activities sometimes seemed to vanish after the state's crackdown, but the seeds of private economy remained. When the political control eased up a bit, the local private economy recovered quickly, which caused headaches for some government officials who wanted to demolish it.[24]

Wenzhou's pioneer role

After the death of Mao Zedong, China shifted its leadership to Deng Xiaoping in 1978. In 1979, China established diplomatic relations with the USA and gradually eliminated the hostility from the West. To change the inefficient and backward economic situation, China tried to explore a new path of pragmatic reformism and opening-up for economic development. Without a well worked out blueprint in the beginning, economic reforms proceeded cautiously intending to solve conspicuous problems and moved forward at the rate that the government considered appropriate. The process was characterised as crossing the river by groping the underwater stones ("摸着石头过河"). Gradually, the household responsibility system was promoted in the countryside and market mechanisms were introduced again. SOEs were reformed concerning their autonomy, taxation, responsibility, management systems and corporate reconstruction. Foreign trade was liberalised and the strategy of bringing in ("引进来") was adopted to attract foreign direct investment (FDI) and advanced technology and management. Foreign firms were encouraged with preferential policies to conduct and establish corporates firstly in Special Economic Zones in Guangdong and Fujian, then in other coastal provinces. The roles of private economy, private entrepreneurs and private property in the national development were officially acknowledged step by step.

When China started the economic reform in 1978, the Wenzhou people's enthusiasm of developing private economy burst out and individual and private businesses sprang up dramatically, especially in the industrial and commercial sectors. Household manufacturing in the form of front shops and back factories was the typical style of production. Local people hired their family members and friends as workers and used basic equipment to mechanically produce small commodities, which then were sold to clients in specialty markets located in different regions within Wenzhou. Moreover, in these markets, Wenzhou fostered market mechanisms to provide firms with production materials and tools, supply and demand information, technology and labour. Near these markets, many industrial firms gradually emerged to specialise in making some parts or the whole body of products for the markets. These firms as well as the specialty markets later formed several producing bases for certain commodities.

The previous travellers became sale agents who overcame massive difficulties in exploring markets and collecting order information outside Wenzhou, organising and coordinating manufacturing within Wenzhou and then selling local products all over China. Private finance was the main financial resource for household firms, including professional money lenders, middlemen, credit associations ("会"), private money houses, urban credit cooperatives, rural credit cooperatives and pawnshops. During the process, the local government usually adopted a hands-off policy ("无为") when the requests of the central government to restrict the private economy conflicted with the local demands of the developing private economy. It in fact tacitly consented to the existence and development of Wenzhou's private economy.

In 1985, the number of Wenzhou's household industries were estimated at 133,000, producing RMB 1.1 billion (USD 379.3 million) in output value (occupying more than 60% of output value in Wenzhou's rural area), and involved a labour force of more than 800,000 (Editing Group of the Book Three Decades' Development of Wenzhou's Private Economy, 2008: 69). Around 120 specialty markets took shape in different towns where businessmen specialised in trading one or several products with customers from places inside and mainly outside Wenzhou. The volume of freight handled in Wenzhou port increased by 65% from 1978 to 2.8 million tons (Statistics Bureau of Wenzhou Municipality, 2011). In 1987, retail sales of the top 10 specialty markets, as shown in Map 3.2, reached RMB 1.7 billion (USD 459.5 million), accounting for about 55% of total retail sales in Wenzhou. For example, the button market in Qiaotou town supplied more than 1,400 kinds of buttons with 1,030 stalls operated by 300 SOEs and collective and private firms, attracted around 3,000 businessmen to trade every day and achieved retail sales of RMB 84.6 million (USD 22.9 million) in 1987 (He, 1989: 19). In the 1980s, more than 100,000 people in Wenzhou's were sales agents (Zhang and Li, 1990). Private finance contributed to at least 80% of capital demands in Wenzhou between 1983 and 1985 (Tsai, 2002: 125). In the mid-1980s, credit associations were most common, involving billions of RMB in capital and several hundred thousands of people.[25]

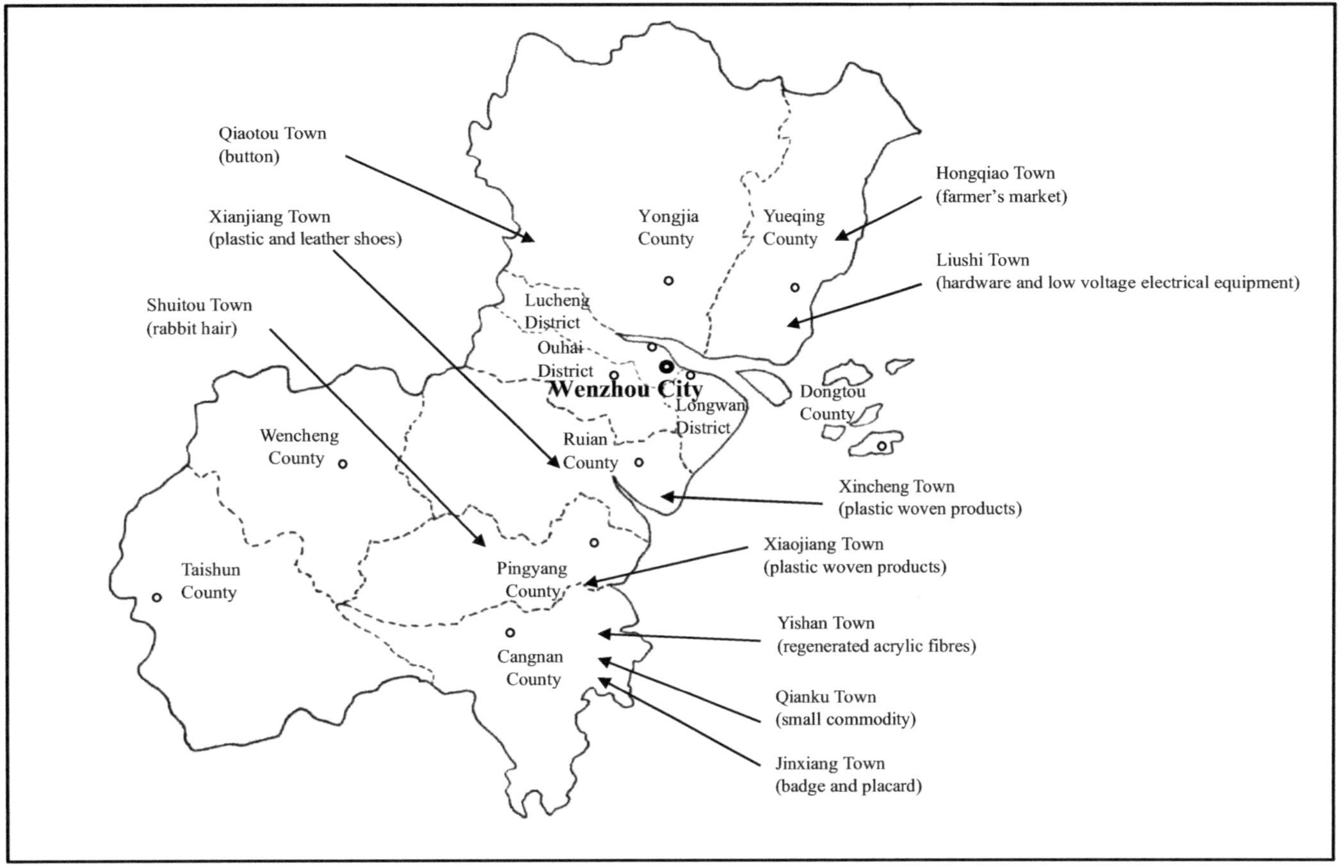

Map 3.2 Map of Wenzhou's 10 specialty market towns in the 1980s

Note: The author drew the map.

The rapid development of the private economy in Wenzhou attracted wide attention. In 1985, *Jiefang Daily* firstly coined the term the "Wenzhou Model" ("温州模式") to describe Wenzhou's economic phenomena. Thereby heated debates arose all over the country over the ideology of the "Wenzhou Model". Some conservatives claimed that the private economy was capitalist and the "Wenzhou Model" was a hotbed of capitalism, which should be prohibited in socialist China. Some researchers and local government officials based on their fieldwork advocated that the "Wenzhou Pattern" might be a feasible approach for economic development.[26] Thanks to the support of a few reformists in leadership positions, the central government finally took a wait-and-see attitude towards the private economy in Wenzhou.[27]

Despite the ongoing ideological debates, Wenzhou's people did not argue, but buried themselves in further developing the private economy. In the 1980s, in order to avoid political strikes and gain operation convenience, they creatively disguised their private companies with public and collective appearances, which featured the wearing of red hats ("戴红帽"). They registered under the name of public firms and township and village enterprises (TVEs)[28] ("挂户经营") and later built shareholding cooperative systems ("股份合作制"), but their firms were independent and privately run in essence. These practices were regarded as institutional innovations of the cooperation between the local government and private firms, which created political protection and survival space for Wenzhou's private firms to grow during China's economic transition to a market economy.[29] At the same time, Wenzhou's people actively speeded up their outward migration and built a larger business network. According to Wenzhou's 1990 census, 407,829 people migrated for business (Statistics Bureau of Wenzhou Municipality, 1990a). They played important roles in bridging Wenzhou's producers and nationwide customers and circulating commodities all over the country, when market mechanisms had not grown and light industrial products were highly needed in most regions of China.

With the hard work of Wenzhou's people, Wenzhou's economy grew tremendously. From 1980 to 1992, the number of individual industrial firms in Wenzhou increased from 1,372 to 19,853 and its proportion in the total volume of industrial firms grew from 21.2% to 47.7%. Their ratio of industrial output increased from 9.2% to 35.6% among all industrial firms.[30] From 1978 to 1992, its agricultural GDP increased by 5 times and the industrial GDP increased by 15 times. A great number of surplus labourers in the rural area were employed in non-agricultural sectors. In 1978, 89% (1.6 million) of Wenzhou's rural people were engaged in agriculture, but in 1985, 63% (1.32 million) were committed in industrial and side-line activities (Nolan and Dong, 1990: 85). Within the 14 years after 1978, peasant income per capita increased rapidly from RMB 113 (USD 66.5) to RMB 1,200 (USD 218.2). The employment of individual businesses in urban areas had a fold increase from 6,200 to 124,000. The urban resident income grew almost six times from 1980 to 1992 (Statistics Bureau of Wenzhou Municipality, 2016). The volume of freight handled in the Wenzhou port increased by 1.5 times from 1978 to 4.4 million tons (Statistics Bureau of Wenzhou Municipality, 2011). The impressive economic growth and improvement of people's living conditions in Wenzhou proved that the private economy was an effective way to reduce poverty, solve unemployment and promote development in China.

Meanwhile, Wenzhou provided valuable experience for China's economic reform. In 1980, the Wenzhou Administrative Bureau for Industry and Commerce issued the first business license in the country for individual industry and commerce. Wenzhou's Jinxiang Town Credit Cooperative took the lead of the reform in the country in adopting financial floating interest rates. In 1984, Wenzhou's peasants built the first town in China that was totally funded by the local people. In the same year, Wenzhou was selected as one of the first 14 coastal open cities to develop foreign economy. In 1986, Wenzhou's people established the Lucheng Credit Cooperative, the first shareholding cooperative financial firm in China. In 1987, Wenzhou became the first experimental city to reform interest rates. Besides, it put forward the first local regulation to manage shareholding cooperative firms in China.

Wenzhou's success and experimental experience helped the nation liberate its thinking from the shackles of ideology and facilitated the state to choose the direction of economic development. In 1992, the Fourteenth National Congress of the CPC affirmed that China would develop a socialist market economy where the individual and private-run economy was the supplementation of the public and collective economy. Wenzhou thereby got rid of ideological criticism and became a development model in the country. Hundreds and thousands of entrepreneurs, officials, researchers and ordinary people inside and outside China came to investigate and learn the "Wenzhou Model". Therefore, the influence of Wenzhou's economic practices rapidly expanded from one city to Zhejiang Province, to the Yangtze River Delta region and to the whole country. Following the example of Wenzhou, many areas developed household industries and private firms. Market mechanisms were spread and adopted rapidly throughout China.

In the upsurge of developing the private economy, Wenzhou enjoyed first-mover advantages and took the lead in economic development within the country. After 1992, more and more of Wenzhou's firms took off their red hats. Many of Wenzhou's household firms changed to modern forms of limited liability companies and shareholding companies. In 1996, shareholding cooperatives decreased to 31,107 from 36,887 in 1993, while limited liability companies reached 8,264 and shareholding companies developed to several scores (Editing Group of the Book Three Decades' Development of Wenzhou's Private Economy, 2008: 267). Some companies even built corporate groups with clear property rights, conducted reforms in share ownership, introduced formal management regulations and employed professional talents for management, research and technology innovation. From 1992 to 1999, the number of Wenzhou's corporate groups increased from 28 to 190 and their impacts on the industries enhanced due to their massive M&A (Editing Group of the Book Three Decades' Development of Wenzhou's Private Economy, 2008: 282). Many large firms built domestic and global retail distribution networks to sell their branded products to customers. These sale networks replaced the previous specialty markets and sale agents, but its operation still highly relied on Wenzhou's migrants.

At this stage, Wenzhou's people were more active in exploring business opportunities outside of local regions. They migrated together with their families and friends and settled down closely to each other in certain regions, where they formed Wenzhou streets, Wenzhou villages and Wenzhou cities to specialise in trading Wenzhou's products and managing Wenzhou's sale networks. In 1995, Wenzhou established the first non-local business chamber in Kunmin in Yunnan Province. In 2003, more than 1.6 million of Wenzhou's people operated business outside of Wenzhou, which created more than 18,800 firms, RMB 160 billion (USD 19.3 billion) of output and RMB 288 billion (USD 34.7 billion) of sale income (Shao, 2006: 57). Despite the fall of local specialty markets, retail sales of consumer goods in Wenzhou increased 7.8 times (Statistics Bureau of Wenzhou Municipality, 2016).

What's more, several IDs took shape. They were mainly funded by indigenous capital, based on local social cooperation, highly oriented to the market, supported by business associations and governmental agencies and were magnets for cheap immigrant labourers from inland China. These IDs engaged mainly in labour-intensive industries, like footwear, LVEE, garments, eyeglasses, locks and metal lighters. In the IDs, large firms played leadership roles in technological progress, organising the production system and building retail networks. Many SMEs in the IDs supplied basic components to large firms and benefited from the flexible production system, scale economy and technological spillover. The IDs made it possible for Wenzhou to manufacture a large scale of low-end products at very low costs. Wenzhou's cheap products were very popular in the market, especially when China was in a shortage economy before the mid-1990s. By 2000, Wenzhou had more than 10 IDs in different regions, as shown in Map 3.3 and Table 3.1. These IDs gathered many firms, produced massive industrial outputs, contributed large export values and occupied big market shares. For example, in the early 2000s, Wenzhou's footwear ID nurtured 5,000 firms, produced RMB 29.6 billion (USD 3.6 billion) in output and USD 0.5 billion in export value and had 20% of domestic market share. Its metal lighter ID gathered 500 firms and occupied 90% of domestic market share. In 2001, these IDs contributed more than 65% of local industrial outputs (Sheng, 2004: 32).

Both the central and local governments facilitated Wenzhou's development at this stage. Many of the most influential national leaders visited Wenzhou, including President Jiang Zemin, Vice-President Hu Jintao, Premier Li Peng and Vice-Premier Zhu Rongji. They gave credit for Wenzhou's achievements, encouraged Wenzhou's private firms to develop stronger and supported Wenzhou in exploring further reform on market economy. In 1997, the central government approved Wenzhou as one of the first four experimental cities that established industrial associations for governance. The local authority launched a strategy of building the market based on product quality and developing industries based on brands ("质量立市, 名牌兴业") to rectify market order and prop up competitive industries. It put forward a "358 Quality Project"[31] from 1992 to 1995 to regulate product

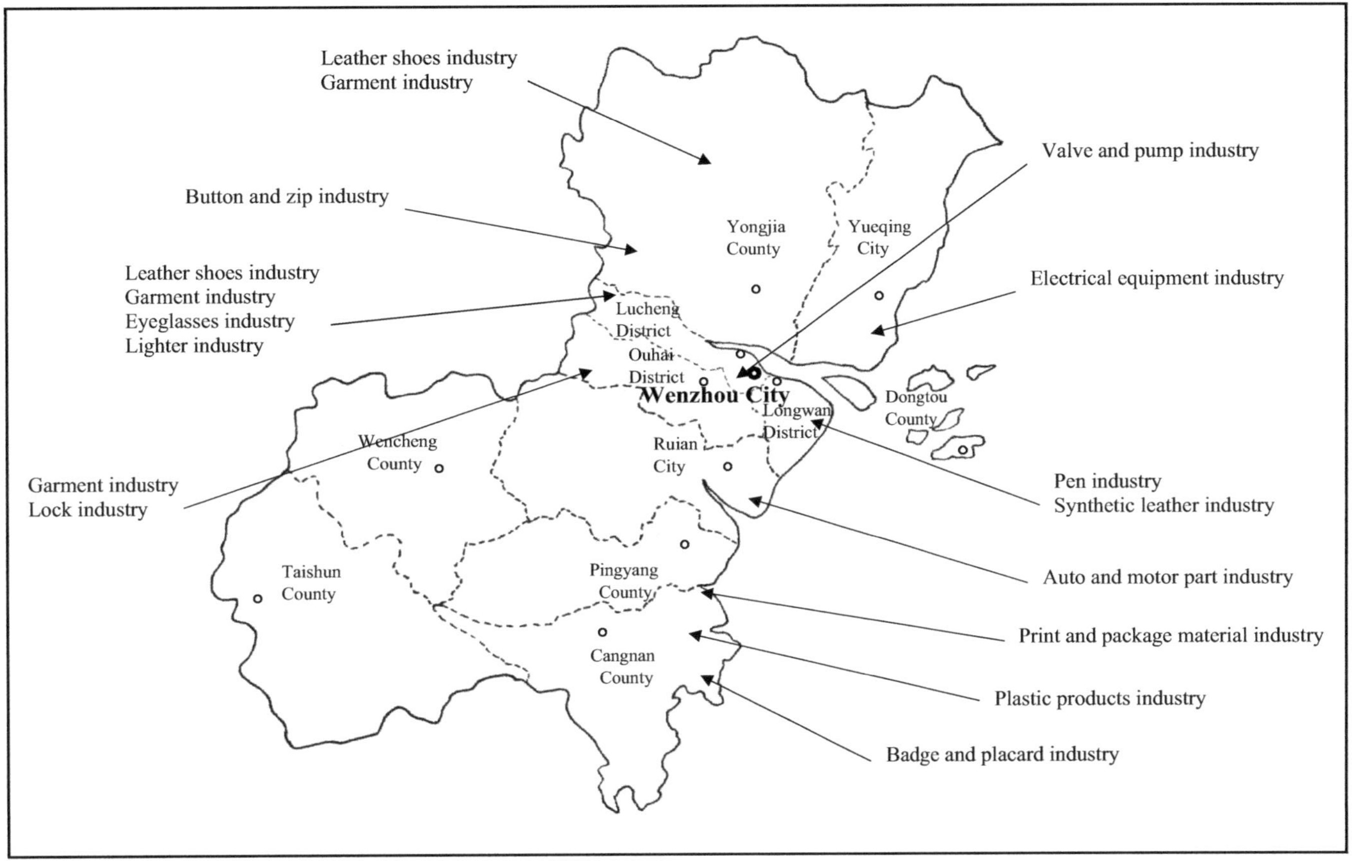

Map 3.3 Map of Wenzhou's IDs in the early 2000s

Note: Map drawn by author

Table 3.1 Wenzhou's IDs in the early 2000s

Industry	*Firm Number*	*Output Value (billion RMB)*	*Export Value (billion USD)*	*Domestic Market Share (%)*
Leather shoes	5,000	29.6	0.5	20
Garment		26.5	0.3	10
Plastic product	450	18	0.1	67
Electrical equipment	1,300	10	0.3	70
Synthetic leather	40	8		70
Lock	200	5	0.2	65
Eyeglasses		4.5	0.5	80
Auto and motor part	700	3.8	0.05	8
Valve and pump		3		20
Metal lighter	500	2		90
Pen	151	1.6	0.3	33
Button and zip	1,208	0.2		
Badge and placard	120	0.9		40

Data source: Sheng (2004), Sheng and Zheng (2004), Wang (2001).

quality. After 1995, it inspired firms to create famous brands and held diverse conferences, seminars and exhibitions around the country to publicise Wenzhou's products. By 2003, Wenzhou had 21 National Production Bases, 7 China Famous Trademarks, 15 China Famous Brands, 52 Products Exempt from National Inspection and 87 Provincial Famous Brands. It owned 1,650 firms with ISO9000 Quality Certificates (Statistics Bureau of Wenzhou Municipality, 2004). In addition, it initiated an "828 Infrastructure Project"[32] to boost Wenzhou's infrastructure. In 1998, Wenzhou achieved the first railway in China that was invested by a joint venture of privately held companies and government-owned corporations. From 1992 to 2003, Wenzhou's number of telephones owned per 100 persons increased to 81.75 from 1.46, the volume of freight handled in ports grew by 4.1 times and the volume of passenger traffic increased by 78%. The improvement of infrastructure greatly facilitated Wenzhou's connection with the outside world and enriched its means of transportation, which paved the way for its further economic development.

From 1992 to 2003, Wenzhou's GDP growth rate[33] was 16.4%, 3.2% and 6.5% higher than the Zhejiang's and national levels correspondingly. Its GDP per capita got to RMB 16,369 (USD 1,972) which was 53.5% higher than the national figure. Its rural and urban resident incomes became 2.1 times and 1.9 times the national levels (Statistics Bureau of Wenzhou Municipality, 2016; National Bureau of Statistics of China, 2016). Wenzhou's FDI in actual use grew 3.8 times, from USD 24.9 million to USD 119.7 million and export value increased 32.8 times from USD 101.4 million to USD 3,424 million. In 2003, Wenzhou's private enterprises reached the volume of 34,975 and had 364,974 employment, 103,187 investors and RMB 4,667,859 (USD 562,393) in registration funds. The private economy accounted for 79.9% of Wenzhou's GDP. Wenzhou was one of the cities in the country that cultivated the most numbers (up to 33) of China's Top 500 Private Enterprises. Among these firms, 3 were listed in China's Top 500 Firms (Statistics Bureau of Wenzhou Municipality, 1993 and 2004). In 2002, the United Nations Industrial Development Organization (UNIDO) evaluated Wenzhou to be one of the Most Dynamic Cities in the world as a place for starting new business and industries.

The development of the private economy in Wenzhou as well as other places further drove the changes in the economic system, political institutions and the government–business relationship in China. In 1997, the Fifteenth National Congress of the CPC claimed that China's fundamental economic system at the initial stage of socialism was keeping public ownership as the mainstay of the economy and allowing diverse forms of ownership to develop side by side. Private economy as an important component of the socialist market economy would be encouraged and guided for healthy development. These statements were confirmed in China's Constitution in 1999. In 2001, Jiang Zemin, the General Secretary of the CPC, putting forward the idea of "Three Represents" ("三个代表"),[34] declared that private entrepreneurs were also builders of socialism with Chinese characteristics and should be allowed to become members of the CPC, although they had been prohibited before. In 2004, China's Constitutional Amendment wrote that the state would encourage, support and guide the development of the private economy and protect the legal rights and interests of private property.

As the restriction on private economy relaxed, private business and firms revived quickly. *China's Private Economy Development Report No. 1* (2003) pointed out that by 2002, the private economy had hired 90.3% of employees in society, 84 in the secondary and tertiary sectors and 70% in urban areas. The private economy contributed 48.5% of domestic GDP, 37% of national revenue, 50% of retail sales and 40.3% of total investment in fixed assets (Huang, 2004: 2).[35] According to China's 2004 economic census of individual and private economy, private firms contributed 65.6% of the number, 22.4% of the output and 11.9% of the export value in the industrial sector. The number of registered private business corporations reached 1,980,000, accounting for 61% of the volume of total registered business corporations in China (Huang and Hu, 2006). In the Yangtze River Delta, the private economy developed even more rapidly and outstandingly. It nurtured 327 firms listed on China's 2004 Top 500 Private Firms and these firms accounted for 67.8% of the total revenue of the Top 500 firms (Huang and Hu, 2006). The private economy in Zhejiang Province even contributed 91.4% of the employment in the secondary and tertiary sectors, 70.1% of provincial GDP of RMB 680.3 billion (USD 82.0 billion), 57.4% of the total investment in fixed assets and 36.5% of the export value by 2003 (Huang, 2004).

The boom of the private economy brought rapid growth of the regional economy and national income. Although the Yangtze River Delta accounted for only 2.2% of China's land area, it increased its GDP percentage from 14.2% to 21% in China from 1978 to 2003 (Statistics Bureau of Jiangsu Province, 2016; Statistics Bureau of Zhejiang Province, 2016; Statistics Bureau of Shanghai Municipality, 2016; National Bureau of Statistics of China, 2016). The fast development of the private economy within the Yangtze River Delta and other broader regions made an indispensable contribution to the rise of China's economy. The World Bank (2017) estimated that from 1992 to 2003, China's GDP per capita ascended from 22% of the world's average to 44.8% and the figure of gross national income (GNI) per capita grew to USD 3,940, from 22% of the global average level to 45%. In the 25 years after 1978, China's GDP increase rate was 9.6% and its share of world's GDP improved from 1.8% to 4.3%. Its share of world's merchandise export value enhanced from 0.8% to 2.7%. UNIDO's data indicated that China's shares of world manufacturing value added increased from 4.5% to 10.8%.[36]

Wenzhou's current predicaments

In the late 1990s, China decided to make further progress in its economic development by becoming deeply involved in globalisation. It aimed to make full use of domestic as well as international resources and markets to advance healthy growth and structural reforms. However, in the beginning many people worried that globalisation would bring in massive foreign products and firms, which might be like wolves ("狼来了") to devour Chinese firms and industries. Expecting both opportunities and challenges, China, on one hand, actively negotiated to enter the WTO. It cut tariffs, broadened trading rights, liberalised the FDI regime and promised to conduct further liberalisation reforms to meet the WTO's regulations. On December 11, 2001, it succeeded in entering the WTO after tough and long-lasting negotiations. Afterwards, the Chinese state expanded the scope of business open to both private firms and FIEs by gradually reducing restrictions on entry and encouraging their investment in many sectors previously reserved exclusively for SOEs. The pre-WTO and post-WTO reforms arguably made China the most open large developing economy in the world. Globalisation also thrust China into international networks of production, R&D and retail in a wide range of industries.

On the other hand, China persisted in building large firms to increase the competitiveness of Chinese industries in the globalised market. After the Fifteenth Central Committee of the CPC in 1997, it adopted a new policy of grasping the large and letting the small go ("抓大放小") to focus on large SOEs and relinquish control over small ones. It tried to nurture dozens of national champions mainly owned by the state with preferential policies in strategic industries where private firms and FIEs had negligible assets and market shares. In 2000, it pronounced a national strategy of "going out" ("走出去") that encouraged competitive firms to operate transnational operations. In the early 2000s, it valued this strategy as being as important as "bringing in" and further supported firms of various ownerships to operate multiple forms of cooperation, optimise the allocation of resources and conduct multinational production and operation all over the world. What's more, national leaders brought along commerce and trade missions consisting of government officials and entrepreneur representatives when they visited foreign countries, to boost the strategy of going out.

When China began to embrace globalisation, the Chinese private economy was not regarded as the main force to participate in global competition. Before 1999, a wide range of regulations on trading rights, export quotas and entry barriers restricted private firms from international involvement. In 2000, there were 13 collective and private firms among China's Top 500 Firms with most trade value, accounting for only 2.6% of the total firm volume. However, after the early 2000s, the international trade and outward direct investment (ODI) of the Chinese private economy developed so rapidly that they started to attract wide attention. Take Zhejiang Province, for example. From 1999 to 2003, its private firms established 516 operations in about 70 countries, which occupied 60.2% of the total volume of newly added Chinese overseas firms (Zhao, 2007: 47). What's more, from 2000 to 2011, in the USA, Chinese private companies achieved 461 deals amounting to USD 4,754 million in investment, accounting for 68.8% of the number and 34.2% of the value of Chinese total ODI (Rhodium Group, 2017). In Europe, private firms made 359 deals (63%) and USD 5,807 million (28%) in Chinese ODI (Hanemann and Rosen, 2012: 46). From 2002 to 2010, private firms increased their export from 4.3% to 30.5% of China's total export value (Huang, 2004 and 2011). By 2010, private firms contributed to 8.2% of the number of all Chinese investing entities and 1.5% of accumulated net stock of Chinese ODI. In the non-financial investment field, more than 70% of the private investors were from Zhejiang and Fujian Province (Ministry of Commerce of People's Republic of China, 2011). Last but not the least, in 2003, five Wenzhou's entrepreneurs from footwear, EE, printing and other industrial sectors joined in the commerce and trade mission of Premier Wen Jiabao to visit Africa, which broke the tradition that only SOE entrepreneurs could participate in the past. Since then, an increasing number of private entrepreneurs have joined in these missions and played growingly important roles in China's economic diplomacy. The private entrepreneurs from the Yangtze River Delta were the most active among their peers, accounting for 20% to 30% of the number of all entrepreneurs who participated in the missions by 2015 (Vista, 2016: 78). In 2010, the number of private firms listed on China's Top 500 Firms increased from 144 in 2005 to 172 and further increased to 207 in 2015 (Zhang and Sun, 2005; Wang, 2010; Yu, 2015).

In the post-WTO period, China witnessed a dramatic economic boom. From 2003 to 2010, according to the data of the World Bank (2017), China's GDP grew at a rate of 11.2% and its share of world GDP increased from 4.3% to 9.3%. Its GNI per capita increased from 44.9% to 72.5% of the world average. Its share of the world's merchandise export value grew from 2.7% to 10.8%. Its share of world manufacturing value added increased from 10.8% to 18.7% (UNIDO, 2016). By 2010, China was the largest recipient of FDI among developing countries, with a value of USD 105.7 billion (UNCTAD, 2011: 189). At the same time, more than 13,000 Chinese investing entities had established about 16,000 overseas firms in 178 countries (regions). Its ODI net flows and accumulated net stock volume stood at USD 68.8 and USD 317.2 billion individually, globally ranking 5th and 17th respectively (Ministry of Commerce of People's Republic of China, 2011: 2). In 2010, China had 48 firms (23 firms in the mainland) in the list of Global 500 firms ranked by the *Financial Times*. For the first time, a Chinese company, PetroChina, overtook Exxon Mobil as the world's most valuable company (Financial Times, 2010). In 2011, China's number of Fortune 500 firms jumped to 69 (61 firms in the mainland), the top Chinese firm, Sinopec Group, ranked the 5th, and China excelled Japan to be the second largest owner of Fortune 500 firms, following the USA with 133 firms (Fortune, 2011). In 2009, China replaced Germany as the world largest merchandise exporter with a value of USD 1,201.6 billion. In 2010, China overtook Japan to be the second largest economy in the world with GDP of USD 6,100.6 billion. In 2010, China's manufacturing value added of USD 1.92 trillion exceeded the American figure of USD 1.81 trillion (The World Bank, 2017) and China regained its reputation as globally the largest manufacturer after the USA had held this position for nearly 110 years (Marsh, 2011).[37]

Keeping with the pace of China's involvement in globalisation, Wenzhou also accelerated to integrate its economy with the world. In the second half of the 1990s, China got rid of the shortage economy and the supply and demand in the domestic market turned to be more balanced. Besides, an increasing number of foreign products imported or locally produced by FIEs provided Chinese customers with more choices, especially in the higher-end market. Wenzhou's products could not compete in the high-end market and thereby Wenzhou's firms took the initiative or were forced to go global to sell their cheap products and sustain their large manufacturing capabilities. They adopted diverse strategies, such as building specialty markets in foreign countries, adapting Wenzhou's overseas migrants as franchisers to sell existing products, conducting OEM for global buyers, seeking for technological cooperation with foreign companies, building joint venture companies, advertising brands and establishing overseas retail networks.

From 2003 to 2010, Wenzhou's export increased from USD 3.4 billion to USD 14.5 billion. By 2010, Wenzhou had 7,009 firms owing the rights of self-managed import and export, and it established trading partner relations with more than 200 countries (regions) (Statistics Bureau of Wenzhou Municipality, 2011). By 2008, Wenzhou had 529 private firms conducting ODI of USD 1.5 billion, which accounted for 1/3 of the numbers of total Chinese private investors and 8.07% of their accumulated net stock volume. Between 2006 and 2010, Wenzhou's ODI increased 23 times over the period between 2000 and 2005, reaching USD 0.41 billion (Shi, 2013; The Editorial Office of Southern Weekly, 2011; Ministry of Commerce of People's Republic of China, 2009). By 2008, Wenzhou had more than 440 private firms setting up international trade divisions in more than 50 countries (regions) and established 15 overseas specialty markets that brought more than 1,000 of Wenzhou's operations out of China. One footwear firm named Kangnai even opened more than 30 shops in the USA, France, Italy, Spain, Greece, Portugal and Belgium with the cooperation of Wenzhou's migrants to specialise in selling its branded products (Wang and Zhang, 2008).

Wenzhou's private entrepreneurs also actively used multiple governmental and civil organisations to boost their economy. Firstly, they expressed their interest appeals to the government through formal platforms of the People's Congress, the Chinese People's Political Consultative Conference (CPPCC) and Federations of Industry and Commerce. In 2008, 2 Wenzhou's entrepreneurs participated in National People's Congress and 3 entrepreneurs were the members of the National CPPCC (K. Chen, 2008). In 2010, 6 entrepreneurs acted as executive members and 4 as the members of the standing committee in Zhejiang Provincial Federations of Industry and Commerce (Local Annals Office of Wenzhou Municipal Government, 2011: 488). Secondly, they joined in the commerce and trade missions of national leaders to foreign countries and took the chances for commercial opportunities. Since 2003, more than 100 of Wenzhou's private entrepreneurs had accompanied national leaders on overseas visits, accounting for 10% of the number of all entrepreneurs in the missions (Zhong, 2013). Thirdly, they used industrial associations to maintain the competition order within Wenzhou and organise collective actions to increase their competitiveness over outsiders. By 2010, Wenzhou had more than 500 industrial associations, and 148 of them were at the municipal level (Jiang and Yu, 2011: 14). Fourthly, they founded more than 192 non-local commerce chambers throughout China and the world to facilitate Wenzhou migrants' business in respective regions and communication inside and outside Wenzhou (Local Annals Office of Wenzhou Municipal Government, 2011: 561). Lastly, they held regular World Wenzhou People's Conferences and World Wenzhou's Businessmen Conferences to bridge the connections and networks among Wenzhou's entrepreneurs and social elites. By 2013, Wenzhou had 0.6 million people in 131 countries and 1.8 million people throughout China doing business (Wu, 2013). In this year, around 1,500 guests in various fields from more than 100 countries (regions) and 211 domestic cities participated in the World Wenzhou People's Conference (Pan and Weng, 2013).

Wenzhou's IDs experienced restructuring in various aspects. Firstly, their production and products were improved. Most firms introduced more advanced equipment and production systems from developed countries to refine manufacturing process and improve product quality. Several large firms conducted technological innovations, enriched product categories and increased more added values to their production. Secondly, industrial concentration accelerated. After several waves of M&A, large firms greatly enhanced their power over SMEs in the production system. Some of them extended their backward and forward linkages to the whole industrial chains. Some even became involved in the fields of other related manufacturing industries and tertiary industries. From 2003 to 2010, large and medium-sized firms expanded their percentage of the total number from 0.2% to 0.4% and their proportion of industrial output jumped from 18.9% to 33.7% among all industrial firms (Statistics Bureau of Wenzhou Municipality, 2004 and 2016). Thirdly, the IDs were further integrated into GVCs. Some firms built or purchased manufacturing factories in Southeast Asian and African countries to use cheaper labour and resources. Some established R&D and sales divisions in several global cities of developed countries and purchased foreign brands for more advanced technologies, frontier designs and powerful sale networks. Besides, a few global firms entered Wenzhou's IDs for component supply, OEM outsourcing and strategic cooperation with local large firms. Fourthly, spatial relocation emerged. Some firms moved or built their manufacturing factories outside of Wenzhou to inland

China. Others relocated their headquarters, R&D and sales divisions to larger domestic cities, such as Shanghai and Hangzhou. Given the relocation, Wenzhou's facilities and networks remained the key nodes of corporate command and control in most of the firms.

Wenzhou's government successively put forward three industrial strategies to guide economic development. From 2002 to 2005, it set the development goal of a Global Light Industry City ("国际性轻工城"), which aimed to build Wenzhou as the important basis of production, collection, distribution and innovation for light industrial products in the world. It raised a "Ten Batches" Project[38] and focused on the development of a few selected outstanding firms in the key light industrial fields. It encouraged outstanding firms to use their advantages of capital, technology, talents and brands to cooperate with large domestic and global firms, to lead and support the development of their industries as a whole.

From 2005 to 2010, it conducted a strategy of boosting development by opening-up ("开放带动"). Setting the No. 1 Project of drawing FDI and foreign business, it tried to attract FDI and foreign firms, especially Global Top 500 firms, to build joint ventures and strategic cooperation with local large firms, to help local firms integrate and upgrade in GVCs and improve Wenzhou's existing industries to more advanced levels. It also endeavoured to build high technology industries, such as new material, IT and bio-medicine industries.

After 2010, it followed the policy of vacating the cage to change a bird ("腾笼换鸟"), which wanted to move out backward traditional industries for new strategic industries and develop service industry to replace manufacturing industry. It gave the priority to developing modern service industries, such as commerce, trade, logistics, finance, tourism and IT and encouraged capable firms to shift from manufacture to service industry. It focused on the new strategic fields of advanced equipment manufacturing, new energy, new materials, new generation of IT, energy saving and environmental protection. In addition, it attempted to cultivate several traditional industries to increase their production scale to above RMB 100 billion (USD 15 billion). Within these IDs, the government wanted to attract transnational corporates to build production bases, R&D centres, procurement centres and regional headquarters, encourage local large firms to forge a few leaders by M&A and nurture about 1,000 outstanding SMEs with expertise.

Despite these efforts, Wenzhou's economic performance after the twenty-first century posed a striking contrast with its past. From 2003 to 2010, Wenzhou's GDP growth rate was 7.7%, 3.5% lower than the national level. Its annual growth rates continuously ranked at the bottom 3 out of the 11 cities in Zhejiang Province. In 2003, Wenzhou's urban resident income was 21.7% higher than the Zhejiang level and 89.3% higher than the national level, but it narrowed to only 2.3% and 46.4% separately in 2010. It attracted in total USD 2.4 billion of FDI within the seven years, which was only 16.8% of Wenzhou's export value in the one year of 2010 (Statistics Bureau of Wenzhou Municipality, 2016). Besides, most of the FDI was from Wenzhou migrants rather than real foreign investors. Between 1998 and 2009, more than 250 firms moved whole companies out of Wenzhou, 1,000 firms moved some divisions, and more than RMB 100 billion (USD 15 billion) in capital outflowed from Wenzhou (Yang, 2009: 81). The number of firms headquartered in Wenzhou and listed on China's Top 500 Private Firms decreased from 33 in 2003 to 22 in 2010, then to only 9 in 2015. The rank of top 1 Wenzhou's firm declined from 13th to 30th and to 89th among China's Top 500 Private Firms (Chen, 2004; Li, 2010; Li and Zhuang, 2015).

In addition, given their considerable market shares, most of Wenzhou's private firms had not built strong brands and could not gain rich profits from their products. Regular disputes and diverse barriers of international trade also heavily attacked Wenzhou's economy. For instance, Wenzhou's metal lighter industry accounted for 70% of the global market share and 85% of the domestic market share with more than 500 firms and 0.5 billion of production volume in 2001. Most of these lighters were sold without brands at the factory price of about USD 2.5, but their final market price reached USD 65 or even higher. In this way, Wenzhou's firms only earned very limited profits while retailer giants had the major profits. What's worse, by 2010, most of these lighters were prohibited from entering the markets of the USA, Europe and Japan because they did not meet the technological standards required by the Child Resistance Laws in these countries. It resulted in overproduction of the ID, the decline of firm numbers by 86% and the drop of export value by 35% within the decade since 2004. The remaining firms struggled to find international customers and tried to survive in extreme difficulties (Local Annals Office of Wenzhou Municipal Government, 2002: 110; Local Annals Office of Wenzhou Municipal Government, 2005: 164; Wang and Ye, 2002; Local Annals Office of Wenzhou Municipal Government, 2015).

Moreover, in 2011, Wenzhou suffered from a serious financial crisis in its private borrowing and lending market, which involved around RMB 110 billion (USD 15 billion) in capital, 59% of firms and 89% of families and individuals (Wenzhou Government's Official Web Portal, 2011). The development of the financial crisis had deep economic, political and social roots and exercised far-reaching influence on Wenzhou's economy. As discussed, Wenzhou's private finance was very resilient and played indispensable roles in supporting local industrial development in history. After the 2000s, private finance was still the main resource for most SMEs (the main body of Wenzhou's firms) to fund their businesses. Formal institutions, like banks, were reluctant to lend money to SMEs due to the difficulty of supervision and the high possibility of their operational failure. Different from formal agencies, private finance operated in informal ways based on local people's social networks and interpersonal trust. It was common for local entrepreneurs to temporarily lend their money to friends or relatives to alleviate the short-term financial shortage of their firms. In the future, they could get support back from these firms when they needed money. Because of the frequent money exchange, some entrepreneurs even lent and borrowed money without formal receipts for loans.

After the mid-2000s, due to the profit decrease in their manufacturing business, many of Wenzhou's entrepreneurs allocated many funds to speculative fields, like property, copper, coal and steel, for quick gains of profits. Between 2008 and 2009, the State Council invested RMB 4 trillion (USD 580 billion) to stimulate the domestic economy and deal with the international financial crisis. Some banks in Wenzhou thereby relaxed their lending policies and encouraged firms to borrow loans if they could provide liability guarantees. Many of Wenzhou's entrepreneurs took advantage of the policy change and weaved a chain of liability guarantees ("担保链"). For instance, the entrepreneur of firm A became the guarantor for firm B, the entrepreneur of firm B became the guarantor for firm C, and the entrepreneur of firm C became the guarantor for firm A. In this way, all of them got access to loans from different banks and could support each other by robbing Peter to pay Paul. However, the operation of the chain highly depended on relaxing monetary policy and was very fragile to external and internal changes.

In 2011, when the government tightened monetary policy, many firms had difficulties in running capital flows. Once some firms were not able to pay back their loans, the firms of their guarantors were in trouble. Then domino effects happened in the whole chain quickly, which caught more firms that had backward and forward linkages with them in a wide range of industries in the trap. After the crisis, the central government set up Wenzhou as an experimental zone for financial reform. It put forward a series of measures to regulate informal finance, widen the scope for private investment and facilitate fund lending for SMEs. Although these measures helped alleviate the bad situation of financial crisis to some extent, the reform achievements were much less than expected. Many measures were difficult to realise in practice and the barriers for SMEs to get financial support still existed. The shortage of finance made it very difficult for SMEs to upgrade and further develop their businesses.

Because of the above phenomena, a succession of criticism on Wenzhou's economy emerged in the first decade of the twenty-first century. Some people claimed that the "Wenzhou Model" had been out of date and Wenzhou had fallen behind the times when China gained tremendous economic development. Some people thought that Wenzhou would not be important anymore to China's economic development in the new century because developing a market economy had already been a widely recognised goal. Some argued that Wenzhou's economic miracle in the 1980s and the 1990s was a coincidental result when its tradition of developing private economy happened to meet China's economic transition, but Wenzhou could not continue its glory in the 2000s because special historical conditions and its first-mover advantages had gone. Some people put forward that traditional industries that required low technology yet much labour brought the rise of Wenzhou's economy in the past, but they also resulted in its decline after the 2000s because Wenzhou was locked in low-end manufacturing and its production advantage of low cost faded. Given diverse opinions, most people shared the view that Wenzhou had encountered severe challenges and it needed economic transformation and industrial upgrade for further development.

In fact, many of Wenzhou's problems also appeared in similar ways in China's economy. Firstly, China's economic growth slowed down. In 2012, China's GDP annual growth rate dropped from 10.1% in 2004 to 7.9%, which was the first time that the rate was below 8% in the twenty-first century and the lowest point after 2000. Since then, the growth rate continuously went down every year and reached

6.9% in 2015 (The World Bank, 2017). Secondly, excessive capacity became a remarkable issue in various traditional industries. For instance, the State Council pointed out that by the end of 2012, the capacity utilisation rates in China's industries of iron and steel, cement, aluminium, sheet glass and ship were only 72%, 73.7%, 71.9%, 73.1% and 75% respectively. Firms in these industries suffered from a large drop of profits for a long time (The State Council, 2013). Thirdly, manufacturing cost increased dramatically. The Boston Consulting Group estimated that from 2004 to 2014, China's productivity-adjusted manufacturing wages increased by 187% to USD 12.47 per hour, industrial electricity costs grew by 66% to USD 11 per kilowatt hour (kWh), industrial natural-gas cost increased by 138% to USD 13.7 per million British thermal units. At the factory gate, China's manufacturing-cost advantage over the USA has shrunk to less than 5% (Sirkin et al., 2014: 4 and 10). China's cost advantages faded to other developing countries, like India and Mexico.

Fourthly, international trade frictions and disputes heated up. By 2016, China had continuously been the country that encountered the most anti-dumping investigation for 21 years and the one with the most anti-subsidy investigation for 10 years. Most of these investigations negatively affected China's labour-intensive industries. From 2011 to 2015, China had USD 55 billion involved in the cases of trade remedy investigation, which impacted about USD 140 billion to USD 150 billion of China's international trade (Zhao, 2016). Fifthly, capital outflow accelerated. From 2010 to 2015, China's ODI increased by 85% to USD 127.6 billion, while FDI grew by 18.2% to USD 135.6 billion (UNCTAD, 2005 and 2016). Its ODI exceeded its actual use of FDI at the first time. In 2015, China overtook Japan to be the country with the second largest ODI net outflow and it ranked the 8th in terms of accumulated net stock volume in the world (Ministry of Commerce of People's Republic of China, 2016). In 2014, non-SOEs increased their proportion of accumulated net stock volume in the non-financial sectors from 19% in 2006 to 46.4%, reaching USD 345.7 billion (Ministry of Commerce of People's Republic of China, 2015).

Besides these problems, the apparent success of China's economic achievement faded after a closer observation. Concerning technology innovation, despite big progress, most Chinese firms have not forged strong capacities. In 2015, only four Chinese firms were listed among the World's Top 100 Companies ranked by R&D. The total R&D investment of these four companies was only 75% of the volume of the German firm Volkswagen, the global top company in R&D expenditure (IRI-Economics of Industrial Research and Innovation, 2015). As to Fortune Global Top 500 Firms, most Chinese firms listed are SOEs supported by the state. In 2015, only six private firms from mainland China (excluding Hong Kong) were listed, accounting for 5.7% of the volume of all Chinese firms listed (Tang, 2015). These SOEs have large market shares in strategic industries, but their operation efficiency and technical capability are still not competitive with foreign firms, especially in technology-intensive sectors and high value-added segments. When it comes to FDI, it has brought instability and frailty to the local economy. In recent years, some FIEs started to move their factories outward from coastal China to Southeast Asian countries for lower manufacturing costs, which negatively affected China's regional economy. For example, the export and import of FIEs in Guangdong, the province receiving the most FDI in China, turned to continuous decline after 2013, from USD 357.3 billion and USD 234.8 to USD 333.0 and USD 209.7 in 2015 individually (Statistics Bureau of Guangdong Province, 2016). In terms of ODI, the total volume and influence of China's investment are not as strong as those of developed countries. In 2015, its accumulated net stock volume was only 18.4% of America's number. Besides, China's ODI in the high-income countries is negligible. Most investment was in developing countries (83.9%) and Hong Kong (59.8%) (Ministry of Commerce of People's Republic of China, 2016). As to export, Chinese firms are not competitive with FIEs. As Nolan (2014: 158) wrote, "China's exports of manufactured goods to developing countries mainly come from firms in the non-state sector. They mostly export low-technology, low value-added and non-branded goods or cheap counterfeit global brands. . . . China's exports of high-technology goods are mostly produced by the subsidiaries of global firms within China."

As development pioneers, Wenzhou's firms encountered development challenges of globalisation earlier than the firms in many other regions of China. They have already taken corresponding actions to respond to these issues, which provide relevant cases to examine the current challenges for Chinese private manufacturing firms. The following two chapters will focus on two pillar industries of Wenzhou's economy – the footwear industry and the EE industry. They will discuss in detail the global competition situation, firms' pressure in the competition, firms' response to the pressure and firms' difficulties in handling global competition. These two chapters will lay a solid foundation and reveal important insights for the conclusion of the study.

Notes

1 The Song dynasties include the Northern Song (960–1127) and the Southern Song (1127–1279). The Northern Song came to an end when enemies from the north conquered its capital Kaifeng (in current Henan Province). The Southern Song dynasty started when the provisional capital was founded in Yingtian (current Nanjing in Jiangsu Province). After 1138, the Southern Song moved the capital further to Lin'an (current Hangzhou in Zhejiang Province).

2 Maddison referred Intl$ to 1990 international Geary-Khamis dollars. See Table 2 in Appendix for more details. Given the advantage of quantification, the accuracy of Maddison's calculation was questionable, especially in the early periods of Chinese history when reliable statistical data were very rare. Maddison (2007a: 149) admitted that "[f]or the period before 1890, estimates of Chinese GDP can only be very rough judgements."

3 Quanzhou is a city in Fujian Province located beside the Taiwan Strait. It was China's major port for foreign traders during the eleventh and the fourteenth centuries. Marco Polo visited it and praised it as the largest trade port in the world.

4 Mingzhou is current Ningbo in Zhejiang Province. It played as a major port, along with Yangzhou and Guangzhou in the Tang dynasty and a major port for foreign trade in the Song dynasties.

5 The lines were written in the poem titled *Yong Yongjia* [An Ode to Yongjia], quoted from Zhou (1990: 8).

6 The definition of Jiangnan is diverse in different research. See Li (1991) for more discussion. This study refers Jiangnan to the broad area of the Yangtze River Delta, including Shanghai, Zhejiang and Jiangsu Province at present, covering around 219,000 km^2 of land area.
7 Data are quoted from Zhou (1990: 12).
8 Data are quoted from Zhou (1990: 14).
9 Wenzhou customs administration was revoked in 1293, but much evidence indicated that its foreign trade and communication continued afterwards. For instance, it was recorded that many famous Japanese Buddhist monks, such as Yuan Xuan, Yuan Tong and Zu Neng, successively took commercial ships to visit Wenzhou. In 1296, Yuan's diplomatic corps departed from the Wenzhou port for Cambodia and sent many Longquan celadons as gifts to Cambodian King.
10 The lines were written in the book titled *Beishan Xiao Ji* [Beishan's Little Collection], quoted from Teng (2013: 23).
11 The lines were written in the paper titled Yongjia Xian Chongxiu Haitang Ji [Notes on the Reconstruction of Sea Walls in Yongjia County], quoted from Chen (2005: 99).
12 The Yongjia School was originated in the Northern Song dynasty and matured in the Southern Song. Among all typical representatives, Ye Shi comprehensively expressed the ideas of the School and expanded its influence nationwide. See Zhou (2005) for more discussion.
13 According to Maddison, China's GDP per capita was stagnated at Intl$ 600 from 1300 until 1820 and then reduced to Intl$ 552 in 1913 and Intl$ 448 in 1950. However, many scholars based on diverse evidence believed that China's economy continuously developed rather than stagnation or decline. For example, Li (1998, 2000) revealed that during the Ming and Qing period, the productivities of both land and labour in Jiangnan's agriculture increased. By the 1930s, Jiangnan had been one of the most industrialised and commercialised areas in the world and one of the global centres for textile and fibre industries. Xu and Wu (2000) described that during the early and middle Qing, Chinese maritime trade was very prosperous. There were 5,000 sea-going ships in the ports of Shanghai and Zhapu, with burdens ranging from 100 to 150 tons. Some large merchants owned more than 100 large ships and employed over 2,000 people. Data source: Xu and Wu (2000: 362–364). Wagner (1997) quoted that in 1890 Foshan was called as the city of iron and steel wares where had almost one million working people. Data source: Wagner (1997: 73). Dawson (1964: 7) wrote that "[a]s late as 1798 Malthus declared that China was the richest country in the world." According to Rawski (1989: 344), "[b]etween 1914–18 and 1931–36, total output, as measured by gross domestic production, rose by two-fifths, implying an increase of 20–25 percent in inflation-adjusted output per head."
14 See Table 3 in Appendix for more details.
15 The putting-out system was a production system in which merchant-employers put out materials to rural producers who usually worked in their homes but sometimes laboured in workshops or in turn put out work to others. Finished products were returned to the employers for payment on a piecework or wage basis.
16 The lines were written in the book titled *Wenzhou Zhuzhici*, quoted from Chen (2005: 91).
17 The *Chefoo Convention* was an unequal treaty between the Qing and British empires. The official reason for the treaty was to resolve the "Margary Affair", but the final treaty included several items that had no direct relation to the killing of Margary. The "Margary Affair" was a crisis in Sino-British relations, which followed the murder of British official Augustus Raymond Margary in 1875.
18 Data are quoted from Cai (2010: 64).
19 These figures were official estimates based on the government's austere poverty line equivalent to USD 0.66/day (in constant 1985 PPP [purchasing power parity] dollars). Data source: The World Bank (2001: xiii).

20 The figures were estimated by the World Bank based on poverty headcount ratio at USD 1.90 a day (2011 PPP). Data source: The World Bank (2017).

21 Japan, South Korea, Singapore, Taiwan and Hong Kong experienced high and sustainable economic growth in the two to three decades after World War II and transformed from developing economies to newly industrialized advanced economies. Their achievements were known as the "East Asian Miracle". See The World Bank (1993) for more discussion.

22 See Table 4 in Appendix for more details.

23 The Nationalist Party of China overthrew the Qing dynasty and established the Republic of China in 1912. It was the ruling party of China until 1949, when it was defeated by the CPC during the civil war and retreated from the mainland to Taiwan Province. It was not until 1979 that military battles within the Taiwan Strait ended.

24 Very rare documents recorded the details of Wenzhou's private economy during this period, but the author's interviews with local government officials supported the view.

25 With the increase of capital scale, the uses of credit associations changed from financing consumption and production to serve as a profitmaking end, which thereby resulted in collapse and brought a series of financial and social chaos. Therefore, the government strictly prohibited all forms of credit associations. Other forms of private finance finally retreated due to the political and economic repression in 1989, were banned by the government or supervised by official financial organisations. Some research pointed out that although its overt prosperity existed only in a short period of time, private finance was resilient in Wenzhou, running in a more covert way afterwards until now. See M. Chen (2008) for more discussion.

26 See Nolan and Dong (1990) for more discussion.

27 The central government's attitude in fact was back and forth due to the conflict between the reformers and the conservatives. Wenzhou's development was interrupted by several episodic ideological campaigns, such as the "rectification of companies" campaign in early 1985 and the "anti-bourgeois liberalism" campaign in 1986–1987. See Liu (1992) for more discussion.

28 Since the 1980s, China's TVEs grew quickly because the SOEs were reformed and non-SOEs were permitted to enter many fields that were previously monopolised by the SOEs. Jiangsu Province used to take the lead in building TVEs for local development, which was known as the "South Jiangsu Model". After the mid-1990s, however, most TVEs in China were privatised because their collective ownership could hardly adapt to the development of market economy.

29 See Wu (2006) for more discussion.

30 Considering the firms with red hats, the actual numbers of private firm and their output were much larger than these figures. In 1992, the number of shareholding cooperative firms was 12,185, contributing to 29.7% of the total firm volume. Data source: Statistics Bureau of Wenzhou Municipality (1993).

31 The "358 Quality Project" aimed to spend three years in improving the quality of Wenzhou's products to provincial level, five years to achieve national level and eight years to reach international level.

32 The "828 Infrastructure Project" aimed to accomplish 28 important items of infrastructure within eight years.

33 The GDP growth rate refers to compound annual GDP growth rate adjusted for inflation.

34 The "Three Represents" referred to the goals that the CPC must always represent the requirements of the development of China's advanced productive forces, the orientation of the development of China's advanced culture and the fundamental interests of the overwhelming majority of the Chinese people.

35 This report calculated private firms, individual business and collective firms as private economy.

36 See Table 5 in Appendix for more details.

37 According to the estimate of IHS (Information Handling Services) Global Insight, China's global share of manufacturing output value reached 19.8% and the American share was 19.4% in 2011, so China became the largest manufacturing country in the year.

38 The "Ten Batches" Project refers to making an overall plan and separate plans for a batch of industries, accelerating to build a batch of featured industrial parks, facilitating a batch of leading firms in light industries, nurturing a batch of famous brands, creating a batch of information and R&D centres, cultivating and introducing a batch of talents with management and technical skills, establishing a batch of expert colleges and departments of light industries, improving a batch of market retail networks, organising a batch of product test centres and nurturing a batch of industrial intermediary institutions.

4 Case study I

Footwear industry

This chapter will discuss the first case study on the footwear industry. It will introduce the industry, reveal its global competition and display China's and Wenzhou's competitiveness in the industry. It will analyse three case studies of leading firms and discuss in detail their practices and development challenges.

Brief introduction of the footwear industry

Footwear is the garment that people wear on feet. Its history can be traced back to approximately eight thousand years ago, based on the discovery of sandals in what is now Missouri in the USA. Since then, footwear of various designs and materials has been developed in different civilisations all over the world. Footwear has dual aspects of practicality and indulgence. Shoes are outer coverings to keep feet warm and dry and provide comfort and protection from rough terrain. Also, they might be embellished with all manners of decoration to satisfy the indulgence of their wearers. In ancient times, shoes were status symbols to distinguish the wealthiest and highest-ranking members of society. At present, although shoes are affordable by ordinary people, they continue to reveal a great deal about people's identities. Shoes represent not only wearers' perception of themselves, but also how they would like others to perceive them and their roles in society.

The basic anatomy of modern shoes is recognisable and stable. A shoe mainly consists of a sole, heel and upper. The sole is the bottom of a shoe, composed of an insole, midsole and outsole. The insole sits directly beneath the foot under the foot bed and is attached to the lasting edge of the upper. The midsole is between the outsole and the insole, typically for shock absorption. The outsole is the layer contacting with the ground. The heel is the bottom rear part of a shoe to support the heel of the foot. The upper helps hold the shoe onto the foot. The inside part of the upper is lining to cushion, improve fit or reduce abrasion. The outside part of the upper is decorated. The upper usually has a mechanism, like a lace, to tighten the upper on the foot. The upper with the lace usually has a tongue that helps seal the laced opening and protects the foot from abrasion. The upper is connected to the sole by a welt that is stitched between it and the sole. The vamp is the front part of the shoe, starting behind the toe and towards the back part of the shoe.

In history, footwear was handmade by skilled craftsmen. Individual shoemakers, perhaps with the aid of apprentices, operated in small towns or villages where they made handsewn footwear for the local market. In large cities, firms operated with several shoemakers working together. It was not until the mid-nineteenth century that footwear production stepped into an industrial age. The second half of the nineteenth century witnessed some of the most significant changes. The USA took the lead in innovating and exporting shoemaking machinery. For instance, the Singer Sewing Machine, initially used to sew cloth, was modified in 1856 to sew leather and it enabled the stitching tougher of shoe uppers. Another machine was the Blake Sewer, invented in 1864, which made stitching soles onto shoes possible. The development of specialised shoemaking machinery promoted the establishment of modern factories in the USA and Europe, which tremendously enhanced footwear output. Since then, the mass production and industrial revolution of the footwear industry has spread all over the world.

The footwear industry has been traditionally regarded as a low technology intensive industry. However, many new technologies have facilitated the industrial development and accelerated the evolution of production mode. For example, IT is used to communicate product information globally and has further internationalised supply chains. Computerised cutting and stitching have greatly improved efficiency. Injection moulding enables the mass production of synthetic soles and heels. Tag-less labelling technology allows for increased consumer comfort, branding, cost savings and security management. In recent years, a series of more advanced technologies have made it possible to produce shoes in a more rapid, customised, diverse, energy-saving, labour-saving and eco-friendlier way. These technologies include computer-aided design, 3D printing, body scanning technology, wearable technology, nanotechnology, green manufacturing techniques and robotic automation. The development of these technologies might bring revolutionary changes to the footwear industry in the future.

Despite the innovation of advanced technology and machines, footwear production is still labour intensive in most countries at present. This is because to date, the expenditure of adopting advanced technologies is more expensive than the cost of using human labour in developing countries. Although many firms in developing nations have introduced some technologies and machines into their production, most procedures of their manufacturing still need to be operated with human intervention.

In factories, workers are often allocated into five departments to accomplish about 200 processes of footwear production. The first department is the clicking room, where workers cut shoe uppers from fine leathers using knives with very sharply pointed blades. The second is the closing room, where workers complete numerous processes required on the uppers. These processes include marking stitching lines, skiving, recording sizes, fittings, lasts and shoe numbers on linings, decorating the uppers, edging, binding and inserting eyelets. The third department is the rough stuff room, where workers cut heels, soles and welts. The fourth department is the lasting room, where the soles and uppers are jointed together using foot-shaped lasts, and heels are fastened in place. The fifth department is the finishing room. Workers trim, smooth, colour and poll heels, insert socks inside shoes to cover the insoles, attach trimming, thread laces and stamp shoes with size information and other labels. Once all the processes are finished, then shoes will be finally checked and polished before being placed into boxes.

During the past two centuries, commercialisation and consumerism propelled the development of the footwear industry. On one hand, footwear firms supplied a wide range of shoes in shops and made them available and affordable to almost everybody. Craftsmanship and designs were exhibited at global fairs and fashion shoes were widely advertised in media by stars and celebrities. Firms tried to promote shoes as a panacea to everyday problems: shoes could make people more fit, successful, attractive and as cool as sporting heroes and celebrities. On the other hand, consumerism rose along with economic growth and social liberation. Since the end of the nineteenth century, national wealth has increased greatly and rapid urbanisation has upgraded living standards. As a result, people became more willing and able to purchase shoes. Besides, social liberation stimulated more footwear consumption. For instance, the introduction of machines endowed people with more leisure time to do sports and outdoor activities, so the rubber footwear industry developed rapidly. In addition, the movements of women's emancipation improved females' social status and helped them go out of homes and take professional jobs. Thereby, women became important consumers with increasing purchasing power.

Nowadays, the global footwear industry is mature. Data from *World Footwear Yearbook 2015* (APICCAPS, 2015) show that the worldwide production of footwear reached 24.3 billion pairs in 2014. The international trade of footwear is highly developed and the number of pairs exported exceeded 16 billion with USD 133 billion of value. From 2004 to 2014, the quantity of exported footwear increased by 79% and its value grew by 144%. The world average export price increased from USD 5.79 to USD 8.12. In terms of materials, leather footwear contributed the most value, which reached USD 59.35 billion with 2.35 billion pairs in 2014. Rubber and plastic footwear accounted for the most quantity, with 9.4 billion pairs and USD 40.89 billion of value.

Since the 1970s, the global footwear market has increased dramatically, closely related to the growth of population and household disposable income. Population growth is a key driver in this industry. A higher global population leads to a larger demand for consumer products, particularly basic footwear. Household disposable income is influential on the quantity, quality and frequency of footwear purchases. From 1970 to 2014, footwear consumption per capita grew from 1.3 pair to 2.7 pair. From 1990 to 2015, the world's footwear expenditure per capita increased from USD 30.3 to USD 54.1. In 2014, the world consumed 19.39 billion pairs and USD 360.92 billion of shoes. These shoes were distributed mainly through three channels in the market: apparel and footwear specialist retailers (56% by retail value in 2015), department stores (13.1%) and online retailing (10.6%).[1]

In general, footwear consumers are sensitive to the aesthetics, quality, durability, comfort, function and price of shoes. However, specific consumption preferences vary from people to people. Based on consuming capabilities, consumers can be divided into high-, medium- and low-end groups. High-end consumers often pursue footwear with frontier fashion, big labels, customised service, luxury materials, profound meanings, high comfort and ultimate quality. Their consumptions of volume and value are high. Medium-end consumers like footwear with well-known brands, decent designs, reasonable price, good quality and good comfort. Their shoe expenditure is medium. Sometimes, they trade off between footwear price and quantity. Low-end consumers often choose shoes at low price. They don't care much about brands but expect shoes to have a nice appearance, a certain comfort and durability. Their footwear expenditure is low and often fluctuates with their disposable incomes. To medium- and low-end consumers, regular footwear is not a luxury item, but a rise in personal income can lead to increases of their demands for more expensive and a higher volume of shoes.

The gap of footwear consumption among different households is large. Take the largest developed country, the USA, and a developing nation, China, for examples. In 2015, the lowest 30% of households by income accounted for 13.6% of the consumer expenditure on clothing and footwear in the USA and 8.4% in China, but the highest 30% of households had 53.2% and 60.4% in the USA and China respectively. In the USA, the consumption of the highest 10% group on clothing and footwear was 6.7 times that of the lowest 10% group. In China, the consumption of the highest 10% income group was 23.7 times that of the lowest 10% group.[2]

When it comes to geographical difference, market demands vary in different regions. In 2014, footwear consumption per capita in North America and Europe was 4 times and 2.7 times the global average, but the Asian level was only 50% of the global average and the level of Middle East and Africa was only 42% of the average. Although people from developing countries have lower average expenditure than those in developed world, their total consumption volumes are large and increasing. In 2014, Asia consumed 52% of the global volume and 32% of the expenditure, followed by Europe with 17% (by volume) and 29% (by value) and North America 15% (by volume) and 23% (by value). With the rapid economic growth of developing countries after the 1980s, consumption capability of the Global South increased rapidly. In 2014, China, Brazil and India ranked as the top 10 global footwear consumers by both quantity and value. The three countries in total accounted for 33.5% of the volume and 21.5% of the value of global footwear consumption.[3]

As to gender difference, men and women have non-identical preferences. Men usually attach more importance to the quality and durability of shoes and their shoes are more similar in style. They are more likely to buy a few good-quality products than many low-quality shoes. In contrast, women are more aware of fashion and their shoes regularly change in style. Females are more likely to compromise high quality and durability with diversity and quantity. Nowadays, women's footwear accounts for the largest market share by value. With the rising purchasing power of women, the quantitative and qualitative demands of female shoes are expected to continuously increase.

In terms of product categories, leather and rubber shoes are the two most popular types. *World Footwear Yearbook 2015* (APICCAPS, 2015) displays that the average export price of leather shoes is USD 25.16, which was 5.8 times rubber footwear's price of USD 4.33 in 2014. Although leather shoes have been welcomed since the olden times, rubber shoes have gained popularity in recent decades, due to the rising awareness of sustainability and fascination of physical exercise. In 2004, leather footwear represented more than 60% by value and 30% by volume of the global exports and rubber footwear had more than 22% by value and 46% by volume. Ten years later, leather footwear accounted for 45% by value and 15% by volume of the global exports, and rubber shoes had about 30% by value and 60% by volume.

Global competition in the footwear industry

Industrial concentration

The global competition in the footwear industry is fierce and industrial concentration has been increasing in the recent decade. From 2006 to 2015, the top 10 largest firms by retail value increased their shares by 5.9% to 22.1% (Euromonitor, 2017). Although these comprehensive figures seem to be low, the levels of concentration greatly increase when taking a closer look at market segments of shoes with different categories, functions, qualities, materials and technologies. For example, in terms of occasions, footwear can be divided into athletic shoes and life-style shoes. In 2015, the global top 5 athletic footwear companies had about 45% of the market share, Nike ranking the first with 22.9% (Statista, 2017). The global top 5 lifestyle footwear companies accounted for 56.8% of the market share, Clarks ranking the first with 18.4% in 2011 (Di Maria and Webster, 2012: 3). The increasing concentration was due to massive M&A among industry participants. For instance, in 2015, New Balance Holding along with Berkshire Partners acquired the iconic comfort brand Rockport from Adidas Group with a deal of USD 280 million (Schneider-Levy, 2015). In addition, Sycamore Partners bought the luxury company Stuart Weitzman in its USD 2.2 billion acquisition of the Jones Group in 2014 and then sold its footwear brand for USD 574 million to Coach (Intrepid Investment Bankers, 2015: 2). The trend of M&A and concentration is expected to go on in the future.

Competition factors

In the global footwear industry, firms continuously compete in production cost, product quality, customer service, brand influence and R&D. In terms of production cost, the persistent chase for cheap labour has driven the global geographical shifts of footwear production. Before the 1950s, American firms produced the majority of shoes in the world. However, the increasing domestic labour costs forced them to outsource manufacture overseas and build offshore factories in less developed regions. In the 1960s, Italian firms emerged as competitive producers and exporters. As labour costs grew in Italy, Japan and South Korea showed their strengths in succession in the 1970s. After the 1980s, footwear firms continuously shifted manufacturing activities from South Korea to Taiwan. Since the mid-1980s, footwear manufacturers in developing countries, especially Asian countries, have gained their comparative advantages of mass production at low costs. Many footwear companies from developed countries outsource their products to these countries with a typical way of OEM. In 2014, Asia produced 88% of global volume and accounted for 62% of global export value of shoes (APICCAPS, 2015: 5 and 12). Take Deichmann, from Germany, the largest shoe store chain in Europe, for example. In 2016, it sold 173 million pairs of shoes at low price in 3,857 branches worldwide with 5.5 billion euros (EUR) (USD 6.1 billion) of turnover.[4] In 2014, it had approximately 100 direct suppliers, of which about 70% from China and 10% from Vietnam. The 10 largest suppliers of the company accounted for 80% to 90% of its outsourcing orders (Aronsson, 2014: 18). Another example is Yue Yuen, the globally largest footwear manufacturer, owned by Pou Chen Group from Taiwan. In 2015, it produced 317.5 million pairs of shoes with USD 8.4 billion of revenues, among which 42% of the volume was made in Vietnam, 32% in Indonesia and 25% in China (Yue Yuen Industrial [Holdings] Limited, 2016: 2 and 12).

When it comes to product quality, high-quality shoes are the concerted results of good materials, decent design, dedicated production and effective management of corporate and supply chain. Although the manufacture of low-end shoes mostly shifted to developing countries, firms from developed countries still conduct the production of high-end shoes. They devote themselves in exploring new materials, innovating advanced machines, improving process methods, creating trendy styles and enhancing chain management. All these activities contribute to high price tags of their products. Among all the firms in advanced countries, many Italian companies stand out by their high-quality products, such as Salvatore Ferragamo, Gucci, Prada and Tod's. They created the label of "Made in Italy",[5] which conveys ideas of quality, innovation, creativity and culture, especially for foreign buyers and markets. In 2014, the average export price of Italian footwear reached USD 50.92/pair, which ranked at the top among all exporters (APICCAPS, 2015: 17). Italian firms as well as other firms from developed countries gain more profits than manufacturers in developing countries within the production chain.

As for customer service, customers want to have more choices of shoes, access to more knowledge of the shoes and their companies, achieve more pleasure of selection, trying on and comparison, enjoy more convenience of payment and delivery and gain more responsive and friendlier service for feedback, complaints and refunds. To offer good service, footwear companies should supply a wide range of products with diverse styles, gain expertise in products and production, manage orders and stocks in real time, control the supply chain effectively and spread retail network widely. Take Clarks, from the UK, the globally largest player in casual lifestyle footwear, for example. It adopts multichannel strategies to take products to customers. It has opened Clarks stores in over 75 countries which offer customers great product range and personal service. It has also launched online shops and enabled customers to access products via Internet at any time. Besides, it has outlets, where customers gain generous discounts compared with normally high street prices. In addition, it has around 680 franchise stores around the world, so that it can use partners' local knowledge to delight customers (C&J Clark International, 2016). Moreover, it works with thousands of wholesale retailers to share products with all sorts of different customers.

Concerning brand influence, there are sets of marketing and communication methods that help to distinguish companies from competitors and create a lasting impression among customers. Customers usually evaluate brands through their price, quality and service, but they are also influenced by advertising and marketing. Customers' recognition of and loyalty to brands contribute to their added value and market shares. In 2015, companies from developed countries swept all the global top 10 footwear brands, Nike ranking the first. Nike, from the USA, the globally largest footwear brand, has committed high investment, continuous efforts and diverse strategies to advertise, maintain its reputation and enhance its brand image. It built deep brand connections to consumers by endorsements from high-profile athletes and sports teams, high-impact marketing in global sporting events and digital marketing (like social media and online campaigns). In 2015, its expenditure on advertising reached USD 3.2 billion, up to 10.5% of its revenue (Nike Inc., 2015: 80 and 86). Its brand value was estimated by WPP to be USD 29.7 billion, ranking at the first among the Top 10 Global Most Valuable Apparel Brands (WPP, 2016: 97).

As far as R&D is concerned, the competition exists in a wide range of aspects, including appearance designs, structure designs, material innovations, manufacturing techniques and production mode. R&D makes the shoes more durable, fashionable, comfortable and aesthetic, and makes the footwear manufacturing eco-friendlier, more energy-effective and time-saving. For example, Adidas Group from Germany has massive investments of funds and efforts in R&D. Its R&D on products is closely integrated with sourcing, design and marketing. Its R&D process engages not only internal resources, but also long-term and exclusive partnerships with well-established third parties, including athletes, partners, customers, universities, industry-leading companies and national and international governments. It has continuously invested in sports science, sensor technology and digital communication platforms, to be a leader changing the industry through technology. In addition, it attaches equal importance to the commercialisation of technological innovations. In 2015, 81% of its brand sales was from the latest product offerings launched in the same year. In 2015, its R&D expenditure increased by 10% from the previous year and reached EUR 139 million (USD 154 million), up to 8% of its net sales (Adidas Group, 2016). It positioned at the 681st in the world and the 188th in the European Union (EU) among top companies by R&D expenditure (IRI-Economics of Industrial Research and Innovation, 2016). In 2016, it successfully built a Speedfactory[6] in Germany which combined the R&D of sporting goods with an automated, decentralised and flexible manufacturing process. In the factory, high-performance sporting shoes are created faster than ever before and made almost entirely by robots. The intelligent robotic technology not only offers outstanding performance quality but also presents unique designs to shoes. What's more, the factory is greener by reducing the use of adhesives and shipping emissions.

China's footwear industry

In the global competition of the footwear industry, China has stood out as a very important player since the 1980s. It increased its production, consumption and international trade dramatically in the past few decades and its development situation has and will continuously shape the landscape of the global footwear industry.

Development history

China has a long history of shoemaking. The current archaeological finds discovered in Loulan of Xinjiang Province indicated that the first Chinese shoes traced back to at least four thousand years ago. Since then, Chinese shoes developed diverse functions, styles, materials and cultural meanings to meet the demands of their wearers from various backgrounds. For thousands of years, females made shoes at home for their family with their own handsewing skills. It was not until the Tang dynasty that shoemaking became commercialised and shoes became commodities in the market. After the nineteenth century, Chinese footwear manufacture stepped into industrial times. In 1853, the first factory, named Neiliansheng, was launched in Beijing to mass-produce textile shoes with machines. The modern leather shoes were firstly introduced into China in the 1830s and the first leather footwear factory was founded in Shanghai in 1876. In 1919, the first Chinese rubber shoes were produced successfully in Guangdong and a few factories were established in Shanghai to specialise in producing rubber shoes afterwards. During the early twentieth century, Shanghai was China's manufacturing centre of light industry products, including shoes. In 1937, there were more than 200 leather footwear factories in Shanghai and the number increased to 800 in 1945. Between the 1950s and the 1970s, the central planned economy regulated the Chinese footwear industry, and most private shoe companies were transformed to be SOEs. These firms obeyed state monopoly of purchase and sale and produced very limited categories and volumes of footwear. It was reported that at one time all soldiers, 90% of workers and 40% of farmers wore the same kind of sneakers called Jiefang shoes (Sa, 2016).

After 1978, the Chinese footwear industry started to develop rapidly. This was because footwear manufacture has comparatively low technological barriers and China had large resources of cheap labour and rich resources of raw materials. Also, there was a big footwear demand in the domestic market after a few decades of insufficient supply. What's more, Japan and South Korea's experience showed that developing an export-oriented footwear industry was a good way to engage in the global economy. To utilise these comparative advantages, improve domestic employment, satisfy residential needs and become involve in the global economy, China completely liberated its footwear industry and encouraged private and foreign capital to play in the field. Thereby, an upsurge of the developing footwear industry in coastal China appeared and Chinese footwear production and export increased quickly in the 1980s. In 1981, China exported USD 11.6 million of leather shoes and USD 73.61 million of rubber shoes. In 1990, the former figure increased more than 36 times to USD 427.91 million, and the latter grew 7 times to USD 540 million (National Bureau of Statistics of China, 1982 and 1991).

During the 1990s, China witnessed an explosive growth of the footwear industry and gradually developed into the world footwear manufacturing centre. From 1985 to 1995, China's footwear production increased from 1.6 billion pairs/year to 5.7 billion pairs/year (Xinmin Evening News, 2007). In 1997, China overtook Italy to be the largest global exporter by value with USD 8.5 billion (UN Comtrade, 2017). In 2000, its leather footwear export increased to 828.96 million pairs and USD 4.4 billion and rubber footwear export grew to 734.84 million pairs and USD 1.2 billion (National Bureau of Statistics of China, 2001). Moreover, three large footwear IDs took shape in Guangdong, Fujian and Zhejiang Province.

Guangdong is geographically close to Hong Kong and Macau, which had a more developed market and open economy than mainland China at that time. Besides, it enjoyed preferential economic policy as a Special Economic Zone, which provided exclusive benefits for foreign capital to invest in the local economy. Consequently, many foreign footwear companies chose Guangdong as the primary destination to undertake the global shift of footwear production from Taiwan. Guangdong thereby cultivated a footwear ID centred in Dongguan City, attracted many foreign firms to outsource a wide range of shoes, and developed export-orientated industrialisation and processing trade.

Fujian is the province inhabited by relatives of many overseas Chinese and returned overseas Chinese. When China launched its opening-up policy, many overseas Chinese were encouraged to invest in their hometown for local economic development. In the early 1980s, Jinjiang City in Fujian already had rich experience at making rubber slippers. With the help of overseas remittances, Fujian firstly developed its business of producing OEM rubber shoes for foreign brands. In the 1990s, it continued to specialise in rubber shoes and developed an ID centred in Jinjiang, but it started to nurture its own brands at the same time.

Compared with Guangdong and Fujian, Zhejiang has a more profound tradition of handcrafting shoes. In history, private and household factories of shoemaking flourished, and Wenzhou was famous for its leather products within and outside China. As soon as China reformed its planning economy, the local footwear industry revived quickly in the 1980s. Residents collectively funded their footwear firms based on their kinship and social networks. In the 1990s, these companies gradually expanded their scales from household factories to modern firms and made various categories of shoes with their own labels and sold them to both domestic and foreign market.

Since the twenty-first century, as labour costs have increased in coastal China, there have appeared geographical shifts of footwear production from the eastern region to inland China and Southeast Asian countries. Although in the early period, the phenomenon only adapted to a few firms, the shifts became prevailing and remarkable after 2005. In terms of domestic migration, many Chinese footwear firms in Guangdong, Fujian and Zhejiang moved or built their production bases in Sichuan, Chongqing, Henan, Anhui and Jiangxi provinces for cheaper labour. The preferential policy on lands, funds, taxes and public service from inland local governments accelerated the movements. Take Belle for example, China's largest footwear firm. In 2009, it made a contract with the Suzhou city government to build a new production base and planned to gradually move its production from Guangdong to Anhui Province. The project was supposed to be the globally largest leather footwear production base, with USD 0.1 billion investment and 533,360 m^2 of land, which was expected to hold 30,000 workers and produce 48 million pairs of leather shoes every year in the future (Belle International, 2014). Take Sichuan Province as another example. From 2006 to 2010, its increased figures of firms (above designated size[7]) and industrial value for garments, shoes and hats production reached 60 and RMB 9.8 billion (USD 1.4 billion), although the numbers were only 4 and RMB 876 million (USD 106 million) from 2003 to 2005 (Statistics Bureau of Guangdong Province, 2007–2011).

As for international movements, many global companies evaluated that Southeast Asian countries had developed their capabilities of production, logistics and material supply and their labour costs were much cheaper than the cost in eastern China. Therefore, they reduced orders from Chinese firms and shifted some outsource business, especially cheap footwear orders, to Southeast Asian countries, especially Vietnam. For instance, Nike steadily changed its primary destination of outsourcing from China to Vietnam during the 2000s. In 2008, it outsourced 36% of its footwear from China and 33% from Vietnam, but in 2015, its contract factories in Vietnam accounted for 43% of its outsourcing and Chinese factories only had 32% (Nike Inc., 2009: 5 and Nike Inc., 2016: 67).

Current situation

After more than three decades' development, China's footwear industry is mature at present. It has forged much strength, but it also encountered many challenges. On one hand, China has a large scale of production, market and export. As for production, China has been the global footwear manufacturing centre. It has cultivated a few footwear production bases in both the eastern and inland regions. As Table 4.1 shows, all these bases have forged their strength in different footwear segments. It was estimated that in 2015, China had more than 4,505 firms above the designated size and 3 million employees in the footwear manufacturing industry and created USD 121.4 billion of industrial revenue.[8] It was globally the largest producer and made 15.7 billion pairs of shoes, accounting for 64% of global output volume (APICCAPS, 2015: 5). When it comes to consumption, China is the largest consumer by volume and the second largest by value in the world. In 2014, its consumption reached 3.6 billion pairs (18.8% of the global volume) and USD 48.9 billion (16.1% of the global value).[9] Concerning export, as Table 4.2 displays, China has been globally the largest exporter since 1997 until now. In 2014, it exported 12 billion pairs, up to 74.1% of the global volume to more than 210 countries. It contributed 40.5% of the global export value with

Table 4.1 China's main footwear production regions, year 2013

Province	*Main Area*	*Industrial Output Value* (billion RMB)*	*Number of Firms above Designated Size*	*Main Products*	*Main Features*
Fujian	Jinjiang	267.26	–	Athletic shoes	Create own brand (medium-end) Flexible marketing strategy OEM for global brand (low- and medium-end)
Guangdong	Dongguan	205.11	1,773	Athletic shoes Leather shoes	R&D capability Latest information OEM for global brand (high-end)
Zhejiang	Wenzhou	150.93	1,780	Leather shoes Casual shoes PU women's shoes Export oriented safety shoes Rubber shoes Injected shoes	Create own brand (medium-end) Well-developed supporting industries OEM for global market (low-end) OEM for domestic market (low-end)
Jiangxi	Yingtan Shangrao	40.10	168	PU shoes	Cheap labour, raw materials and resources OEM for foreign market (low-end)
Anhui	Suzhou	33.52	256	Leather shoes PU shoes	Cheap labour, raw materials and resources OEM for domestic market (medium-end) OEM for foreign market (low-end)
Sichuan	Chengdu	28.04	156	Women's PU shoes	Cheap labour, raw materials and resources OEM for domestic market (low-end)

Data source: Statistics Bureau of Fujian Province (2014), Statistics Bureau of Guangdong Province (2014), Statistics Bureau of Zhejiang Province (2014), Statistics Bureau of Jiangxi Province (2014), Statistics Bureau of Anhui Province (2014), Statistics Bureau of Sichuan Province (2014).

Note: * Data of leather, furs, down and related production, shoes manufacturing.

Table 4.2 Global top 10 footwear exporters (by value, million USD), years 1990–2014

Rank	*1990*	*1995*	*2000*	*2005*	*2010*	*2014*
1	South Korea 4,307.1	Italy 8,091.8	China 9,850.2	China 19,052.5	China 25,633.9	China 56,248.7
2	Spain 1,524.0	Hong Kong (China) 7,790.2	Italy 7,135.9	Italy 9,138.4	Italy 9,852.1	Italy 12,290.8
3	Portugal 1,307.5	China 6,661.7	Hong Kong (China) 6,495.9	Hong Kong (China) 6,144.5	Hong Kong (China) 5,576.9	Vietnam 10,690.5
4	Brazil 1,183.6	Thailand 2,158.3	Spain 1,885.2	Vietnam 3,078.6	Vietnam 5,229.8	Germany 5,815.3
5	West Germany 1,179.2	Indonesia 2,055.2	Indonesia 1,672.1	Germany 2,530.3	Germany 3,942.0	Belgium 5,584.6
6	Thailand 790.8	Spain 1,960.4	Brazil 1,617.8	Belgium 2,528.6	Belgium 3,682.8	Hong Kong (China) 4,341.3
7	Indonesia 569.5	Portugal 1,846.8	Portugal 1,476.9	Spain 2,189.2	Spain 2,593.0	Indonesia 4,108.4
8	India 506.7	South Korea 1,505.9	Vietnam 1,471.7	Brazil 1,984.5	Indonesia 2,501.9	Spain 3,689.3
9	Switzerland 215.6	Brazil 1,498.8	Belgium 1,426.5	Portugal 1,599.1	Netherlands 2,443.3	Netherlands 3,623.6
10	Denmark 140.0	Germany 1,445.0	Germany 1,302.0	Romania 1,589.0	France 2,081.7	France 3,214.6

Data source: United Nations Comtrade database, DESA/UNSD, 2017.

Note: The statistics are based on the trade products with the commodity code of 64.

USD 53.84 billion, among which Guangdong exported USD 14.7 billion, Fujian USD 12.2 billion and Zhejiang USD 9.5 billion (APICCAPS, 2015; Statistics Bureau of Guangdong Province, 2015; Statistics Bureau of Zhejiang Province, 2015; Statistics Bureau of Fujian Province, 2015).

On the other hand, given its large scale, China's footwear industry is not strong. Firstly, most of the shoes made in China are low-end. One evidence is the low price of Chinese exported footwear. In 2014, China's average export price of shoes was only USD 4.44/pair, which was only 55% of the global average and 8.7% of the Italian level. The export price of the second globally largest player, Vietnam, was USD 16/pair, 3.6 times as high as the Chinese level (APICCAPS, 2015: 19).

Secondly, most of the Chinese footwear firms sit in the low value-added segments of the GVC and suffer from low profits. Most Chinese firms concentrate on the supply of raw materials and components and footwear manufacture, but they don't have sufficient capabilities of R&D, sales, marketing and branding. It was estimated that the production can create only 10% to 20% of the added value in the footwear industrial chain, but the operation of sales can make 30% to 40%

and R&D and branding achieve 40% to 50% (Guan, 2012). By 2015, no Chinese footwear firms had ranked as the world's top 10 sales or R&D companies. Most Chinese footwear firms in production gain much less profits than their peers in developed countries committed in sales, marketing, branding and R&D.

Thirdly, due to the increase of labour costs, China's advantages of cheap manufacturing have faded. Take Guangdong and Sichuan Provinces, for example. The footwear export volume in Guangdong continuously reduced after 2011 from 4.23 billion pairs to 2.96 billion pairs in 2014. Its export volume of 2014 was only slightly larger than the figure of 2.91 billion pairs in 2005 (Statistics Bureau of Guangdong Province, 2006–2015). In Sichuan, given its growth in the 2000s, the industrial value of garments, shoes and hats production continued to decrease from RMB 32.6 billion (USD 5.0 billion) in 2011 to RMB 27.5 billion (USD 4.5 billion) in 2014 (Statistics Bureau of Sichuan Province, 2012–2015).

Fourthly, the high-end footwear products in the Chinese market mainly rely on import or are produced by FIEs. China has an increasing high-end market, but domestic products can hardly supply it. The high-end market shares are dominated by mainly foreign global brands. After 2010, China's footwear imports from Italy increased rapidly from USD 80.8 million in 2010 to USD 267.5 million in 2015 (ITC, 2017). Table 4.3 indicates that in 2014, China ranked number 13 among the 15 globally largest footwear importers by value and its average import price reached USD 28.7/pair, ranking the highest among the top 15 largest importers.

Table 4.3 Global top 15 footwear importers (by value), year 2014

Rank	*Country*	*Value (million USD)*	*World Share (%)*	*Average Import Price (USD)*	*Average Import Price Rank*
1	USA	26,595	21.8	11.32	11
2	Germany	10,028	8.2	15.83	4
3	France	7,437	6.1	14.61	5
4	UK	7,110	5.8	10.47	12
5	Italy	5,504	4.5	16.48	3
6	Japan	5,452	4.5	9.24	14
7	Russia	4,318	3.5	13.87	7
8	Hong Kong	4,288	3.5	13.28	8
9	Belgium	3,676	3.0	13.01	10
10	Netherlands	3,621	3.0	13.02	9
11	Spain	3,175	2.6	10.03	13
12	Canada	2,408	2.0	14.17	6
13	China	2,031	1.7	28.70	1
14	Arab Emirates	2,008	1.6	4.82	15
15	Austria	1,868	1.5	21.50	2

Data source: APICCAPS, 2015.

Fifthly, Chinese firms have not forged brand influence in the world. By 2014, no Chinese footwear brand had been listed in the Global Top 10 Apparel Brands by WPP. Although Belle and Anta were ranked in the list of global top 20 brands by retail value estimated by the Euromonitor, they are not global brands because their revenues are mainly from the domestic market and their brand influence is limited within China. Take Nike and Belle for comparison. Nike's overseas business reached 54% of its revenue, but Belle's global business only accounted for 1.6% in 2014 (Nike Inc., 2015: 66; Belle International, 2015: 9).

Future trend

In the future, the footwear market will increase, the global shifts of footwear production will continue and R&D, sales and marketing and branding will be increasingly important for firm competition. With their strength and weakness, China's footwear firms are facing opportunities and challenges.

Firstly, the footwear market will increase. Many market reports estimated that the growth rate of the Chinese footwear market will be much higher than the global average from 2015 to 2020. What's more, with the rise of the middle class, the market for high- and medium-end footwear will increase. *Footwear Consumer 2030* (APICCAPS, 2014: 10) reports that the global number of middle class people will grow from 2.5 billion to 5 billion from 2015 to 2030. In 2030, the Asian and Pacific region is expected to have 66% of the global middle class, among which China will have a big share. The middle class usually prefers shoes with good quality, so the demand for medium- and high-end shoes will increase, but the market for the low-end shoes will decrease. With the optimistic market prospect, Chinese footwear firms have much space for further development. Big firms in mature IDs particularly have many advantages to produce a large scale of shoes efficiently. However, the changing market preferences put forward more requirements for firms to upgrade their products and improve their production. Only if they forge their capabilities of supplying good quality shoes can they share the promising market profits in the future.

Secondly, global shifts of footwear production might continue. Since footwear production is still labour intensive to date, firms have a consistent impetus of seeking for cheaper labour all over the world. The geographical shifts of footwear production from China to other less developed countries will be unavoidable, especially the production of low-end products. However, this is not to say that the future for China's footwear industry is doomed to be gloomy. History indicates that the global movements of footwear production did not destroy footwear industries in all countries and they did not happen overnight either. A few European nations, like Italy and Germany, survived from the shifts and maintained their export competitiveness. They delicately keep their strength by improving production techniques, leading design fashions and producing and supplying high-end products. Moreover, during global shifts, footwear firms from both developed and developing countries coexist and produce different kinds of shoes. If Chinese firms can improve their design, technology and management, they can upgrade their business to more sophisticated, innovative and value-added products and processes. If they fail to upgrade, then the future of the firms and the country will not be promising. In the recent years, some Southeast Asian countries, especially Vietnam, have displayed their comparative advantages quickly. In addition, some European countries, like Germany and Italy, aimed at rebuilding their power in footwear manufacture with Industry 4.0[10] strategy. Squeezed by the double pressure, Chinese firms for footwear manufacture are facing unprecedentedly stern challenges.

Thirdly, R&D, sales, marketing and branding are increasingly crucial for firm competition. The business of R&D, sales, marketing and branding put forward high demands to firms' capabilities of operation, finance, sales and marketing and challenge their knowledge and skills to influence and interact with customers. New business forms, such as Internet retailing, will bring more opportunities as well as competition to traditional operations. It is highly important for firms to accurately manage and rapidly adjust their products and production chains based on the changing market preferences. For most Chinese firms, all these tasks are tough, but they are also opportunities for further development. For export-oriented firms, improving their design capability and expanding their sales channels are necessary to gain stable orders and maintain their business. Creating company brands to attract international buyers is also a good way to increase their bargain powers over buyers for more profits. For the firms that serve the domestic market, leading domestic fashion, mastering their sales network and creating their brand influence are effective approaches to resist the pressure of increasing production costs and invasions of global brands. Since manufacturing costs are increasing, firms must increase the added value of brands to maintain reasonable profits. Moreover, many large domestic firms have wide sales networks within China and have good local knowledge. It will be a tough mission for them to learn how to improve their brand into the higher-end market and extend their brand impact to foreign customers.

Wenzhou's footwear industry

Among all the footwear production bases in China, Wenzhou has been honoured as China's Shoe Capital since 2001 and it has been famous for producing leather shoes for hundreds of years. As Table 4.4 shows, it produced RMB 86.5 billion (USD 14.2 billion) of industrial output, 12.4% of China's footwear output volume, 8.9% of China's export value and 5.7% of China's footwear export quantity in 2014. It was estimated that 65% of Wenzhou's footwear industrial revenue was from domestic sales and the other 35% from export business. It had 8 national honours in the shoemaking field, produced the most diversity of footwear in the country and created more than 350,000 jobs. It had 3,647 enterprises producing shoes for both the domestic and international market. Most of these firms are totally invested by local entrepreneurs and operated by the private sector. Some of them have good competitiveness in the domestic and international market. As a pioneer and most influential player, Wenzhou provides important reference to studying China's development challenges in the footwear industry.

Table 4.4 Development indices of Wenzhou's footwear industry, year 2014

Indices	*Data*
Output quantity (billion pair) (year 2011)	1.6 (leather shoes 1, rubber shoes 0.3) 12.4% of China's footwear output
Output value (billion RMB)	86.5
Employment	350,000
Enterprise number	3,647
Number of enterprises above designated size	742 77.1% of Wenzhou's footwear output value
Number of enterprises above RMB 100 million	80+ (year 2013)
Number of enterprises above RMB 1 billion	6 (year 2013)
Number of high-technology enterprise	13 (year 2013)
R&D investment (billion RMB)	6.41 (year 2011)
Number of listed enterprise	2
Tax (billion RMB)	State 2.38 Top 2 highest among Wenzhou's total industries Local 0.79
National honour	China's Shoe Capital China's Synthetic Leather Capital China's Casual Shoes Producing Base China's Rubber Shoes Famous City Women's Shoes Base of China's Shoes Capital Men's Shoes Base of China's Shoes Capital China's Leather Capital China's Shoe Capital Safety Shoes Famous City
Domestic market share	12.78 % (year 2013)
Terminals and point of sale	70,000+
China's Famous Brand	7 (year 2013)
China's Famous Trademark	92 (year 2013)
China's Famous Export Brand	3 (year 2013)
Firms awarded as China's Genuine Leather Shoes Leader King	5 (year 2015) Account for 5/15 of the list
Firms awarded as China's Genuine Leather Shoes King	4 (year 2015) Account for 4/10 of the list
Firms awarded as China's Genuine Leather Famous Shoes	5 (year 2015) Account for 5/15 of the list
Export quantity (billion pair)	0.694 5.7% of China's footwear export quantity
Export value (billion RMB)	29.57 8.9% of China's footwear export value 25.94% of Wenzhou's total export value
Average export price (USD)	6.94 1.6 times than China's footwear export average
Exported destination country	150+
Main export destination	EU, USA, Russia, Africa

Data source: The author's summary.

Development history

Wenzhou has a profound tradition of footwear making. Its development history can be divided into the following five stages.[11]

Embryonic stage (before 1978)

The history of Wenzhou's footwear production can be traced back to the Southern Song dynasty when Wenzhou's households specialised in making leather shoes. In the Ming dynasty, Wenzhou's leather production was famous around the country and its leather was listed as an imperial tribute due to their excellent quality and handicraft. During the following hundreds of years, its leather shoemaking continuously developed despite ups and downs. In the 1920s, there appeared streets for making leather and leather shoes, and the leather manufacture industry took primary shape in Wenzhou's downtown. In the 1930s, Wenzhou's leather products spread over the country and were exported to some Southeast Asian countries, like Singapore, Philippines and Indonesia. Household workshops gradually became the basic formation of footwear firms. In the 1950s, Wenzhou had 43 footwear workshops with 103 employees. In the following two decades, however, most private firms and factories were closed or nationalised because of the socialist reform of industry and commerce and the movement of rural cooperative transformation. In 1978, only 19 footwear firms remained in Wenzhou.

Rise stage (1978–1987)

Thanks to the economic reform and opening-up, Wenzhou's footwear industry regained its vitality and developed rapidly. Many employees of pervious SOEs and collective firms started to build private footwear firms after the 1980s. Meanwhile, a great number of Wenzhou people, working as salesmen, travelled around the country to sell Wenzhou's shoes and bring back orders. With the huge domestic demand, Wenzhou's footwear industry developed dramatically. At one time, there spread the upsurge of shoemaking from one household to the whole village and from one village to the whole country. The number of footwear firms increased from 19 in 1978 to more than 6,000 in 1987. At that time, most of the firms were very small and had backward producing facilities, so many of their products were low quality and substandard. In some extreme examples, their shoes would be worn within one week or even one day. In 1987, 5,000 pairs of Wenzhou's low quality shoes were burned in the Wulinmen Square of Hangzhou, which gave Wenzhou a notorious reputation all over the country, which was regarded as a quality crisis of Wenzhou's footwear industry.

Growth stage (1987–1999)

To deal with the crisis, 30 large firms in Wenzhou spontaneously organised an industry association in Lucheng District in 1988, aimed at managing product quality and competitive order. In 1993, the local government put forward the strategy of "building market based on product quality and developing industries based on brands" and published the first local regulation on quality management in China, proposing specific measures to guarantee product quality. Due to the diverse pressure from the market, the government and the industry association, footwear firms were forced to improve their product quality. Some firms started to specialise in certain processes of shoemaking and commit to providing supporting components. Thereby, Wenzhou steadily cultivated a footwear production chain on a small scale and wide cooperation. For example, there appeared the production of shoe soles in Baishi Town of Yueqing County, shoe decoration in Huangtian Town of Yongjia County and the leather specialty market in Shuitou Town of Pingyang County. In addition, Wenzhou's salesmen enhanced their retail network all over the country and even expanded it to foreign countries, especially Russia. After more than 10 years' effort, Wenzhou's footwear finally improved their quality and rebuilt its public trust.

Mature stage (1999–2008)

In 1999, Wenzhou's entrepreneurs burned 2,000 pairs of bogus imitations of Wenzhou shoes in Hangzhou. This event was a milestone for Wenzhou's footwear industry and it entered the mature stage afterwards. In 2001, the China National Light Industry Council and the China Leather Association awarded Wenzhou the title of China's Shoe Capital. Despite the shrinkage of the total number of footwear firms, dozens of large companies emerged in Wenzhou with their production capabilities and domestic brand influence. During the stage, Wenzhou nurtured a series of brands with domestic influence, like Aokang, Kangnai and Red Dragonfly. Moreover, several of Wenzhou's large firms got in contact with global retailers and built steady and long-time relationships with them by their competitive price and reliable product quality. Wenzhou's footwear was widely exported to the EU, America and Russia and became a pillar exporting industry in the city. In 2008, Wenzhou had 770 footwear firms above the designated size and developed a mature industrial system with a wide range of supporting industries, such as machine manufacture and chemical leather, in different regions of the city.

Transformative stage (2008–present)

Since 2008, Wenzhou's footwear industry has encountered a series of difficulties and entered its transformative stage. After the 2008 global economic crisis, the growth of the global footwear market slowed down, and some developed nations therefore adopted trade protectionism to support domestic industry. Many global retailers and footwear companies outsourced more products from Southeast Asian countries due to their lower labour cost. With the declining number of global orders, production overcapacity in Wenzhou became notable. What's worse, the labour cost in Wenzhou increased greatly especially after the implementation of the New Labour Law in 2008 and thus the profit of making low-end footwear became very thin. According to one survey conducted by the Lucheng Footwear Association in July 2015, the number of footwear firms in Lucheng, the most important region of Wenzhou's footwear industry, dropped from more than 500 in 2008 to about 170 and it would be very likely to further decrease by 30 to 40 firms per year. Moreover, less than 37% of investigated firms were in good operation and most of them, especially SMEs, were teetering on the brink of ruin. In addition, some previously well-known large firms were also at the edge of bankruptcy. Therefore, the issue of transforming and upgrading the footwear industry became a remarkable task for Wenzhou at the transformative stage. The Wenzhou government released a few project plans, aiming at tackling these problems and upgrading the footwear industry.

Current situation

At present, Wenzhou's footwear industry has its diverse strengths as well as many predicaments.

Wenzhou's footwear industry has its strengths of a developed production chain, broad sales network and thriving self-owned brands.

Firstly, Wenzhou has formed a mature industrial chain of footwear production with complete backward and forward linkages.[12] As Figure 4.1 illustrates, it includes three main manufacturing industries of footwear, leather and leather goods and a range of supporting industries of shoe materials, moulds, decorations, lasts, leather chemical and synthetic leather. These industries contain more than 2,000 firms and almost one million employment. Map 4.1 indicates that Wenzhou has

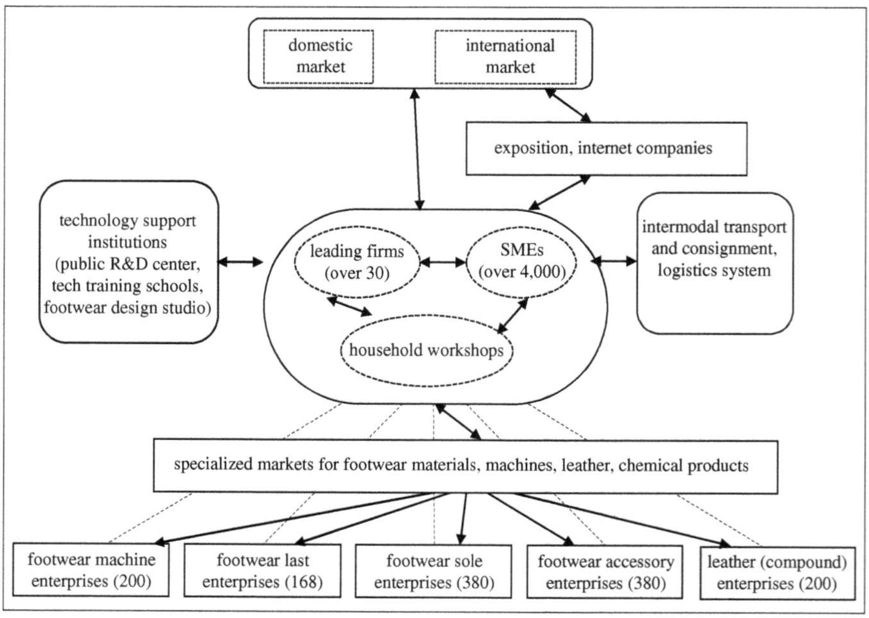

Figure 4.1 Structure of Wenzhou's footwear production chain

Note: The author drew the figure. Data source: Huang et al. (2008: 411).

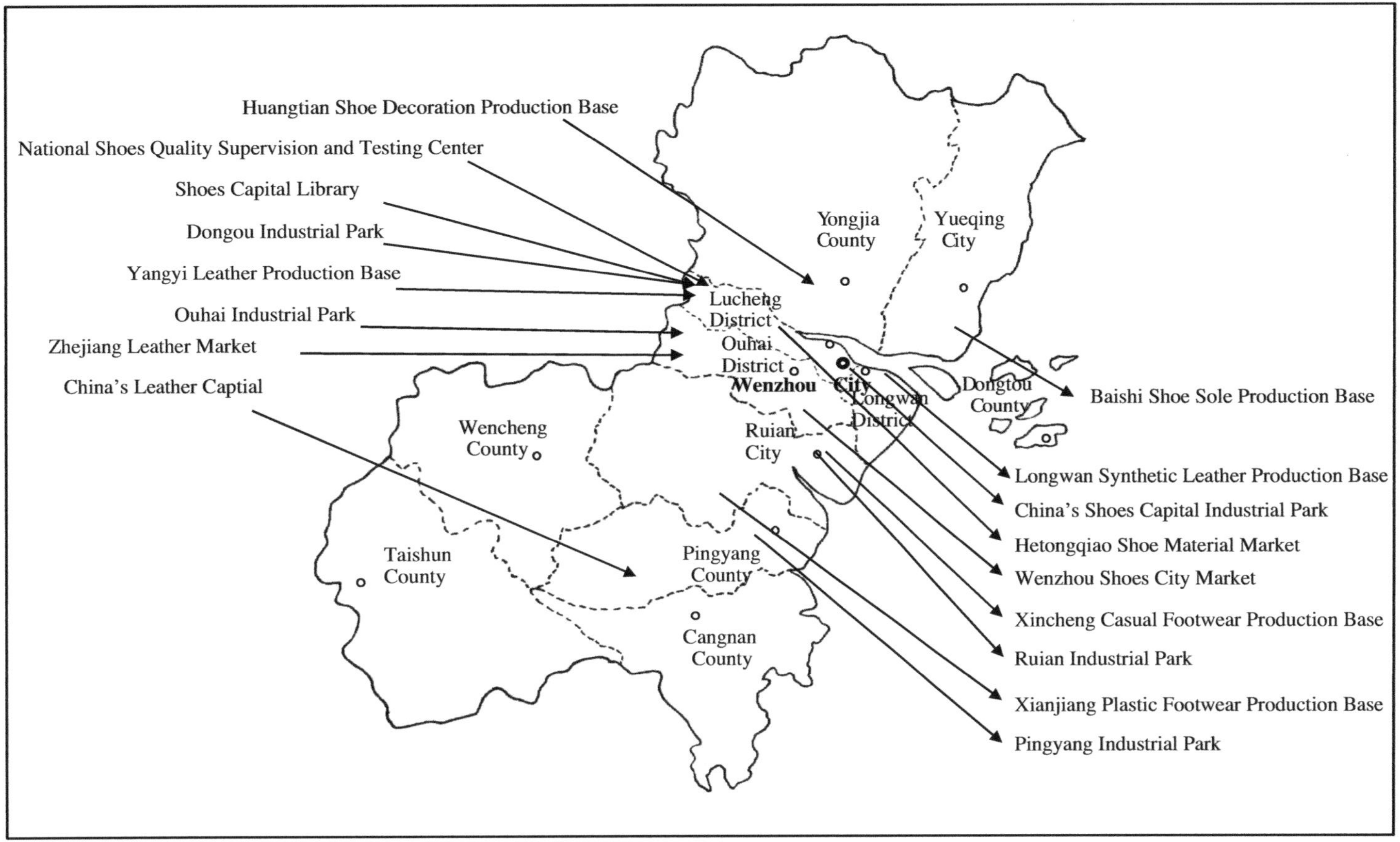

Map 4.1 Geographical distribution of Wenzhou's footwear industry

Note: The author drew the map. Data source: Gao and Zhang (2002).

developed about 6.5 km^2 of footwear industrial parks and several large industrial regions in Lucheng District, Ouhai District, Longwan District, Yongjia County, Ruian County and Cangnan County. In addition, it built dozens of specialty markets and public organisations, such as the Wenzhou Footwear City Market, National Footwear Quality Supervision and Testing Centre, Leather Research Centre, Footwear Library, Footwear Culture Museum, National Footwear Production Standardisation Technology Council and Public Bonded Warehouse. Many R&D agencies were established and provide technological support for firms. In 2011, Wenzhou invested RMB 6.41 billion (USD 986.2 million) on footwear R&D and possessed 730 footwear innovation patents (Wenzhou Municipal Government, 2014b). Moreover, since 1995, Wenzhou has held the Global Leather Exhibition every year to advertise Wenzhou's shoes and promote the exchange of information and technology among footwear firms within and outside China.

Secondly, Wenzhou has built a comparatively broad sales network. For the domestic market, its network mainly consists of chain stores, specialty markets and retail points. Among them, chain stores are the most popular. Most of the retail stores are independent agents developed by branch offices of Wenzhou's footwear companies all over the country. For the global market, OEM for transnational retailers and supply for Chinese overseas footwear stores are the most common forms. Nowadays, Wenzhou's footwear has more than 70,000 retail terminals and 12.78% of the market share in China, and 150 export destinations all over the world. Additionally, with the rise of Internet sales, some of Wenzhou's firms have developed their online sales channels and are trying to build a united system for online and offline sales.

Thirdly, Wenzhou's firms have a strong awareness of brand making since the 1990s. Currently, Wenzhou has been the place with the highest density of footwear self-owned brands in China. When it comes to brand honours awarded by relevant administrative organisations, in 2013, Wenzhou had 7 China's Famous Brand, 92 China's Famous Trademark, 3 China's Famous Export Brand, 48 Zhejiang Famous Brand and 37 Zhejiang Famous Trademark. What's more, it made 5/15 of China's Genuine Leather Shoes Leader King, 4/10 of China's Genuine Leather Shoes King and 5/15 of China's Genuine Leather Famous Shoes. As to market shares, however, Wenzhou's brands are small currently. In 2015, it had only 1 brand among China's top 10 largest footwear brands by retail value. Aokang had 1.3% of the market share and ranked eighth.[13]

Given its multiple strengths, Wenzhou's footwear industry has predicaments of fading comparative advantages, fragile industrial structure and low-end locking dilemma.

Firstly, in recent years, Wenzhou's comparative advantages of labour cost, export and retail channels have gradually faded. Its labour costs have increased greatly. From 2003 to 2013, the average wage of the footwear industry in Wenzhou increased by 3.5 times to about RMB 3,000 (USD 484)/month. What's more, the New Labour Law imposed on firms more burdens and strict requirements of social security fees for their employees. Thus, the current labour cost in Wenzhou is much higher than the average costs in China and other developing countries.

Secondly, Wenzhou has some disadvantages in exporting tariffs compared with other developing countries. Take Vietnam, for instance. In 2015, with the achievement of the Vietnam-EU Free Trade Agreement, Vietnam was free from the tariff when exporting footwear to the EU. On the contrary, Wenzhou's firms still bear a tariff at the rate of more than 15%, which greatly influenced their competitiveness in the EU, one of their main international markets. Thirdly, new business models have pounded Wenzhou's traditional strength of chain stores. With the rise of business forms like shopping malls and online shopping, chain stores are getting less popular among customers, especially youngsters and the middle class. Product overstock in chain stores becomes a remarkable problem and many firms fall into the throat-cutting competition of low price.

The industrial structure of Wenzhou's footwear ID is fragile. Firstly, the sizes of firms are not very big. In 2013, Wenzhou had 2 listed firms, 6 companies with annual sales above RMB 1 billion, and more than 80 firms reaching sales of RMB 100 million (USD 16 million) (Wenzhou Municipal Government, 2014b), but most firms are SMEs. Compared with other production regions, even the large firms in Wenzhou are also comparatively small. Take Aokang, Wenzhou's largest footwear firm, and Belle, the largest footwear firm in China, for example. In 2014, Aokang's operation revenue was RMB 2,965 million (USD 486 million) and employment was about 7,000, which were only 8% and 35% of Belle's figures separately (Zhejiang Aokang Shoes Limited Company, 2015; Belle International, 2015). The relationship among firms and organisations within the production chain is loose. The R&D platforms are lacking constant support from the government and firms, so that their innovation can hardly transform to commercial products. The coordination among the material production, specialty market and retail channels is poor, so that they cannot reflect the change of the market demand and pass on information and knowledge within the production chain in good time. Moreover, finance has become a big issue in the production chain. Many footwear firms involved in the financial crisis in 2011 and its after-effects have continuously endangered the operation of more firms. The shortage of funds is a great barrier for most SMEs to upgrade and transform their business. Larger firms are also cautious and hesitant to invest in R&D due to the big uncertainty of innovation itself and their pessimistic estimate on the industrial prospects.

Wenzhou is stuck in the dilemma of low-end locking. First, most of Wenzhou's products are low-end and homogenised. Most firms follow designs in the market, use similar materials and even outsource from the same OEM factories. Therefore, the competition among firms is mainly in price. As to the domestic market, even branded shoes are sold at the average price of RMB 200 (USD 29)/pair. For the global market, the average export price is only about USD 6.94/pair. The fierce price competition decreases firms' profits and makes it more difficult for them to improve products. Second, retail channels for Wenzhou's products are low-end. In the domestic market, most of Wenzhou's shoes are sold at small chain stores along streets. In the international market, overseas Chinese sell most of the products in non-branded shops in Chinatowns. These retail channels are not ideal to market and advertise high-end footwear products. Third, although Wenzhou has a couple of thriving self-owned brands, most of them have limited brand influence. Within China, no Wenzhou brand has been regarded by WPP as a Most Valuable Top 100 Chinese Brand. Outside China, Wenzhou's branded sales are almost negligible. In 2014, Aokang's overseas business only accounted for less than 5% of its sales, among which a large part was for OEM orders (Zhejiang Aokang Shoes Limited Company, 2015).

Leading firms

Given the current situation, several firms are exploring pilot strategies to make breakthroughs for the further development of Wenzhou's footwear industry. Among them, the Juyi Group, Zhejiang Aokang Shoes Limited and Menglani Shoes Limited are typical examples.

Juyi group

The Juyi Group was founded by Mrs Li Ailian, who discontinued study in the first year of junior high school due to her poor family background. Thanks to her hard work and strong character, she became the director of a street-run firm, Xiangyang Footwear Factory, in 1979. In 1987, the factory suffered from bleak business because Wenzhou's quality crisis destroyed customers' trust in Wenzhou's shoes at that time. Mrs Li thereby resigned from the factory in 1988 and bought a firm called the Juyi Footwear Factory from the Juyi brigade with RMB 5,000 (USD 1,351) of her savings, aiming at exploring a better way for Wenzhou's footwear industry. After a few years, her factory produced more than 500,000 pairs of shoes and indirectly exported more than 50,000 pairs to Miami in the USA. It then developed from a small household factory to a group firm in 1995. Due to her excellent performance, Mrs Li was awarded a lot of honours, including National Top 10 Famous Female Entrepreneur and National Outstanding Example of the Footwear Industry. She was received by several central government leaders, such as Deng Yingchao and Kang Keqing, and even invited to make a speech to the United Nations' World Conference on Women in 1995.

In 1996, Mrs Li's son, Mr Pan Jianzhong took up the position of General Manager and started Juyi's career with the leadership of the second generation. Due to his expertise in footwear machinery, he introduced the factory to assembly lines and helped it to achieve mechanised production in 1993. At that time, Juyi was the first firm in Wenzhou with assembly lines. In 1995, he amalgamated a Taiwanese-funded footwear enterprise and hired a Taiwanese professional manager, aiming to improve the production management in Juyi. After 1997, Mr Pan started to explore the export business and participate in a lot of international exhibitions. Thereby, Juyi got acquainted and achieved OEM orders from several foreign customers. Mr Pan's efforts helped him to win the honour of Zhejiang Excellent Entrepreneur and Zhejiang Footwear Influential Manager. In 2005, he was invited to visit European footwear firms together with President Hu Jintao.

As an export-oriented firm manufacturing OEM products, Juyi's production process is as follows: a foreign buyer gives shoe samples and order requests, such as volume, quality, purchasing price and delivery time, to its supplier firms like Juyi and asks them to make a bid. The buyer decides the winners of the bid based on their performance-price ratio. It also considers the balance of order distribution in different regions. If Juyi wins the bid, then it will arrange its production process according to the delivery dates. It will analyse shoe samples, purchase related materials, manage labour distribution and confirm its sample products with the buyer. If the buyer is happy with its sample products, then Juyi starts to manufacture the shoe order on a large scale. During the process, it must coordinate production progress, make regular reports to the buyer and most importantly control product quality. Finally, it delivers the products via sea transportation in a good time. Due to the long distance and time of shipping, winter boots must be produced in summer and summer sandals should be made in winter. It is a key task for Juyi to gain large and constant orders so that it can stably feed experienced workers and achieve the best benefits of scale economy. To gain orders, it must make every effort to reduce manufacture cost, maintain product quality and ensure punctual delivery.

Nowadays, Juyi has developed to be one of the largest and most influential export firms in Wenzhou. It has more than 15 assembly lines and achieves the production capability of 15 million pairs every year. It has about 3,000 employees and more than 100,000 m^2 of factory area in Wenzhou. In 2006, it built a second production base in Shangrao in Jiangxi Province to take advantage of cheaper labours in inland China and specialise in producing female polyurethane (PU) footwear. Its OEM products were widely sold in European countries. In 2014, it exported more than 10.23 million pairs and RMB 473.7 million (USD 75.2 million) of footwear, ranking as the second largest export firm in Wenzhou. It has been awarded the honours of Top 500 China's Private Firm, Custom AA Management Firm, National Inspection-free Export Firm, Zhejiang High-technology Firm and the Zhejiang Quality Prize.

Despite its strength, Juyi has encountered increasing pressure in the recent years due to its internal and external challenges. In terms of internal pressure, labour is a remarkable problem. On one hand, it is not easy for Juyi to hire skilled workers and retain existing workers, which challenges the product quality. On the other hand, the employees' wage and insurance expenditure increase greatly and fast. In terms of external pressure, its OEM purchasers demand increasingly higher product quality but offer a lower procurement price. With the threat of order reduction from OEM buyers, Juyi has struggled to take a range of measures for survival.

The first measure was to introduce intelligent machines. In the recent years, it imported a series of intelligent machines mainly from Italy and Japan. They included automatic cutting machines, computer-controlled stitching machines, computer-controlled laser machines, automatic pin buckle machines and 3D printers. These machines helped Juyi achieve automatic manufacture in some of its production processes. Thanks to his expertise in machinery, Mr Pan provided foreign machine companies with detailed parameters and fine-tuning plans for making footwear machines based on Juyi's practical manufacturing experience. Mr Pan was thereby awarded as 2015 China Famous Leader in the Leather Industry and Juyi became an outstanding model to show automatic production in the footwear industry. The adoption of these machines brought various benefits. It increased Juyi's production rate and the rate of good products, decreased energy consumption, production costs, workplace accidents and numbers of labourers.

The automatic cutting machines and computer-controlled stitching machines were the most outstanding examples to explain the advance of automatic production. Traditionally, cutting shoe materials was very time-consuming and labour-intensive. The workers had to arrange and draw the layout of different shapes on every piece of materials, and then cut them with the help of knives under traditional cutting machines. However, the Italian automatic cutting machines introduced by Juyi totally changed the traditional way. Workers just needed to put materials on the machine. Then, the machine scanned the material into a computer, recognised flaws on the materials and provided the tidiest layout plan based on the material's shape and feature. After workers' fine-tuning and confirmation, the machine automatically transmitted materials and cut them with a laser. After using the automatic cutting machines, the working efficiency in Juyi's cutting workshop increased, the material waste rate decreased and the workers and working space in the workshop reduced notably.

Another example was the computer-controlled stitching machines. Stitching and sewing uppers were usually considered the processes demanding a lot of skill and experience. The salary of the workers in stitching workshops was usually 2 times the wage of ordinary workers. Traditionally, it took three to five years for an ordinary worker to cultivate skills for these processes. During the stitching process, the workers had to conduct a very good coordination among hands, feet and eyes based on their personal experience. However, the computer-controlled stitching machines introduced by Juyi made a big difference. After setting a programme in the computers, the machines could automatically stitch certain lengths of threads with very high accuracy and very few mistakes. With them, ordinary workers could do stitching after four hours' training, and their working efficiency would be improved by 5 to 10 times. What's more, the expenditure of hiring skilled workers was reduced and the product quality remained stably good.

Given the advantage of intelligent machines, several problems should be further discussed. Firstly, the utilisation of intelligent machines in China highly relies on import. China has developed the shoe machine industry quickly since the 1980s, introduced related technologies from Italy in the 2000s and nurtured four large bases in Zhejiang, Guangdong, Fujian and Jiangsu provinces. In 2012, Wenzhou had 300 shoe machine firms and they occupied a big share of the domestic market. A few firms, like the Dalong and Oujiang machine companies, gradually become main suppliers for the local market and important players within China. However, most of Wenzhou's as well as Chinese footwear machine firms still have comparatively low technological and innovation capabilities, so that they are not able to provide intelligent machines. On the contrary, a few firms from developed countries, mainly Italy, Germany and Japan, control the core technology of producing high-end intelligent footwear machines and export them globally. Brother Company for example had global sales revenue of Japanese yen (JPY) 616.8 billion[14] (USD 6.3 billion) in 2013 and its overseas business reached 80% of its revenue. Moreover, it was estimated that in 2015, China consumed the largest number of industrial robots in the world, up to 68,600 units and 27% of the global share. Among these robots, more than 70% were from foreign suppliers and only 30% were from Chinese producers (International Federation of Robotics, 2016: 11–12). The dependence of Chinese footwear producers on import machines has negatively affected the independence and flexibility of their production.

Secondly, purchasing imported intelligent machines is very capital consuming. Take the Japanese computer-controlled stitching machines in Juyi for example. The purchase price of a stitching machine in Juyi was 20 times more expensive than traditional sewing machines in 2014. What's more, the maintenance and upgrade of the machines also need further investment in technology and personnel. For many SMEs, adopting intelligent machines is not a feasible task. Although large firms like Juyi can afford machinery purchase and upgrade, they must calculate whether and when their net profits would increase after the replacement of humans with machines.

Thirdly, the usage of intelligent machines puts forward more demands on workers' competency. Although intelligent machines can help less skilled workers handle footwear production in a shorter time, they make other requirements on workers. Ideally, workers should have knowledge of IT, industrial design, software and system integration, so that they can operate and repair the computers independently. However, most workers in the Chinese footwear industry only had high school educations and lacked advanced knowledge on automation. The International Labour Organization (ILO) (Chang et al., 2016: 57) estimated that a significant share of wage workers in the footwear industry in Southeast Asian countries are at high risk of automation, ranging from 64% in Indonesia, 86% in Vietnam, to 88% in Cambodia. China is facing the similar problem. Thus, the footwear firms have to hire external experts to control computers and train workers, which will increase their financial burdens.

The second action was to build a production base in Shangrao of Jiangxi Province. Juyi founded the Jiangxi Oumeiyi Footwear Company in 2006 and it started to produce footwear for export in 2009. The base in Shangrao had five production lines, 1,500 employees and 90,000 m^2 of factory buildings. In 2012, it achieved more than 2.6 million pairs of production, RMB 0.18 billion (USD 26.5 thousand) of revenue and USD 2.1 million of export revenue (Juyi Group, 2017). Although Jiangxi's footwear industry was not well developed, the reason why Juyi chose Shangrao to build the production base was because firstly, the labour cost in Shangrao was cheaper than Wenzhou. In 2005, its average wage of urban workers in private sectors was RMB 806 (USD 98)/month, but the one in Wenzhou was 1.7 times more with RMB 1,370 (USD 167)/month (Statistics Bureau of Jiangxi Province, 2016; Statistics Bureau of Zhejiang Province, 2016). Utilising local labour in Jiangxi could directly reduce Juyi's labour cost. Secondly, Shangrao had a good geographical location. Jiangxi is a middle China province and Shangrao shares borders with Zhejiang Province. Shangrao was the interchange for multiple highways and railways opening out in all directions. With its geographical and transportation location, Juyi could easily transport goods between Wenzhou and Shangrao. It usually took five hours for trucks to commute in a one-way trip. Thirdly, the local government of Shangrao provided preferential policy for Juyi. It promised to provide Juyi with good public service, tax reduction and priorities of land and energy usage.

The initial purpose of establishing the second base was to expand Juyi's production scale as well as take advantage of Shangrao's labour and policy resources. However, the result did not meet Juyi's expectation. These were mainly following reasons. Firstly, the labour cost in Shangrao has increased quickly. In 2014, the local average wage increased to RMB 2,577 (USD 422)/month, which was 3.2 times than the figure in 2005. The growth speed of wages in Shangrao was even faster than the increase rate of 2.9 times in Wenzhou. Although Shangrao's wage level was still RMB 1,443 (USD 237)/month lower than Wenzhou's wage in 2014, the cost advantage of producing footwear in Shangrao faded very quickly (Statistics Bureau of Jiangxi Province, 2016; Statistics Bureau of Zhejiang Province, 2016). What's worse, Shangrao's comparative advantage hardly exists when taking global competition into consideration. Although China still had some advantages of better public infrastructures and labour literacy, its advantage of labour cost already disappeared compared with other developing countries like Vietnam. In 2014, as Table 4.5 shows, the average wage in Vietnam was USD 201/month, which was USD 185/month less than Shangrao's number. For manufacturers of low-end and export-oriented shoes, moving production bases from China to foreign countries for cheaper labour might be unavoidable. For high-end and domestic market oriented producers, however, inland China might still be reasonable places for production due to their closeness to the domestic market and higher labour skills.

Secondly, Shangrao cannot develop a good industrial environment for the footwear industry. When Juyi founded the base in Shangrao, no local firms could supply material for footwear production. Juyi tried to encourage its suppliers in Wenzhou to move together. However, most its suppliers were not persuaded. This is because they are the suppliers of various footwear companies in Wenzhou. If they move to Shangrao, they will lose their business from other firms and Juyi's orders are not big enough for their profits. Moreover, Shangrao's local government only provides supportive policies to big firms like Juyi, yet not to SMEs like Juyi's suppliers. Sometimes, preferential policies for large firms are not stable and they change with the shifts of government officers. The development of an industrial environment involves the formations of cooperative relations among firms, the development of supporting industries, the growth of qualified labour and the improvement of political, social and economic conditions. The formation of an industrial environment is a long-time process and needs joint efforts of the public and private sectors. Very few firms succeed in nurturing a good industrial environment alone. The material procurement is the largest expenditure for most footwear manufacturers, accounting for 60–70% of production cost, while the

Table 4.5 Development indices of China and Vietnam, year 2014

Indices	*East China*	*Middle China*	*West China*	*China*	*Vietnam*
GDP per capita (USD)	8,077	5,304	4,366	7,590	2,050
GDP per capita growth (annual %)	6.68	10.04	8.44	6.73	4.50
Literacy rate	96.43 (year 2013)	96.25 (year 2013)	90.30 (year 2013)	94.60 (year 2010)	93.52 (year 2009)
Freight transported (billion ton-km)	8,298.47 (year 2013)	3,902.32 (year 2013)	2,431.01 (year 2013)		
Railways, freight transported (billion ton-km)	962.72 (year 2013)	935.13 (year 2013)	1,005.30 (year 2013)		
Logistics performance index: Quality of trade and transport-related infrastructure (1 = low to 5 = high)				3.67	3.11
Time to export (days)				21	21
Quality of port infrastructure, WEF (1 = extremely underdeveloped to 7 = well developed)				4.6	3.7
Internet users (per 100 people)	58.48	39.15	40.34	49.3	48.3
Average wage (USD/month)	798	585	654	701	201

Data source: National Bureau of Statistics of China (2016), The World Bank (2017), ILO (2017), UNESCO (2017). WEF = World Economic Forum.

labour alone contributes 15–20%. The large logistics costs of transporting materials from Wenzhou to Shangrao corrode the comparative advantage of labour cost in Shangrao and reduce the profitability of Juyi's business.

Thirdly, it is not easy for Juyi to manage operation in the Shangrao production base. Developing from a family-owned firm, Juyi's owner prefers to handle decisions by himself rather than authorising other professional managers to take part. With the expansion of production scale and geography, it is almost not possible for one person to manage all the business at the same time. The coordination and cooperation among different sectors and different production places are also challengeable. It is necessary for Juyi to adopt a modern firm management institution and build mutual trust with professional managers and employees, to manage and further develop the firm with professional experience and knowledge. The weakness of corporate governance is one of the main barriers preventing Juyi from building new production bases in Southeast Asian countries to utilise cheaper labour in the global field.

The third action was to improve supply chain management. The material quality lays the foundation for shoes quality. The innovation of materials on quality and technical processes usually brings more profits and competitive advantages to not only material companies, but also footwear manufacturers. Therefore, Juyi tried to build a long-time, stable and interactive relationship with its material suppliers. It established a competitive and transparent supplier system. When Juyi got OEM orders, it informed suppliers with its material requirements and asked them to make a bid. Only the firm offering the best quality at a reasonable price could achieve the order. At the same time, Juyi along with several research institutions participated in the R&D process of its suppliers and gave them technical support. It established its own lab to test a range of performance indices of the supplied materials, such as the skid resistance of the soles, weight capability of heels, folding endurance of the uppers and chemical contents of the materials. It held regular meetings with its suppliers to timely communicate foreign customers' demands and check research progress. Additionally, it provided financial support and production management guidance to its suppliers. In this way, Juyi and suppliers became an interest group with a tight vertical cooperation, which ensured the stability of the supply chain and the material quality.

Thanks to the well-developed production chain in Wenzhou, it is very convenient and economical for Juyi to get most its materials locally and communicate with its material suppliers. Despite Juyi's efforts, the technological capabilities of Wenzhou's suppliers are still limited due to various reasons. Some of the suppliers don't have the motivation to improve because their owners are relatives or friends of Juyi's owner. Based on the relationship, they don't need to worry much about their orders. Some small-scale ones are not able to enhance their abilities because of their weak technological and financial abilities. Others are hesitant to change because they think that although a few large firms want high quality materials, most footwear producers in Wenzhou will not buy expensive materials due to their low-end products. Consequently, suppliers compete more on price than technological innovation. Mr Pan realised that facing the rising competitors from Southeast Asia, the competition in the footwear industry was not among individual footwear producers, but among firms' groups linked by vertical production relationship. The comparative advantage of Wenzhou was not cheap labour anymore, but its developed production chain connecting diverse suppliers at an arm's length. It is high time for the strong shoe producers and material suppliers to be united, build mutual trust and fight together to transform and upgrade.

The fourth strategy was to adjust its corporate operation according to buyers' appetites. On one hand, Juyi made a great effort to satisfy buyers' requests on product quality. Since 2013, it launched a very strict quality inspection regulation. It asked the workers to double check the quality of products transmitted from their previous process and ensure the quality of their own products. It also requested inspectors to check the product quality at the end of each production line and at the last stage of footwear package. It stipulated that the workers, team leaders, inspectors, workshop directors and production managers had joint liability on the product quality. In this way, the product quality increased remarkably. On the other hand, Juyi closely followed buyers' preferences. When choosing outsourcing firms, buyers usually prefer to cooperate with firms having proper R&D capability and good factory management. Therefore, Juyi built a special business centre for its largest buyer and set up project teams in its sale, marketing and R&D departments to specialise in analysing and tracking shoe samples. In this way, it could know the buyers' purchasing preference on shoes' design and materials and have higher chance to get orders.

Despite the above attempts, Juyi still faced persistent pressure of order drain. This is because with the development of footwear production in other Asian countries, firms from these countries also improve their quality management and interaction with buyers. Having less cost advantages, Juyi's attraction to buyers is gradually reduced. For its survival in the future, Juyi should enhance its influence and power over buyers rather than relying on buyers. Exploring more and diverse sales channels might be an effective way to reduce its business risks and dependence on a couple of buyers. Forging its capabilities of making more sophisticated products can also enhance its attraction to higher-end buyers and increase its chance of getting more profits. In addition, improving its capability from manufacture to design might be an ultimate but more challengeable choice. The development of Taiwanese footwear firms, such as Yue Yuen, showed that export-oriented footwear firms could still maintain their competitiveness in developed economies if they continuously forged their strengths in the above aspects. In contrast, if firms cannot upgrade from making low-end products to higher-end shoes or more sophisticated business, then they will lose their competitiveness soon.

Zhejiang Aokang Shoes Limited

Unlike Juyi, the Zhejiang Aokang Shoes Limited Company is a domestic market oriented firm focusing on footwear production, retail and branding. Mr Wang Zhentao, who used to be a sales clerk, founded the Aokang Company in 1988. The company was initially a household factory making leather shoes named Yongjia Aolin Shoes Factory with only 10 employees and RMB 30,000 (USD 8,108) of assets. In the beginning, it was not different from other household firms that made poor quality shoes and it experienced Wenzhou's quality crisis as well. In the 1990s, however, it spared no effort to introduce machines and enhance management and finally improved its product quality and brand reputation. In 1998, it introduced franchising into leather shoes retail within China, which had a substantial influence in the reform of sales channels for leather shoes in the country. In 1999, the company was one of the initiators that burned bogus imitations in Hangzhou, aiming to rebuild the public trust in Wenzhou's footwear. In the following two decades, Aokang attached great importance to sales networks and brand influence and expanded its business quickly.

In 2001, the Aokang Group established the Zhejiang Aokang Shoes Limited Company to specialise in operating its footwear business.[15] In the same year, it launched its second brand called Kanglong. In 2002, Aokang became the first brand in Wenzhou to be rated as China's Famous Brand of footwear by governmental authorities. In the same year, it promoted its third brand, MeiRie's. In 2003, it built a footwear manufacturing base in Chongqing to increase its output capacity, diversify its products and reduce its production costs. Moreover, it became the first retail partner of Geox Company, the largest Italian brand for lifestyle shoes, in China and the two companies agreed to share worldwide sales networks until 2008. At the same time, Aokang built one of Geox's largest outsourcing bases in Asia and supplied more than 8.9 million pairs of OEM products from 2003 to 2014. In 2004, the firm put forward its fourth brand, Redess. In 2008, Aokang succeeded in supplying leather products for the Beijing Olympic Games, aiming to improve its brand recognition around the world. In addition, it made a contract with the Italian company Calzaturificio Vallevderde S.P.A. to exclusively operate its global retail business. In 2010, Aokang bought the permanent ownership of the brand Vallevderde within China and was authorised to produce and retail Vallevderde shoes within China. In 2012, the Zhejiang Aokang Shoes Limited Company went public on the Shanghai Stock Exchange. It also won the largest case of anti-dumping against the EU after a six-year lonely battle. It helped Chinese footwear firms be exempt from 16.5% of anti-dumping tariffs imposed since 2009. In 2013, it introduced Load Max,[16] a British retail brand into China's shopping halls and further developed its retail business with the cooperation of Wanda Group.[17] In 2015, the firm made contracts with the American company Skechers and started to retail sports shoes within the Great China Area. It also launched its first shoes shopping mall named AOK-MART in Wenzhou, selling all kinds of shoes with a wide range of brands from both inside and outside the Aokang Company.

As a firm operating self-owned brands, Aokang has a very different business process from export-oriented OEM producers. Its operation is dynamic, with four seasons all year round and interactive with the market, including brand plan, product design, manufacture, outsourcing and sales. Brand planning is the starting point of its operation. Since the firm has multiple brands, it makes differential strategies for each brand to serve different consumers in target market segments. For example, it plans Aokang as a formal shoe brand for the white-collar class, Redess as a young fashion brand for young consumers and Valleverde as an honourable fashion brand for successful people. Brand plans provide guidelines of target consumers, product styles and production costs for the design department. Based on the guidelines, the design department tries to understand the fashion in the coming season and consumer preferences in target market segments and then creates a series of prototypes that can reflect new fashion trends and consumer preferences.

To increase production flexibility, manufacturing is arranged in both internal and external production bases. In some cases, their external production bases will supply products with their own designs. The manufacturing process usually consists of a first batch of orders and supplement orders. The first batch orders are made before the season when retailers and franchisers select certain prototypes and formulate orders based on their predictions. The company arranges these production orders to internal factories or external suppliers and then delivers the orders. The supplement orders are made in the season when retailers and franchisers analyse real-time sales records and make more following orders of popular products. The firm then arranges follow-up production in a short time and delivers the products to retail terminals quickly. Compared with export-oriented firms, Aokang produces more batches of shoes with less volume and more varieties within a shorter period. During the process, it is significant for the company to efficiently manage the information and material flows, so that it can fully understand consumers, quickly respond to market change, flexibly adjust production, accurately arrange stock, promptly deliver orders and effectively improve market competitiveness.

Nowadays, Aokang has become one of the largest Chinese private footwear firms, and it aims to be the leading footwear retailer in China. In 2015, it had 7,300 employees and RMB 3.3 billion (USD 532.3 million) of sales revenue from directly owned stores, franchise stores, online sale, department stores, group purchase and OEM business. Aokang had 2,912 chain stores across China, among which 1,231 were directly owned and 1,681 were franchising stores. It also collaborates with a few e-commerce platforms, such as Tmall.com, JD.com and Vipshop, to manage its online sales business. Aokang sold 19.1 million pairs of shoes and was regarded as the largest Chinese brand for men's shoes by sales revenue within China (Zhejiang Aokang Shoes Limited Company, 2016).

In the past few of years, Aokang was awarded National Quality Prize, Zhejiang Government Quality Prize and Wenzhou Mayor Quality Prize. It was also rated as China Genuine Leather Shoes Leader King, National Important Brand, Zhejiang High-tech Firm, Zhejiang Green Enterprise, Custom AA Management Firm and Top 500 Chinese Private Firm. Due to Aokang's remarkable development, many national leaders visited Aokang, such as President Xi Jinping, the Vice-Premiers of Wang Yang and Wen Jiabao, the President of National CPPCC Li Ruihuan. Mr Wang was elected to be the vice-president of the China Commerce Association for General Merchandise, China Leather Association, Zhejiang Association of Industry and Commerce, Wenzhou CPPCC and the president of the Wenzhou Association of Industry and Commerce and the General Commerce Association.

Despite the above strength, Aokang has confronted increasing pressure to enhance its competitiveness in recent years. Firstly, due to the slowdown of China's economy, the growth momentum of the Chinese footwear industry has declined and many Chinese customers have become more rational about footwear consumption. The strategy of opening many new chain stores can hardly bring firms as good sales performance as before. In contrast, a few leading firms display their strength of innovating products, fine-tuning management and reforming sale operation, so that they increase their market share and gain higher growth. Secondly, customers develop more demands on leather footwear. They would like to buy leather shoes with not only better quality, but also more diversity and fashion. Also, their preference for types and aesthetics of shoes get more diverse and change faster. As a result, footwear firms cannot maintain their competitiveness by providing a few kinds of shoes at a large volume. Instead, they should increase their product diversity, operation flexibility and response to market. Thirdly, new forms of business operation, especially online sales and shopping malls, weaken Aokang's traditional advantages of marketing and selling products through chain stores. Online sales provide customers with much convenience of shopping at any time anywhere, buying at cheaper prices than in stores and receiving products without transportation. Shopping malls enable customers to not only enjoy a one-stop shopping experience, but also to relax among other multiple entertainments. The rise of online sales and shopping malls reduces the attraction of shoe chain stores. Therefore, footwear firms must explore more sales channels of online sales and shopping malls to make up their fading sales performance in shoe stores.

All these changes have brought Aokang unprecedented challenges in the past few years. From 2009 to 2015, although Aokang doubled its revenue from RMB 166.8 billion (USD 26.9 billion) to RMB 3318.8 million (USD 535.3 million), its net profit increased only by 67%. Also, Aokang's gross profit rate was less than global footwear leading firms. Take Geox, for example; its gross profit rate in 2015 was 51.6%, which was 18.5% more than Aokang's number. What's worse, from 2007 to 2015, Aokang's rank of domestic market share declined from the top sixth to the top eighth[18] and the gap of market shares between Aokang and leading firms got larger. In addition, it is not easy for Aokang to spread its brand influence. From 2010 to 2015, Aokang enhanced its revenue mainly in the eastern China region, which accounted for 58.5% of its business growing from 45.4%, while its revenue proportion in other regions could hardly increase (Geox S.p.A., 2016; Zhejiang Aokang Shoes Limited Company, 2011–2016).

Faced with these results, Aokang realised that it was urgent to reform. It believed that only if it understood and satisfied customers' demand could it improve its sales performance and competitiveness. Thereby, it took the following measures to transform and upgrade. The first action was to strengthen retail networks. Aokang spared no effort to forge the scope and efficiency of its retailing network. Firstly, it increased directly operated business. In 2009, 84.6% of Aokang's chain stores were franchise stores and they accounted for 58.3% of its sales revenue. In the following six years, Aokang increased 794 directly owned stores, occupying 42.3% of its chain store numbers and contributing 62.3% of its sales revenue in 2015. Despite the investment of finance and human resources, directly owned stores endowed Aokang with more control over its terminal retail points than franchise stores, so that it could respond to market change quickly. At the same time, Aokang shut down 1,100 small franchise stores with poor sales performance (Zhejiang Aokang Shoes Limited Comany, 2012b and 2016). It reorganised the distributions of stores and products among directly owned stores and franchise stores to effectively improve regional sales performance with less store numbers.

Secondly, it upgraded the product supply and customer service in its chain stores. In the past, one chain store usually sold one brand of products from Aokang Company, like Aokang shoes or Kanglong shoes. After 2013, the company started to launch Aokang Selective Stores and Aokang International Stores in several cities. These stores provided multiple brands of shoes in one store, including Aokang, Kanglong, MeiRie's, Redess and Vallevderde from Aokang and some international brands. In 2015, Aokang spread the reform to a wider range of chain stores. It increased 197 stores providing multiple brands of products and reduced 180 stores that only sold one brand of shoes. These upgraded stores offered customers more choices to select and compare products and gave them a one-stop shopping experience. In some of the flagship stores, Aokang even provided the service of making customised shoes. Consumers could measure their foot shapes with machines and pick the materials, accessories and styles for their shoes. Aokang's reform boosted its sales records to some extent. For instance, it was reported that compared with normal chain stores, Aokang International Stores had 30% more customer volume, 2%–3% more gross profit rate and 2% more sales profits (Zhejiang Aokang Shoes Limited Company, 2016).

Thirdly, it expanded online sales. In 2008, Aokang already set up a small scale of e-business via the Aokang online mall on its official website. After 2011, it started to extend the scale by opening shops in diverse platforms, beginning with T-mall. Its e-business increased quickly from 2011 to 2015. At present, it sells 10 brands of shoes online, including Aokang, Aokang ladies, Kanglong, Redess and MeiRie's from the company and four brands from other companies. In many cases, it provided online exclusive products to avoid internal competition with its chain stores and offered cheaper products to attract customers.

Fourthly, it extended sales networks to multiple channels. Maintaining its advantage in chain stores, Aokang tried to make breakthroughs in other sales channels like department stores and shopping malls to approach a wider range of consumers. Aokang noticed that it was important to supply different products to different channels because customers' preferences differ among channels. Its strategy was to firstly supply Vallevderde to department stores for high-end customers and Load Max to shopping malls for young customers. After it got the experience and credits of sales on these platforms, it then would supply other brands later through these channels.

Despite its efforts, Aokang still faced several problems. Firstly, most of Aokang's products, given their different brands, don't have unique product features. Aokang's diverse styles and large stores might impress customers, but they sometimes realise later that many of the products are similar to each other. Secondly, it is not easy to coordinate mutual growth between online and offline businesses. On one hand, Aokang has developed online business quickly, but its net profit rate of online sales is low. On the other hand, online shoes become internal competitors for Aokang's shoes sold in offline stores. Thirdly, Aokang's brand recognition and trust are still not strong among high-end customers and large retailers. Aokang tried to provide customised footwear, but few customers would like to buy. In addition, in some cases, Aokang is not allowed to supply products to high-end department stores, because they believe that the Aokang brand is not recognised enough to meet their brand management requirements.

The second measure was to enhance product supply management. Mr Wang believed that shoes retail was like selling fruits because both products should be supplied to customers when most fresh. Aokang reformed the traditional product supply frequencies of four times per year to eight times, to ensure its shoes could catch up with the latest fashion in the season. It tried to forge a supply system that could provide products faster and more punctually. The achievement of the goal needed a close cooperation among multiple departments. The design department had to capture the updated fashion the first time and transform it into product design within one day. Then it provided a wide range of product samples for order-placing meetings organised by the sales department. All retailers throughout China would attend the meeting, select products suitable for their regions and make orders with specific styles, volumes and retail time.

The sales department would gather all the orders to the production department. The production department would arrange manufacture in different bases depending on the retailers' geographical locations, selling time and product features. To achieve the fastest speed and most flexibility, internal bases consisted of a series of small factories specialising in making certain types of products, such as men's casual shoes and women's formal shoes, and they could adjust their manufacture procedures and worker arrangement within each factory very quickly based on different orders. The orders of producing and transporting products for different retailers mainly depended on their selling dates. Aokang tried to supply the products at the exact day when retailers wanted to put them into shelves, to reduce inventory time and volume and take full use of available capital and storage space. To support the operation of the whole supply system, Aokang also built digital platforms to connect designers, producers and retail terminals and share information in real time.

When enhancing the product supply system, Aokang faces the below difficulties. Firstly, it is hard to control the consistency of product quality. It tried to carefully select suppliers and gave them requirements, but some external providers still could not ensure their product quality sometimes, especially with the pressure of increasing manufacturing costs and declining profits. Also, the arrangement of internal and external procurement makes it hard for Aokang to achieve identical ranges of products with common design ideas and features. Secondly, production costs have increased greatly. The growth of labourers' wages in eastern China boosted the production costs in Aokang's production bases in Wenzhou. Although it built a base in Chongqing, most its retailers are still in eastern China. The transportation from west to east increases Aokang's costs. Its procurement costs from external bases of Wenzhou and Guangzhou grow as well. Thirdly, it is hard to improve supply accuracy. Despite Aokang's effort to provide products at a punctual time, most retailers cannot give exact dates of selling products. Their management mainly depends on their previous experience other than accurate data analysis. Some of them still follow their traditional management of making order dates earlier than actual selling time. Furthermore, the usage of digital platform during management is still at the primary stage at present. It will take not a short time for all the staff to adapt their work and take full advantage of the digital management platforms.

The third action is to improve product R&D. Firstly, it tried to enhance the comfort level of shoes by increasing its technological capabilities. Aokang built an Aokang Shoes Technological Academy in 2007, named Aokang Comfort Fashion Institute later, and founded a High-tech Digital Research Base in 2010. It also built long-term cooperation with the China Leather and Shoemaking Industry Academy and Zhejiang University to conduct research. At present, the Aokang Comfort Fashion Institute has achieved more than 36 patents. For example, it innovated a comfort breathing technology by adopting nanometre technology, micro-porous technology and microcapsule technology. What's more, it researched the technologies that made shoes more resistant to high temperature and anti-bacteria and made them recyclable and shock-absorbing. Secondly, it made efforts to improve product design. It built design offices in Italy, Guangzhou and Wenzhou aiming to catch up with the latest fashion. Usually, the designers in Italy were responsible for absorbing the frontier fashion information from international fashion shows and passing it on to their colleagues in China. The designers in Guangzhou were responsible for collecting updated fashion in Asia and within China and passing it on to the designers in Wenzhou. The designers in Wenzhou were supposed to transform the fashion information to specific product design. To strengthen its design capability, it introduced designers from Italy and Guangzhou to Wenzhou and planned to take full advantage of local market knowledge and frontier ideas. In addition, it bought product designs from external designers by offering them design ideas and drafts.

Given the above efforts, Aokang's R&D capability is still not as strong as global footwear leaders. Its R&D investment is less. For example, in 2015, Aokang's R&D investment was RMB 33 million (USD 5.2 million), accounting for 1.02% of its revenue. However, Geox invested EUR 16.8 million (USD 18.6 million) and 1.83% of revenue (Zhejiang Aokang Shoes Limited Company, 2016; Geox S.p.A., 2016). In terms of technology, many of Aokang's innovations have not been put into practice. It needs some time to make the technology achievable for commercial value. Furthermore, the technological levels of some patents are still so low that customers cannot fully recognise the performance improvement of its shoes. As to product design, it cannot design products with unique features. Most local designers in Wenzhou focus on fine-tuning existing designs of other famous brands rather than innovating their own designs and leading the fashion. Moreover, the introduced designers found it hard to get inspiration and continuously make creative designs in Wenzhou. They claimed that Wenzhou had very little social atmosphere for aesthetic arts that encouraged creative designs and very few local firms could provide good materials to match their designs.

After trying diverse reforms, Aokang finally realised that the product was the key to the success of competition. No matter how hard it tried to boost the sales network and launch brands, if it could not supply differential products that stood out in the market, then the real achievement of its efforts would not be optimistic. In the past decades, it mainly focused on product sales and forged sufficient strengths on retail. However, enhancing R&D and transforming technologies to products required different sets of capabilities and a lot of time and effort. Aokang has to pay more attention to longer-term rather than short-term sales profits, so that it can really upgrade products and business.

Menglani Shoes Limited

Different from Juyi and Aokang, the Menglani Shoes Limited Company is a small footwear firm in Wenzhou. It had only about 100 employees and less than RMB 50 million (USD 7.9 million) of sales revenue in 2012. During extremely fierce competition, its living situation is harsher than large firms. However, it endeavoured to make product R&D and forged its unique competitiveness and surviving strategy.

Mr Zheng Guohong, who is a leading technician and senior designer in Wenzhou, founded Menglani in 1982. Since its establishment, Menglani specialised in making export footwear and selling to the Russian market through trade companies.[19] During the 1990s, Menglani gained rich profits because of its low production costs and the large Russian market. However, at the end of the 1990s, as more and more firms, mainly from Wenzhou, arrived in Russia, the competition among firms became cutthroat and profits dropped greatly. It was estimated that in the 1990s, the profit for each pair of shoes sold in Russia was USD 3, but after 2000, it declined to about 20 cents. In addition, many footwear firms started to build factories on the border of Russia and China, to get closer to the market and deal with the grey customs clearance. Faced with the harsh situation, Mr Zheng noticed that if a small firm like Menglani still took the old way of footwear production and competed with other firms in the existing mature market, it had very little chance to survive in the end. In 2003, Mr Zheng shut down his firm and travelled to Chile to explore a new market, where very few Wenzhou footwear products were sold at that time. After investigation, he figured that there was a big market for low-end footwear in Chile, but the market was very likely to be carved up by other Chinese firms in about five years. After one month's trip, Mr Zheng still hesitated to shift his export destination. At the same time, he collected a variety of products from other Wenzhou firms, trying to find competitive products for the Chilean market.

During the product collection, from a small firm in Ruian County, he accidently discovered a new technology for footwear production, called the direct injection production (DIP) technology, which is often used to make safety shoes. This technology is very different from the mainstream technology, the cold bounding production (CBP) technology, which is widely used in making daily footwear. Simply speaking, the general process of footwear production with the CBP technology is to make shoe uppers, lasts and soles separately and then bind uppers and soles together with the help of lasts. The process with DIP technology is to produce uppers, lasts and modes according to a united design and then inject materials into soles directly at the bottom of uppers with the help of lasts, moulds and machines. At that time, in the world, only one company, called Ecco Sko A/S, cooperating with a few German companies for machines, materials and foot lasts, had monopolised the method of adopting this technology to make daily shoes since 1980. Within China, only two firms in Wenzhou and Guangzhou were trying to make some breakthroughs in this area, but both were at the very primary stage.

The DIP technology brings a big difference to the footwear production industry. Firstly, it is eco-friendlier. After the adoption of the DIP technology, there is no need to vulcanise shoe uppers and use glue, which are typical ways of making cold bounded shoes and often produce toxic gas and substances. Secondly, it is consumer friendlier. The injected shoes are more comfortable to wear because the technology makes it possible for the shoes to adapt to people's feet more accurately. In addition, wearing injected shoes are healthier. This is not only because they have less toxic materials, but also they are more consistent with physiology. Thirdly, it saves labour. Traditionally, the lasting workshops need 70 to 80 labourers. With this technology and automatic machines, the number of labourers is reduced to 20. Therefore, the labour cost decreases greatly. Fourthly, it is more technology intensive. The production of injected shoes not only needs profound understanding of footwear design, production skills and manufacturing machines, but also the knowledge of physiology and medical science. Injected shoes need more experienced and three-dimensional design skills, but design for traditional shoes only need the knowledge of plane geometry. Last but not least, the DIP technology has much higher requirements on accuracy. The production of injected shoes needs very accurate coordination between shoe uppers, lasts and moulds, with its error margin less than 0.03 cm. If the error margin is larger than 0.03 cm during production, then it is not possible to make even one injected shoe. However, the error margin for traditional footwear production could be 1–1.5 cm.

Mr Zheng was deeply amazed and attracted by the new technology. Based on his expertise and experience, he concluded that it was likely for Menglani to make some progress within five years. Therefore, in 2004, he made up his mind to transform his firm from producing cold bounding shoes to further develop the DIP technology. He sold out all the machines related to the CBP technology with tears and devoted his heart and soul to researching the new technology. When doing research, he not only learnt experience from the small firm in Ruian, but also had the whole world in his mind. He noticed that Ecco was a global leader and global brand in the area. Its founder had a very similar professional background and hard-working spirit like himself. Thereby, Mr Zheng set Ecco as his target, paid close attention and conducted reverse engineering to its products and tried to make further technological breakthroughs.

After 8 years' efforts, Mr Zheng successfully mastered the DIP technology, applied a series of patents and produced his own injected shoes. However, Ecco Company sued Mr Zheng in 2009, claiming that one of his patents of appearance design was invalid. Mr Zheng insisted that despite some similarity, there was actual obvious difference between his design and Ecco's design. He did reference Ecco's product during product development, but he had made innovations rather than copying Ecco's technology. After continuous fighting, the Beijing No. 1 Intermediate People's Court pronounced in the second instance in 2010 that Mr Zheng's patent was valid. Menglani's victory was regarded as a good case for Chinese footwear firms to achieve the success of intellectual property rights (IPRs) disputes. However, the influence of the case on the firm's competition in the global field was very limited. To date, Menglani is still an unknown SME to many footwear firms even in Wenzhou, not to mention its consumers outside China.

Since this victory, Menglani was more confident about its core technology and gained an increasing number of innovations in the following years. Especially in 2011, it successfully combined the technology and the use of automatic footwear production machines. Nowadays, the business process for Menglani is to first design mother lasts by Mr Zheng according to OEM orders and then to outsource son lasts and modes from Shanghai and Wenzhou firms with numerical control equipment. Then it designs and produces the uppers with the guide of Mr Zheng within Menglani. In Wenzhou, currently no firms can provide qualified materials and machines for making DIP shoes, so Menglani imports raw materials and machines from German giant firms.

Although the production of injected shoes involves diverse aspects of technological cooperation, Menglani's core competitiveness is its capabilities of making mother lasts and coordinating them with machines. The traditional footwear production only cared about the front of lasts, but the adoption of the new technology needs very accurate calculation on the whole lasts, especially the heel parts. The mother lasts are the most core parts for producing injected shoes. They change according to the designs and functions of shoes and directly relate to the degree of comfort and qualified rate. Currently, very few people in the world have grasped the skill of making mother lasts, because it is tacit knowledge depending on master technicians' design experience, imagination capability and understandings on manufacturing machines. In most cases, the creation of mother lasts in Menglani is a result of sculpting with exquisite craftsmanship based on Mr Zheng's professional experience, rather than the complex calculation of existing data. After master technicians make mother lasts, ordinary technicians calculate their parameters and then ask workshops for moulds, lasts and uppers to conduct large-scale production according to the parameters. The master technicians are the only people who know the matching parameters for each kind of shoes.

With the capability of making mother lasts, Menglani has controlled the initiative of the whole production chain. If the company was large enough, it could earn profits of the most processes of footwear production. On the contrary, without the ability, no factory can independently produce a pair of injected shoes even though they buy all kinds of advanced machines. In fact, some Chinese firms introduced automatic production lines and German machines to make injected shoes, but very few of them knew the secret of producing mother lasts and most of them had to buy mother lasts from foreign companies. The purchasing was very expensive, usually costing EUR 450 (USD 500) for each pair, but it could not help Chinese firms learn the technology. Thus, foreign companies held up their development.

Based on the core technology of mother lasts production, Menglani has also extended its business to the production and innovation of manufacturing facilities, shoe lasts, moulds, technology and products. It forged its own production chain from material, technology and products. It achieved important innovations in improving breathing functions to greatly enhance the breathing and comfort level of injected shoes, which was usually regarded as a big problem for the DIP technology. Besides, cooperating with the China Leather and Footwear Industry Research Institute, it participated in formulating production standards for breathing shoes in 2012. Its own developed shoe lasts and manufacturing facilities, such as fixture and moulds, had high quality and could be used in both domestic and foreign automatic machines. It applied for more than 30 patents in all the aspects of manufacturing facilities, shoe lasts, moulds, technology and products. According to a patent report provided by the Technology Bureau of Wenzhou Municipality (2013), Menglani ranked at number 8 among the global top 10 firms with the largest number of patent applications in the DIP technology by 2013. Within China, Menglani shared the rank with Ecco Company to be the firms with the most patent applications of DIP technology.[20] Mr Zheng pointed out although Ecco had more patents on shoe appearances, its advantage might fade because appearances usually changed more quickly with customers' preferences. Ecco had not gotten the patents in last design, but Menglani had all aspects of patents in making injected shoes.

Thanks to the technology innovation, Menglani found its way towards a second spring of development. Nowadays, it has expanded its factory building to more than 5,000 m^2. It had 107 employees, among whom 33 people had professional training education background and 28 people had expertise in engineering, shoe design, manufacture and technology. It was a National High-technology Enterprise and its R&D investment reached 9.6% of its total producing cost in 2014. From 2010 to 2012, its annual production capability grew from 1.6 million pairs to 2.9 million pairs and its sales reached RMB 48.9 million (USD 7.8 million) from RMB 18.99 million (USD 2.8 million). From 2010 to 2014, its gross profit rate doubled and the 2014 figure was two times than other large firms producing cold bounding shoes in Wenzhou. Before 2013, since the injected shoes were very popular in the countries with cold weather, Menglani exported OEM products for the Russian market at the average export price of USD 60/pair. Besides its high profits, Menglani gained more power in foreign trade. Its Russia partners for instance had to give advance payment to make orders and total payment when Menglani started to dispatch goods. However, many ordinary OEM exporters usually cannot get payments from their buyers before their products arrive at their destinations.

However, the development of Menglani was not smooth. Due to its heavy dependence on the Russian market, its export orders shrank greatly between 2013 and 2014 after the rouble crisis attacked the Russian economy. Without large orders, it was difficult for Menglani to offer labour cost and research expenditure in the long run. Menglani could not get loans from banks because they were hesitant to lend money to SMEs, especially after the 2011 financial crisis. Without enough finance, the transformation of technological innovation to production capability had to be delayed. It was forced to seek for more customers in the domestic market. Unfortunately, Menglani did not build its brand influence and sales channels in China in the past decade. What's worse, Menglani still did not have the ability to enter the commercial market. This was because the commercial market needed more product diversity, but Menglani could only produce very limited kinds of footwear.

Given the current difficulties, Mr Zheng was optimistic about the future of his firm. He believed that with the increasing demand on footwear quality and public consciousness on the health of people and the environment, the market prospect for injected shoes was very promising. In addition, very few firms could compete with Menglani because most of them did not know the core technology and many did not even have the sense of the new technology. He estimated that Menglani could have the technology monopoly for 5–10 years.

Therefore, his plan for the next five years was not to make further technological breakthroughs, but to achieve a large scale of the automatic production. For the further development, he thought its real competitor in the world was only

Ecco. In 2015, Ecco had about EUR 1.26 billion (USD 1.4 billion) of global sales and 19,109 employees (Ecco Sko A/S, 2016: 2). It regarded China as the largest market in the Asia-Pacific zone and built shoe and tannery factories in Xiamen and a business consultancy company in Dongguan. Although Menglani was tiny compared with Ecco, Mr Zheng was ambitious to compete with it because of his advanced technology and innovation. He said focusing on Ecco had become a compulsory course for every member in Menglani. Catching up with Ecco was the career for the whole crew of Menglani. Excelling Ecco would always be the dream of the people in Menglani. Mr Zheng imagined that Menglani would open its own retail shop just next to Ecco's sales points in the future and compete with its own advantage of comparatively low price and closeness to the local market.

According to his 30 years' plan, Menglani will build up its own brand, AEHV, in the commercial market, remain at its headquarters in Wenzhou, make uppers in inland China and then dispatch them as well as other semi-finished products to different production bases across China and even in Russia and Northern Europe. The footwear production in each production base will not be labour intensive. The main task for Mr Zheng was to control the core technology and pass it to his own son through mentoring. He insisted that his products would be popular in the future because their unique quality could win over their customers.

Mr Zheng argued that the competition of footwear firms in the future would greatly depend on their core technology. As Ecco's history showed, it was not impossible for firms outside Italy, the kingdom of the footwear industry, to make breakthroughs and have great influence. The lesson for Chinese people was that in technological innovation, Chinese people were not less smart but more hard-working than foreign technicians. After comparing the development history of Ecco and Menglani, he realised the development of Menglani was much slower than Ecco. He thought that the main reason was that Chinese labour in the footwear industry had much weaker competency than European workers. Technical talents were badly needed in Wenzhou and the low competency of Chinese workers was one of the most outstanding barriers preventing the Chinese footwear industry from catching up.

In most Chinese people's minds, working in the footwear industry doesn't need good education. Many people regard shoemaking as a dirty and low-end job and they prefer to commit to higher technological industries, like the electronic industry, although in many cases, they do similar low technological tasks, like assembly. What's worse, the professional training for footwear manufacture is far from developed in China. Most of the students attending the professional training schools are not interested in footwear, but they cannot go to universities. Thus, only a few technicians really have enough skills, passion and patience to make technological progress in the footwear industry. In Menglani, Mr Zheng cultivates his technicians for a decade through mentoring. It will be a long-run task for the whole society to change the professional discrimination against footwear workers and develop good technicians for footwear manufacture.

The story of Menglani displayed a new way for footwear firms in Wenzhou to overcome the dilemma of tiny profit. The experience of concentrating on one part of the production chain, devoting itself to technological innovation and gradually forging its irreplaceable capability might be a helpful lesson for other firms. It should not be ignored that Menglani still has many difficulties to overcome in its way ahead, such as talents, IPRs, technology inheritance, capital, productivity, market and brands. Besides, it still has dependency on imported raw materials and advanced machines. The automation of its production was far behind the situation in firms from Western countries, such as the Speedfactory of Adidas Company.

Summary

Since the mid-nineteenth century, the global footwear industry has developed quickly with the introduction of machines, the expansion of commercialisation and the rise of consumerism. Currently, the footwear industry is mature, with large-scale production, market and international trade. Footwear consumers are generally sensitive to the aesthetics, quality, duality, comfort, function and price of shoes, but specific preferences vary from people to people. Based on consuming capabilities, consumers can be divided into high-, medium- and low-end groups. When it comes to geographical difference, people from developing countries have lower average expenditure than those in the developed world, but their total consumption volumes are large and increasing. As to gender difference, females are larger consumers and more aware of fashion. In terms of product categories, leather and rubber shoes are the two most popular types.

The global competition in the footwear industry is fierce. Since the 1970s, M&A has increased the industrial concentration. The trend of concentration is expected to continue and increase in the future. To date, footwear manufacturing is still labour intensive, but the introduction of new technologies and machines has brought great changes to the industry. Footwear firms thereby continuously compete in production cost, product quality, customer service, brand influence and R&D to survive and stand out in the industry. Firm competitiveness differs between developing countries and developed nations. Firms from developing countries have their competitiveness in production scale, but they are not competitive to their peers from developed countries in product quality, customer service, brand influence and R&D.

In global competition, China is one of the largest and most influential players. It achieved dramatic growth and global competitiveness after the 1990s. Since 1997, it has been globally the largest exporter. It nurtured a few footwear IDs in both eastern and inland areas. Nowadays, China has been the largest producer, consumer by volume and exporter in the world. Despite its large scale, China's footwear industry is not strong. Most of the shoes made in China are low-end and most Chinese footwear firms sit in the low value-added segments of the GVC. The high-end footwear products in the Chinese market mainly rely on imports or are produced by FIEs. In the future, the footwear market will increase, the global shifts of production will continue and R&D, marketing network and branding are increasingly crucial for firm competition. With its strengths and weaknesses, China's footwear industry is facing opportunities and challenges.

Among all the footwear production bases in China, Wenzhou has been famous for producing leather shoes for hundreds of years and it has been honoured as China's Shoe Capital since 2001. Wenzhou's footwear industry has its strength of a developed production chain, broad sales network and thriving self-owned brands. However, it also has predicaments of fading comparative advantages, fragile industrial structure and a low-end locking dilemma. As a pioneer and one of the most influential players, Wenzhou provides important reference to studying China's development challenges in the footwear industry.

Several of Wenzhou's firms are exploring pilot strategies to break through the predicaments. Among them, the Juyi, Aokang and Menglani companies are typical examples. Juyi introduced intelligent machines, built a production base in Jiangxi Province, improved supply chain management and trimmed its corporate operation based on buyers' appetites. Aokang endeavoured to strengthen retail networks, enhance product supply management and improve product R&D. Menglani spared no effort to conduct R&D and forged its competitiveness in making mother lasts, improving DIP technology and producing injected shoes. These firms have forged their individual capabilities of production, sales, marketing and R&D. However, none of them is strong enough to have comprehensive competitiveness in all the above aspects at the same time. Consequently, their business is still limited in the Chinese market and they cannot create any influential brand in the world.

Wenzhou's as well as Chinese footwear firms as a whole mainly confront the following challenges. The first issue is human resources, involving both ordinary workers and technical workers. Although intelligent machines help less skilled workers handle footwear production in a shorter time, they put forward more demands on workers' competency. Ordinary workers are expected to have the knowledge of IT and industrial design, so that they can operate and repair computers independently. However, in the Chinese footwear industry, most ordinary workers lack advanced knowledge, and individual firms can hardly afford relevant training. As for technical workers, they are supposed to have more professional expertise and ethics to develop shoemaking technology and cultivate capabilities of making higher-end products. However, currently, very few of them really have enough skills, passion and patience to make technological progress. It will be a long-run task for not only firms, but also the whole Chinese society to nurture good technicians by education and training.

The second is industrial environment. It includes labour quality and costs, transportation conditions and inter-firm cooperation. Currently, the industrial environment is not sufficient to support the upgrade of the Chinese footwear industry. Except for the issue of labour capability, the labour cost has increased quickly. Eastern China has lost its cost advantage and the advantage of inland China is also fading compared with other Southeast Asian countries. Although some footwear production bases came into shape in inland China, local supporting industries are far from developed. It will take time and effort to reduce transportation and logistics costs, nurture relevant firms and cultivate supporting industries. In terms of inter-firm cooperation, most footwear firms don't coordinate with each other for strategic upgrade. Suppliers of footwear firms don't have strong motivation to improve technology due to their weak capabilities, personal relationships and pessimistic evaluation of the industrial situation.

The third is supporting industries. The development of the footwear industry is closely related to many supporting industries, especially the footwear material, machine and fashion industries. However, China has not forged strong capabilities in these supporting industries to back up the upgrading of the footwear industry. Many Chinese firms suffer from high dependence and expenditure on imported materials and machines. Moreover, the Chinese fashion design industry is not advanced. Most Chinese designers still focus on imitating existing designs of famous brands rather than innovating their own designs and leading the fashion. Creative ideas and good materials are highly needed to implement excellent footwear designs and nurture brand culture.

The fourth is the governance of corporates and supply chains. In terms of corporate governance, many Chinese footwear companies are developed from family-owned firms. The personal wills and social networks of the entrepreneurs still greatly influence decision making and staff appointments. The weakness of entrepreneurs in professional experience and knowledge has built barriers to their firms' global competitiveness. It is urgent to build a modern management institution and introduce professional managers to deal with the development challenges. As to chain governance, it becomes significant when firms need to upgrade their businesses from manufacture to higher value-added sections. However, at present, Chinese firms have difficulties in effectively managing internal factories and external suppliers (especially SMEs) to offer consistent quality and accurate delivery of products. The functions of industry associations are not effective to facilitate the cooperation and coordination of firms in the local economy.

The fifth is R&D. Developing high-end products with advanced technology will be an important task for Chinese firms to compete in the future. However, most of them don't have strong capabilities on these aspects. SMEs lack finance and external support for technological upgrade. Large firms hesitate to make large investment due to the uncertainty of innovation as well as the footwear industry and the attraction of other speculative business. Although some large firms have researched several technologies, they can hardly transform the technological patents to commercial profits. Their R&D cannot keep pace with the development of the consumer needs. The Industry 4.0 strategy adopted by the Western countries has brought revolutionary changes to footwear manufacturing. However, to date, most Chinese firms are not capable enough to deal with these challenges because it needs close cooperation and high coordination among firms and their partners in backward and forward relations to make joint efforts on R&D.

The sixth is marketing and branding. Since shoes are consumer products, marketing and branding are crucial for firms to get market shares. Although some Chinese firms achieved a series of official awards, these awards cannot directly transfer to strength of their brands. Real brands should build on the recognition, trust and loyalty of customers, especially for high-end and foreign customers. However, to date, no Chinese footwear firm has forged global influence and been regarded as a global valuable brand. Their business revenue is mainly from the

Chinese market. Their reputation cannot compete with global brands within and outside China. Branding is a comprehensive project that involves not only investment in advertising, but also the understanding of customers, providing high-quality products, portraying brand values and integrating the whole system of firms into their supply chains. Chinese firms currently are still on their way to accomplish all these tasks.

In a nutshell, despite their large production capacity, Chinese footwear firms are not as competitive as global leaders. With the rise of firms in other countries due to cost advantages, there is not much space left for Chinese firms to continuously produce low-end footwear. The only survival way is to forge competitiveness in the higher-end market. High-end shoes are the concerted results of good materials, decent design, dedicated production, effective management and influential brands. Chinese firms are facing a series of challenges to upgrade and transform their business to supply the high-end market. Export-oriented firms which have large production capabilities must find ways to maintain comparative advantages to their competitors and increase their attractions to global buyers. To domestic market oriented firms which have wide local sales networks, the key issue is to effectively supply competitive products. These tasks put forward higher demands on not only firms' capabilities, but also the nation's support for the industry. It might be necessary for the government to cooperate with firms and tackle their bottleneck issues together, to facilitate the further development of the Chinese footwear industry.

Notes

1 The author estimated the data based on the reports of Euromonitor (2017); Mintel (2017); and APICCAPS (2015).
2 The author estimated the data based on the reports of Euromonitor (2017).
3 The author estimated the data based on the reports of Euromonitor (2017); Mintel (2017); and APICCAPS (2015).
4 Data source: Deichmann (2017). The book converted the figures of EUR into USD based on their yearly average currency exchange rates in corresponding years. See Table 1 in Appendix for more details.
5 The history of "Made in Italy" traces back to the second half of the twentieth century. Its link with fashion was evident from the very beginning of Italy's ascendancy to global design leaders. The Anglo-Saxon expression "Made in Italy" was first used in 1951. The development of Italian fashion in the following 60 years relied on the fame of the wider concepts of "Made in Italy".
6 Adidas is constructing a second Speedfactory near Atlanta for the American market in 2017.
7 Enterprises above designated size are firms with annual revenue from principal business over RMB 5 million from 1998 to 2006, and are industrial enterprises with annual revenue from principal business over RMB 5 million 2007 to 2010, and are industrial enterprises with annual revenue from principal business over RMB 20 million since 2011.
8 The author estimated the data based on the reports of IBISWorld (2017) and China Leather Industry Association (2016).
9 The author estimated the data based on the reports of Euromonitor (2017); MarketLine (2016a); MarketLine (2016b); and APICCAPS (2015).

10 The concept of Industry 4.0 was first coined in Germany in 2011. It is also called as the Fourth Industrial Revolution, Internet of Things or the Industrial Internet. The first industrial revolution from the end of the eighteenth century saw the birth of manufacturing using machines powered by water and steam. The second came at the beginning of the twentieth century, when mass production lines were powered by electric energy. The third came with the change from analogue and mechanical production to electronic and digital technology from the 1970s onwards.

11 The author mainly refers to Gao and Zhang (2002), for the information of Wenzhou's development history of footwear industry before 2002.

12 As Albert Hirschman (1958) pointed out, backward and forward linkages are very important to economic development and they can be modified to maximise the advantages of external economies, complementarities and cumulative causations.

13 The author estimated the data based on the reports of Euromonitor (2017) and Mintel (2017).

14 In 2013, the yearly average currency exchange rate of US dollars to JPY was 97.6. Data source: The World Bank (2017).

15 After 2001, Aokang Group also involved in other investment and management business, such as property and bio-medicine.

16 Load Max is a store brand as well as product brand. It sells shoes, garments, leather products and accessories. In the store, Aokang can supply self-owned brand products as well as introduce other brands of products. Aokang introduced buyers to plan and select a range of products from other brands.

17 Wanda Group is a Chinese multinational conglomerate corporation and the world's biggest private property developer.

18 The author estimated the rankings based on the data of Euromonitor (2017) and Mintel (2017).

19 There were many reasons why Menglani chose Russia as its main export destination. Firstly, Russia is China's neighbour with good diplomatic relationship, so it was cheap and convenient to transport shoes there. Secondly, Russia had a big market for low- and medium-end footwear that was the main products of Wenzhou's firms. Thirdly, the existence of grey custom clearance could help firms get more profits, despite big risks. Grey custom clearance refers to the practice by some government-connected clearance companies in Russia, pushing imported goods into the Russian market at a tax rate far lower than the official level.

20 The number of patent applications does not necessarily mean the quality of these applications and the patents. It still needs a lot of effort and luck for firms to turn these patents to commercial profits.

5 Case study II

Electrical equipment industry

This chapter will show the second case study, on the EE industry. After a brief introduction, it will display the global competition in this field. Then, it will discuss the development history and current situation of China and Wenzhou in the industry. It will concentrate on one leading firm to analyse its diverse approaches towards industrial upgrade and reveal its development challenges.

Brief introduction of the electrical equipment industry

Electricity is the set of physical phenomena associated with the presence and flow of electric charge. It was not until the late nineteenth century that engineers were able to put electricity to practical use. In the past more than one hundred years, with the rapid development of electrical technology, electricity gradually became one of the most important powers, which transformed industry and society. Nowadays, electric power has been the backbone for modern life and used in a wide range of applications everywhere. In homes, it lights rooms, works fans, heats electric stoves and powers televisions. In factories, it drives large machines, powers computers and controls robots. On the road, it enables quick means of transportation, such as electric trains and battery cars. As industry and society progress, the need for electric power is increasing day by day, in terms of not only its volume, but also its security, efficiency, productivity and sustainability.

Before its practical usage, electric power usually experiences the processes of electricity generation, transformation, transmission and distribution. Electricity is often generated at power stations by fuel combustion, nuclear fission, flowing water, wind, solar photovoltaic, geothermal power or electrochemical batteries. After generation, it is usually transformed to high voltage (HV) and transmitted from power stations to electrical substations through transmission networks. Electrical substations then lower the transmission voltage to medium voltage (MV) and carry electricity from transmission systems to individual consumers via distribution networks. Primary distribution lines carry MV power to distribution transformers located near the customers' premises. Distribution transformers reduce the voltage again to low voltage (LV) and then secondary distribution lines supply electricity to residential, commercial and industrial customers. Customers demanding a much larger amount of power might be connected directly to the primary distribution level.

During electricity utilisation, EE plays indispensable roles. A wide range of EE products are applied for electricity generation, transformation, transmission, distribution and usage. They consist of generators, wind turbines, photovoltaic panels, batteries, cables, transformers, switchgears, surge arresters, inverters, motors, contactors, meters, bulbs, switches, plugs, sockets and so on. Given its large number of categories and specifications, EE can be classified as LV, MV and HV apparatus based on different voltage levels during their use. According to the Institute of Electrical and Electronics Engineers, HV refers to a class of nominal system voltages equal to or greater than 100 kilovolt (kV), MV refers to voltages greater than 1 kV and less than 100 kV, and LV refers to voltages 1 kV or less.

The EE industry came into being in the mid-nineteenth century. At that time, a series of electrical technology and products were invented and many EE companies were established in Europe and America. In the following 150 years or so, the spread of electricity usage and the increase of manufacturing, construction and electricity consumption drove the development of the EE industry. In the recent half-century, the industries of global electric power and EE increased dramatically. The electricity consumption per capita increased 2.6 times from 1,201 kWh in 1971 to 3,105 kWh in 2013 and the world's electricity generation grew 3.8 times, from 6,131 terawatt-hours (TWh) to 23,322 TWh from 1973 to 2013 (The World Bank, 2017). In addition, the electricity industry in developing countries increased tremendously. In 1973, the developing world only accounted for less than 30% of the world's electricity generation, while it contributed to more than 53% in 2013 (IEA, 2015: 26). As Table 5.1 indicates, The developing world consumed less than 15% of the global electricity in 1964 but used more than 55% of the volume in 2014. The International Energy Agency (IEA) forecasted that the global electricity demand would reach 32,150 TWh in 2035 and over 63% of the volume would be from non-OECD countries (IEA, 2013: 172).

Table 5.1 Electricity consumption by regions, years 1964 and 2014

Region	*1964*	*2014*
	Percentage (%)	*Percentage (%)*
North America	40.60	21.52
Europe	44.57	22.01
Latin America	3.01	6.28
Asia	10.13	45.92
Africa	1.69	2.97
Oceania	1.30	1.31
World	100.00	100.00
World Volume (TWh)	2,759.4	20,301

Data source: Guyol (1969), IEA (2015). Based on IEA data from 2015 Key World Energy Statistics © OECD/IEA 2015, Licence: www.iea.org/t&c; as modified by Routledge.

The EE industry is usually regarded as a medium technology-intensive sector. However, the technological intensity differs among specific EE products. Products with different functions have different technological intensity. For example, an electricity generator is much more complex than a plug. The former needs a series of components and good coordination of these components, but the latter combines only a few parts. The technological intensity can also be different among products with similar functions. For instance, an LV circuit breaker[1] for the protection of individual household appliances is much simpler than an HV circuit breaker for the protection of the circuits feeding an entire city. Generally, the HVEE industry is more technology intensive than the LVEE industry. HVEE products are physically more massive and technologically more complex than LVEE ones. The production of HVEE products relies more on machinery, while the production of LVEE products needs more labourers. The development of HVEE products needs tremendous investment of R&D and finance and their quality has a much wider and larger influence on the effectiveness, efficiency and safety of electricity utilisations in society.

Due to the importance of electricity to national security and development, the EE industry is under various regulations. Most countries put forward formal rules to regulate industrial operations. Several international organisations and industry associations also set up behaviour standards for participants and provide certificates on quality, safety performance, environmental impact and energy efficiency of products. Although specific rules and standards differ from nation to nation, a few standards and regulations made by several professional and reliable organisations are well recognised in many countries and are adopted for international trade. For example, the National Electrical Code is a regionally adoptable standard made by the American National Fire Protection Association for the safe installation of electrical wiring and equipment in the USA. It is often regarded as a globally advanced standard which has the strictest requirements. The International Electrotechnical Commission (IEC) collaborating with the International Organization for Standardization (ISO) and the International Telecommunication Union publishes standards for all electrical, electronic and related technologies, which influence almost the whole world.

The global EE market is large at present. According to the estimate of IEA (2009: 102–103), the global projected capacity addition in power infrastructure was 1,522 gigawatt (GW) from 2008 to 2015, and the figure will increase to 3,277 GW from 2016–2030. The cumulative power-sector investment over 2008–2030 will reach USD 13.7 trillion, USD 7.2 trillion for generating plants, USD 2 trillion for transmission and USD 4.5 trillion for distribution. In the world, the Asia-Pacific region has a large and growing market nowadays. The region is home to more than half of the world's population, with a sizable portion of these people living in rural areas that currently have limited access to electricity. Robust economic growth combined with rapid urbanisation and growth in fixed investment boost the installation of new electric power systems and EE products. In 2013, the Asia-Pacific region contributed 35% of the global EE market value (MarketLine, 2014b: 10). On the contrary, North America and West Europe have large and mature markets, with most of their inhabitants already living in urbanised areas. Even rural inhabitants typically have ready access to national electric grid supplies. These markets rely on replacement and maintenance of EE products and existing systems. Also, rising ecological concerns and investment in power generation from sustainable sources increase the EE market. In 2013, the Americas and Europe made up 32% of the global EE market (MarketLine, 2014b: 10).

EE products are capital goods. They are often sold through intermediaries to end customers. The channels consist of distributors, contractors, specialists, electricians, DIY (do-it-yourself) stores and direct retails. End customers are numerous, ranging from large- to small-scale business. The large customers are energy utility companies and industrial power users, and the small customers are households, offices and SMEs in various industries. According to their expectation on products, customers are often divided into high-, medium- and low-end users. High-end users have strict requirements on technological properties and product reliability and they do not compromise good product performance with low price. They often are products with good brands for their technological advancement and product reliability. On the contrary, low-end users are sensitive to product price. They want products with certain durability, but their requirements on product technology are comparatively low. They attach more importance to product utility and cost than brands. Medium-end users have certain requirements on product technology and prefer to buy products with a good performance-price rate. Product brands appeal to them when the prices are reasonable.

Global competition in the electrical equipment industry

Industrial concentration

In the EE industry, global competition is fierce. Since the mid-nineteenth century, thousands of companies have collapsed due to competitive pressures, unfavourable economic conditions, world wars and inability of technological advancements. However, a few companies from Europe, America and Japan did survive, stand out and play pilot roles. In the past half-century, they have devoted themselves to improving technology, innovating products, reducing costs and expanding market, which drove massive M&A all over the world.

For example, in 1987, ASEA from Sweden and Brown Boveri from Switzerland, two fierce competitors in the heavy-electrical and power-generation fields, merged to be a new company, ABB, in Switzerland. In 1997, Siemens from Germany took over the non-nuclear power equipment business of Westinghouse in the USA, paying USD 1.5 billion, which represented the rapidly developing groups of powerful global players in strategic industries. In the same year, ABB and GEC-Alsthom[2] from France merged their power generation businesses and created a new company, which had annual sales of USD 11 billion and 25% of total world orders (quoted from Nolan, 2001: 338). After 2000, Schneider Electric from France conducted a series of acquisitions to improve its business structure and strength. For instance, it built an alliance with Toshiba from Japan in industrial control and automation in 2000, enhanced its position in customised sensors by acquiring BEI

Technologies from the USA in 2005, strengthened its renewable energy solutions with the acquisition of Xantrex from the USA, a worldwide leader in the inverter market in 2008, acquired Leader Harvest Power Technologies, one of the leading players in MV drives in China. In 2012, Mitsubishi Electric Corporation from Japan acquired the Messung Group from India, a manufacturer of programmable logic controllers and human machine interfaces, to accelerate its industrial automation systems business. In 2015, Furukawa Electric from Japan reached agreement to take over the overseas commercial rights of underground and submarine power cables from VISCAS Corporation, a joint venture of Furukawa and Fujikura from Japan. General Electric (GE) from the USA completed the acquisition of Alstom's thermal, renewables and grid businesses by paying USD 10.1 billion (General Electric, 2017a: 34).

After intensive M&A, some of these companies developed into global giants, such as ABB, Schneider, Siemens, GE, Alstom, Mitsubishi, Furukawa and so on. These giants occupy advanced technology, global brands, wide product ranges and geographical coverage. In 2011, the global EE market share by value of the top 4 global giants reached more than 42%, GE 17.5%, Siemens 8.6%, Alstom 8% and Schneider 8% (MarketLine, 2012: 11). Considering the market segments of specific products, the industrial concentration is even higher in more technology-intensive sectors. For example, in the global heavy EE industry, 76.5% of the market share was occupied by only four companies in 2010, namely, GE (31.9%), Alstom (19.3%), Siemens (12.8%) and Mitsubishi (12.5%) (Datamonitor, 2011: 13). On the contrary, in the global electrical components and equipment field, the top four companies only had about 27% of the market share in 2013, Schneider 9.9%, ABB 9.7%, Siemens 5.3% and Furukawa 2.4% (MarketLine, 2014a: 11). Despite such difference, the concentration in the EE industry in general will continue to increase in the future.

Competition factors

Firms in the EE industry compete in technological ability, financial strength, service capability, product quality and production cost. In terms of technological ability, it is the key to product safety, reliability, efficiency and productivity. The more complex the products, the more important the technological capability. Firms invest large funds, human resources and persistent efforts in R&D for technological innovation, new products and optimum solutions. For example, ABB has dedicated around USD 1.5 billion (close to 4% of revenues) to R&D with 8,200 technologists every year (ABB Group, 2017b: 8). In 2015, GE invested USD 4 billion to build out analytics software and machine learning capability and USD 2 billion to build leadership in additive manufacturing, equipment and services (General Electric, 2017a: 13). Siemens invested USD 5 billion, 5.9% of its revenue, on R&D, held 56,200 granted patents and had about 33,000 R&D employees (Siemens AG, 2017a: 4). With such large investment, these companies keep pace with the technological and market changes, safeguarding their competitiveness in the industry.

When it comes to financial strength, it is crucial to support R&D and long-term business. In the EE industry, firms take much risk to invest in R&D and make many strategic decisions, such as M&A, bids and project construction, which put forward high requirements on financial strength and operation. For example, in 2015, GE completed its acquisition of Alstom's power and grid businesses by EUR 9.2 billion (USD 10.1 billion), which was GE's largest-ever industrial acquisition. In 2014, GE reached an agreement with Alstom to purchase its power and grid businesses for EUR 2.35 billion (USD 16.5 billion). However, it took GE eight months to negotiate with the European Commission for approval. The Commission finally approved the deal on the condition that Alstom divest central parts of its heavy-duty gas turbines business and key personnel to Italian energy giant Ansaldo Energia. GE's transaction had not completed until it got regulatory approvals in over 20 countries and regions, including the EU, USA, China, India, Japan and Brazil (General Electric, 2017a). Without strong financial strength, it will not be possible for firms like GE to achieve such M&A deals for long-term strategic growth.

As to service capability, it has been increasingly important for competition. EE customers often need professional guidance, advice, solutions and service when they select, purchase, install, use, repair and replace EE products. Firms can gain competitiveness if they are able to provide professional solutions and comprehensive service. For example, Schneider devotes itself to being a global specialist in energy management and automation. In 2015, solutions represented 44% of its sales, including equipment, projects, software and services. Its solutions facilitate the integration of its products, speed up project design, address the efficiency needs of its customers, allow complete but simple control of their operations and enhance their productivity. Schneider has developed an extensive range of digital and maintenance services delivered by a wide network of 37,000 qualified technicians (Schneider Electric, 2017a: 17). Such services help firms like Schneider develop great customer intimacy and close interaction with final end-users, which in turn help their own continuous innovation.

Considering product quality, it is the main concern of customers and the fundamental task for firms. It involves various factors and procedures to improve product quality, including raw materials, processing technics, labour skills, design, production, service and management. For example, ABB is committed to a series of quality objectives to its customers. They include delivering on-time and on-quality products, systems and services that meet or exceed its customers' expectations; identifying and understanding customers' expectations, measuring their perceptions and implementing improvements to increase their satisfaction; enabling and engaging its people at all levels to improve operational performance along the value chain from suppliers to customers; leveraging its partners' and suppliers' strengths to improve its products and businesses from product design to production, installation and operation; continually improving environmental, health and safety performance through all its products, operations, systems and services.

As far as production cost is concerned, it becomes increasingly relevant nowadays. In some sectors, technologies are relatively mature and breakthrough innovations are not expected to take place often. End-users, especially medium- and low-end ones, are not sensitive to minor technological differences, but are continuously looking for cheaper products. Firms therefore have outsourced more and more components to cheap suppliers or shifted their production to low-cost locations in developing countries. Among all the developing countries, China has been one of the most popular destinations for many global giants. For example, nowadays, ABB has 40 joint ventures and 17,000 employees in 139 cities of China. Siemens has 65 companies and 30,000 employees. Schneider has 30 firms and 28,000 employees. GE has 34 joint ventures and 30 production bases and 22,000 employees in 40 cities (ABB Group, 2017a; Siemens AG, 2017b; Schneider Electric, 2017b; General Electric, 2017b). By building joint ventures and production bases, these global giants want to not only establish low-cost bases for components supply, but also capture local market share.

China's electrical equipment industry

In the fierce competition, China has been one of the most important battlefields for EE firms throughout the world. Since the late 1970s, China's EE industry has developed quickly due to its dramatic growth of electricity consumption for industrialisation and urbanisation. As Table 5.2 indicates, its electricity consumption increased more than 10 times from 411.76 TWh in 1985 to 5,638.37 TWh in 2014. From 1980 to 2014, its installed capacity of power generation increased more than 14 times from 65.87 million kW to 1,370.18 kW and total investment in fixed assets grew from RMB 91.1 billion (USD 60.7 billion) to RMB 51,202.1 billion (USD 8,258.4 billion). As the largest emerging market, China has attracted almost all global giants to its domestic market as well as nurtured many local EE firms. In 2015, the revenue of China's EE industry reached RMB 5,351.7 billion (USD 863 billion), employment was 5.5 million and the number of firms above

Table 5.2 China's total investment in fixed assets, installed capacity of power generation and electricity consumption, years 1980–2014

Year	*Total Investment in Fixed Assets (billion RMB)*	*Installed Capacity of Power Generation (million kW)*	*Electricity Consumption (TWh)*
1980	91.1	65.87	–
1985	254.3	87.05	411.76
1990	451.7	137.89	623.04
1995	2,001.9	217.41	1,002.34
2000	3,291.8	319.32	1,347.24
2005	8,877.4	517.18	2,494.03
2010	25,168.4	966.41	4,193.45
2014	51,202.1	1,370.18	5,638.37

Data source: National Bureau of Statistics of China, 1981–2015.

the designated size was 29,578 (National Bureau of Statistics of China, 2016). The import value was USD 51.2 billion and exports got to USD 103.7 billion (China Electrical Equipment Industry Association, 2016: 49–50).

The electric power industry is often regarded as the fundamental and strategic sector for China's national economy. Before the 1980s, only SOEs monopolised China's EE supply system from electricity generation to usage. However, these monopoly firms confronted increasing difficulties in operation and technology as EE demands grew explosively. Thus, the Chinese government gradually broke the monopoly and introduced market reform in the industry after the 1980s. At the same time, it used national industrial policies to facilitate the investment and technological development of key fields within the industry, like electricity generation and ultra-high electricity transmission and transformation. Nowadays, different segments of China's EE industry have different market openness, among which the LVEE segment has developed to be the field with the freest market competition. All firms, regardless of their sizes and ownerships, are permitted to participate after they achieve certain production and quality certificates. Independent industrial associations conduct self-regulation of the industrial competition. Most of Chinese private firms in the EE industry develop their business in the LVEE field. The LVEE industry provides important reference to observe the development situation of Chinese firms in the EE industry.

The LVEE in China is defined as the electrical apparatus that controls and protects the usage of electricity in a circuit where alternating current (AC) voltage is below 1,200 V or direct current voltage is below 1,500 V. It comprises a great range of apparatuses, such as breakers, contactors, switches, relays and meters. It distributes and manages 80% of generated electric power and is widely used in almost every industry and home. The demand of LVEE is considerable. The installation of every 10,000 kW of new electricity generation equipment will bring the demand of 40,000 LVEE products. Besides, most LVEE products need to be replaced or maintained after five years, which creates stable and continuous market demands. The high-end customers in the LVEE industry are mainly large firms from industries which have certain and high technological requirements on the products, such as the telecommunication, electric power, metallurgical, petrochemical, industrial control and high-end real property industries. The medium- and low-end customers are mainly SMEs who do not have high requirements on product technology. The development history, current situation and future trend of Chinese LVEE industry are as follows.

Development history

The development of China's LVEE industry can be divided into four stages.[3] During the process, four generations of China's LVEE products took shape. As Table 5.3 indicates, their classification is based on their invented time, technical performance, functions, dimensions, quality and reliability.

The first stage is before 1979. From 1882 to 1949, the total installed capacity of power generation in China was only 18,500 kW and production capacity was

Table 5.3 Four generations of China's LVEE

Generation	*I*	*II*	*III*	*IV*
Research period	*1960s–1970s*	*1980s–1990*	*1990–2005*	*After 2005*
Market level	Low	Low	Medium	High
Technical performance	Poor	Low	Ordinary	Advance
Function	Few	Basic	Many	Versatile
Dimension	Large	Large	Medium	Small
Quality	Low	Low	Medium	High
Reliability	Low	Low	Medium	High

Data source: The author's summary.

43,000 kWh. By 1948, only 625 firms and 31,712 workers produced the electrical apparatus and very few of them made LVEE. After the establishment of the People's Republic of China in 1949, China's LVEE industry broke the ice, starting from fixing and assembling basic apparatus. During 1949 and 1958, the First Ministry of Machine-building of China founded a team in the Shenyang Low Voltage Switch Factory to survey and imitate 10 series of products from the Soviet Union. In 1958, the Shanghai Electrical Apparatus Research Institute (SEARI) set up a lab to R&D LVEE products. The SEARI was responsible to provide united designs for the industry and assign manufacturing tasks to SOEs in several cities, such as Shenyang, Beijing and Shanghai. By the mid-1970s, it developed the first generation of LVEE products, which met basic domestic needs. In 1979, 600 firms manufactured LVEE and produced 30,530 items and RMB 1.21 billion (USD 756 million) of industrial output. Thereby, China's LVEE industry took its initial shape. However, these products had poor performance, big volume, limited specifications and large material consumption. They were only comparable to the products of developed countries in the 1950s.

The second stage is the 1980s. In 1987, China's installed capacity of power generation reached 0.1 billion kW, so the demand of LVEE increased rapidly, especially between 1985 and 1986. The First Ministry of Machine-building (restructured as the State Machine-building Commission after 1985) launched projects to develop the second generation of products. From 1978 to 1990, 125 series of products were developed, among which 56 were newly invented, 34 were imported from Western countries, and 40 were improved based on the first generation. SOEs in the producing bases of Shanghai, Beijing and Tianjin, Northeast, Zunyi and Tianshui manufactured the products. At the end of the 1980s, the second generation of products took shape. Compared with the first generation, they had higher performance, smaller volume and better structure, but they could nearly match the products of developed countries in the late 1970s and the early 1980s.

The third stage is between the early 1990s and the early twenty-first century. The industry witnessed three climaxes, in 1991, 1998 and the beginning of the 2000s. By 1995, more than 2,000 firms produced LVEE and made 0.5 billion items and

RMB 8 billion (USD 952.4 million) of industrial output. The programmes for upgrading urban and rural grids in 1998 and the large construction of the electric industry in the early 2000s further stimulated the development of the LVEE industry. In addition, since the Fourteenth National Congress of the CPC claimed to develop the socialist market economy in 1992, many private and FIEs entered the industry. The competition among private, SOEs and FIEs formed. Many SOEs were shrunk, reformed or closed, while private firms rose dramatically and plenty of foreign companies came to China.

Private firms were mainly from Wenzhou, such as Chint, Delixi, Tengen and the People Appliances Company. They had broad sales networks and low price and took over the low-end market. SOEs were reformed from the previous planning system, like the Changshu Switchgear Factory and the Shanghai Renmin Electrical Apparatus Works. They had strong technology foundations and occupied the medium-end market. Foreign firms were mainly global giants, like Schneider, ABB and Siemens. They had strong brand influence and technological advantages and occupied the high-end market. In 2000, private firms occupied about 50% of the LVEE market by value, the SOEs had 30% and foreign companies had 20%. By 2005, the third generation of products was developed by the cooperation of the government and firms. Specifically, after the government set up a national plan, the SEARI and a few leading firms collaborated to research and then spread their designs to the whole industry. Besides, other companies were also approved to design their own products based on the market demands. This generation of products had even higher performance, smaller volume and more intelligence with electronic functions and could be modularised and combined. They could match the products of advanced countries in the early 1990s.

The fourth stage is after 2005. In 2005, private firms occupied about 60% of the LVEE domestic market, SOEs had 10% and foreign companies had 30%. However, with the increasing costs of material and labour and demands on products technology and quality, the competition in the industry enhanced greatly. The foreign companies expanded their market share quickly and sought for ways into the medium- and low-end markets. Almost all global giants set up their business, added their investment and introduced new products into China. They cooperated or merged Chinese firms, built local R&D centres and components manufacturing centres, and developed not only high-end products but also economical products for the Chinese market. For instance, in 2015, GE had 22,000 employees, more than 30 plants, 60 technology labs and 34 joint ventures in China (General Electric, 2016: 4). In 2014, Siemens had EUR 6.6 billion (USD 8.8 billion) of sales, 44 factories, 76 enterprises, 33,300 employees, 4,500 sales staff in 60 sales offices, and 4,500 R&D experts and engineers in 20 R&D hubs within China (Siemens AG, 2017b). Several SOEs survived by focusing on a few kinds of competitive products with their profound technology. On the other hand, Wenzhou's private firms suffered from increasing manufacturing costs and poor profits. A lot of firms had to conduct throat-cutting price battles. A few large firms with technology and capital abilities started to develop high- and medium-end products for more profits.

Along with the competition, the fourth generation of products was developed. The previous method of exploring united designs for the whole industry could not continue anymore because the SEARI was not able to independently invent a series of products and its designs were not able to keep pace with the changing market. Therefore, the SEARI selected four series of products and cooperated with eight outstanding firms in 2006 to invest and research together. They agreed to have common IPRs of the new products. In 2010, the R&D for the fourth generation was accomplished. Compared with the third generation, they had more independent design, better structure, technology and performance and all added communicating functions. It caught up with the latest technologies of foreign countries, which were firstly released in the mid-1990s. However, there were still big gaps in the technology applications, manufacturing capability and products maturity between the products from Chinese firms and foreign firms.

Current situation

Currently, China has been the largest LVEE producer in the world. According to the survey of China's Electrical Equipment Industry Association, in 2014, its LVEE industry had more than 1,500 firms, 1,000 series of products, RMB 73 billion (USD 12 billion) of industrial revenue, RMB 1.72 billion (USD 282.0 million) of added industrial value and RMB 5.2 billion (USD 838.7 million) of profits. Its main products were air circuit breakers (ACB), moulded case circuit breakers (MCCB), miniature circuit breakers (MCB) and knife switches.[4] In 2014, LVEE component export reached USD 2.9 billion (Sun, 2015). According to the statistical data of UN Comtrade, shown in Table 5.4, China was the largest global exporter by value in 2015 for the LVEE of switches, connectors and so on. From 2005 to 2015, China's export value increased from USD 3.8 billion to USD 13.8 billion and its global share grew from 6.57% to 15.10%.

Given its large scale of production and export, China's LVEE industry is not strong. In the domestic market, indigenous firms mainly produce most medium- and low-end products. These products have weaker technological performance than foreign products or the ones made by FIEs. In the low-end market, products homogenisation and large excess capacity are common phenomena. In contrast, foreign companies, based on their brand influence, innovation capabilities and advanced products, tightly hold the Chinese high-end market. In 2015, China was the largest global importer of LVEE of switches, connectors and so on, reaching the total weight of 170 million kg and the value of USD 14.2 billion, which was USD 391 million higher than its export. China's average import price was USD 83.18/kg, which was four times than its export price of USD 20.75/kg. From 2005 to 2015, China's share of global import increased from 9.6% to 14.8% (UN Comtrade, 2017).

In addition, some foreign firms even invaded the medium-end or lower-end market with economical products or by purchasing local brands. The battle between indigenous firms and foreign firms in the Chinese medium-end market become the fiercest. The profits for Chinese firms become less and less. According

Table 5.4 Global top 10 exporters and importers of LVEE, years 2005 and 2015

Year	*Rank*	*Exporter*	*Weight (million kg)*	*Value (million USD)*	*Average Value (USD/kg)*	*Importer*	*Weight (million kg)*	*Value (million USD)*	*Average Value (USD/kg)*
2005	1	Germany	170.3	8,192.2	48.12	USA	–	7,115.6	–
	2	USA	235.0	6,576.6	27.98	China	–	5,849.0	–
	3	Japan	96.4	5,719.8	59.33	Germany	115.6	4,528.5	39.16
	4	Hong Kong	182.0	4,707.5	25.86	Mexico	436.2	4,269.9	9.79
	5	France	114.6	3,816.9	33.30	Hong Kong	190.1	3,996.2	21.02
	6	China	161.5	3,804.2	23.56	France	81.0	2,365.6	29.17
	7	Mexico	351.4	3,164.0	9.00	UK	941.3	2,308.5	2.45
	8	Singapore	105.4	2,265.8	21.51	Japan	49.2	2,203.8	44.79
	9	Italy	93.8	2,113.9	22.54	Singapore	83.8	1,847.9	22.06
	10	UK	49.7	1,786.5	35.95	Canada	–	1,826.7	–
		World		57,927.0		World		60,671.6	
2015	1	China	664.2	13,784.1	20.75	China	170.4	14,175.5	83.18
	2	Germany	204.2	11,809.9	57.83	USA	–	10,187.3	–
	3	USA	–	10,414.1	–	Hong Kong	162.4	7,425.6	45.73
	4	Hong Kong	147.4	8,098.3	54.96	Germany	161.4	6,848.3	42.43
	5	Japan	102.5	6,961.7	67.93	Mexico	430.4	6,097.1	14.16
	6	France	151.3	4,279.7	28.28	France	100.8	3,014.1	29.90
	7	Mexico	829.0	3,370.3	4.07	Japan	49.3	2,738.5	55.52
	8	Italy	89.1	2,505.2	28.11	UK	110.8	2,717.5	24.53
	9	Singapore	–	2,237.8	–	Singapore	–	2,148.3	–
	10	Czech	103.1	2,202.6	21.36	Italy	61.2	1,961.8	32.07
		World		92,432.4		World		95,600.5	

Data source: United Nations COMTRADE database, DESA/UNSD, 2017.

Note: The statistics are based on the trade products with the commodity code of 8536.

to an investigation conducted by the China Electrical Equipment Industry Association in 2015, 30% of LVEE firms reported profit drops and 10% reported deficits in 2014 (Sun, 2015: 17). What's worse, compared with foreign companies, the domestic large firms are losing their market shares. According to the research of the Top 100 EE Enterprises in China, as Table 5.5 shows, from 2004 to 2014, the number of foreign companies in the list increased from 18 to 34, while the figure of domestic firms decreased from 72 to 66. Schneider group was the largest winner in the LVEE field. Its number of firms in the list increased from five to nine and sales income increased by 422.81% from RMB 3.455 billion (USD 416.3 million) to RMB 18.062 billion (USD 2.9 billion). Its income percentage

Table 5.5 Top 100 firms in the EE industry in China, years 2004 and 2014

	2004				*2014*			
	Firm Number	*Sales Income (billion RMB)*	*Percentage of Total Sales (%)*	*Profit Rates (%)*	*Firm Number*	*Sale Income (billion RMB)*	*Percentage of Total Sale (%)*	*Profit Rates (%)**
Domestic	72	71.54	78.86	7.85	66	264.12	77.59	4.88
Foreign	28	19.18	21.14	18.38	34	76.30	22.41	17.2
Wenzhou's firms	9	10.64	11.73		11	29.94	8.79	
Schneider's firms	5	3.46	3.81		9	18.01	5.30	

Data source: Dianlaohu (2016).

Note: * Data from year 2013

among the total income of the top 100 firms increased from 3.81% to 5.3%. On the contrary, Wenzhou's private firms grew their sales income by 181.35% from RMB 10.643 billion (USD 1.3 billion) to RMB 29.944 billion (USD 4.8 billion), but their income percentage among the top 100 firms dropped from 11.73% to 8.79%.

In the international market, China's strength is endangered by both developing and developed countries. To date, most Chinese firms have not built their own international sales networks and mainly export medium- and low-end OEM products at low price. They are facing increasing competition on quality and price. On one hand, as Table 5.4 indicates, from 2005 to 2015, although China increased its position from the top 6 to the top 1 among the globally largest exporters, the gap between China and developed countries on average value of export products expanded. In 2005, China's figure was USD 23.56/kg, 49% of the number of Germany, the largest exporter. In 2015, Germany became the second largest exporter and increased its figure by USD 9.7/kg to USD 57.83/kg, but China decreased its average value by USD 2.81/kg to USD 20.75/kg, which was only 35.9% of the German figure. On the other hand, China's advantages of cheap products are challenged by other developing countries. In 2005, China and Mexico (ranking the 7th) were the only two developing countries among the top 10 largest exporters. Mexico's average value was 38.2% of Chinese figure. In 2015, the Czech Republic became the third developing country among the largest exporters, ranking in the top 10 with an average value of 21.36/kg (slightly higher than the Chinese figure). Mexico still held the same position, but it increased its total weight to 829 million kg (164.8 million kg more than the Chinese figure) and reduced its average value by almost USD 5/kg to USD 4.07/kg (only 19.6% of Chinese figure).

Future trend

China's EE industry will experience continuous growth and change in the future. Firstly, both China's and the world's electric industries will increase. In 2014, China's electricity production reached 5,545.9 billion kWh and installed capacity got to 1.36 billion kW, which ranked the first in the world. It was estimated that China would continuously be the globally largest electricity producer until 2030 (China Energy Research Society, 2015). As a result, the demands for LVEE products will also increase in terms of volume and quality. The previous low-end and old generation of products might not be able to meet the requirements of the market, but the medium- and high-end products will expand their market share. Thereby, the firms making low quality products with low technological capabilities will lose their competitiveness in the future. On the contrary, the firms with advanced technology, persistent R&D investment and good quality products and service will win the market.

Secondly, the rapid growth of renewable energy will extend more fields for the LVEE industry. As Table 5.6 shows, in 2014, the installed capacity of renewable energy achieved 435.76 million kW, which accounted for more than 30% of total installed capacity in China. The percentage is expected to increase to 42.9% in 2020 and 60% in 2030. With the development of new energy, the LVEE industry can develop into new domains, such as controlling and protecting systems for new energy, photovoltaic generation inverters and energy storage facilities. Moreover, providing solutions and EPC (engineering, procurement and construction) service for the management of new energy is also newly created business for most firms. Yet, the fast expansion of new energy also presents more requirements to EE products on their reliability and technology. Therefore, it also brings challenges for firms to invent new products and develop new technology.

Thirdly, the construction of a smart grid will create new chances. According to China's Thirteenth Five Year Plan, China will invest RMB 384.1 billion (USD 61 billion) for smart grid construction to manage the energy unitisation more effectively and efficiently (State Grid Hubei Electric Power Company, 2013). By 2020, China is planning to develop its smart grid to an advanced level. The smart grid construction will put forward more requirements for EE products, especially their intelligent, modularised and communicating functions. The fourth generation of products with new technology and better performance will be popular soon. Firms with stronger R&D capabilities will be endowed with bigger space and opportunities to develop and compete in the new development domain of the fourth

Table 5.6 China's installed capacity of power generation, years 2005–2030

Year	*Total (billion kW)*	*Renewable Energy (billion kW)*	*Percentage (%)*
2005	0.52	0.12	23.3
2010	0.97	0.25	26.1
2014	1.36	0.44	32.1
2020	2.0	0.86	42.9
2030	2.4	1.44	60.0

Data source: National Renewable Energy Centre (2015), China Energy Research Society (2015).

generation. At the same time, they are facing more and new difficulties. To make the fourth generation of products, firms should not only improve their manufacturing ability, but also forge their competency in the electronic and software fields.

Fourthly, Industry 4.0 might bring revolutionary changes to the industry. The development of Industry 4.0 projects digitizes the manufacturing sector, with embedded sensors in all product components and manufacturing equipment, ubiquitous cyber-physical systems and analysis of all relevant data. The mind-set and business model that firms need to succeed will be different. There will be a greater need for the type of industrial digital services. The stream of data will be a rich source of business intelligence. There is enormous opportunity to analyse data and feed the resulting digital insights back into machines and systems, to make them more efficient, powerful and reliable. There will be more need for software-differentiated services. The industrial and financial foundations of Chinese firms are much weaker than their competitors from developed countries for these Industry 4.0 changes. However, if they don't participate in the new battle now, they will be further behind their competitors in the future.

Confronting promising markets as well as fierce competition, Chinese firms are facing unprecedented difficulties for further development. It is high time that Chinese firms, especially Wenzhou's firms, took the chance to upgrade and transform, so that they can change their disadvantage situation and get rid of development predicaments.

Wenzhou's electrical equipment industry

The EE industry is one of the most famous and largest industries in Wenzhou. Its development is closely related to China's EE industry.

Development history

The development history of Wenzhou's EE industry can be divided into five stages: embryonic stage (before 1978), rise stage (1978–1991), growth stage (1992–2001), mature stage (2002–2006) and transition stage (2007–present).[5]

The first stage was the embryonic stage before 1978. The development of Wenzhou's EE industry started from the LVEE field. It originated from a 49.88 km^2 town called Liushi. In most of its history, Liushi was a poor place due to regular intrusions of typhoons and pirates. After 1949, residents could hardly feed their children because Liushi had very limited farming lands and little national assistance. In 1965, except for the town centre, there was no electricity in the town and villages nearby. People had to collect scraps, keep bees, fix shoes and be hired as contracted labour outside Liushi for survival. In 1969, the Liushi Repairing Technology Agency produced the first batch of LVEE battery lead plates in Wenzhou. In 1970, a local farmer named Chen Qingyao happened to hear the news that contact terminals of AC contactors were badly needed. This was because many LVEE factories were closed in the Cultural Revolution and SOEs were not allowed to sell components. Mr Chen therefore made the contact terminals with simple and crude tools in Liushi and succeeded in making profits. In 1972, he and a dozen farmers established a factory named Mingdong Electrical Hardware Manufacturing. They borrowed money from relatives, hired them as workers, produced components of electrical apparatus and engaged salesmen to sell their products. Inspired by the Factory, many villagers nearby also built factories to produce LVEE products. In 1975, the Mingdong Factory expanded to more than 100 employees and their average income was five times more than local farmers'. Unfortunately, the Liushi Illicit Trading Office claimed that the Factory conducted illegal private business in the planned economy and shut it down with the accusation of "the capitalist tail". Other LVEE firms thereby had to shut down or turn to operate underground.

The second stage was the rise stage from 1978 to 1991. After 1978, as government control of household firms declined, Liushi's LVEE industry grew quickly, but it also encountered a series of crises. In 1978, the first LVEE salesroom opened its business publicly in Liushi. The number of LVEE salesrooms increased to 54 in 1980 and firms increased to 300 in 1981. With the rapid expansion, many LVEE firms could not get enough raw materials, especially silver. Silver was the most important material for LVEE, but the government strictly regulated it and private trade was not allowed legally. Consequently, some firms used brass to replace silver and some even made fraud products. The quality of Liushi's LVEE was very poor and it even led to big losses of property and life. In 1982, the State Council focused on Liushi and attacked its illegal economic activities. Eight businessmen who operated the largest businesses in different fields were claimed as economic criminals. As a result, Liushi's industrial output dropped by 53.8% compared with 1981. In January of 1984, the central government rehabilitated the eight businessmen and clarified their supportive attitudes towards village firms. Two months later, more than 1,000 salesrooms of LVEE appeared again and 10,000 salesmen and 50,000 employees were involved in the industry.

Despite their large number, most of Liushi's household factories were very small and many of them made unqualified products. In March of 1984, the First Ministry of Machine-building as well as many newspapers criticised Liushi's LVEE products. The town government attacked illegal business in 1984 and 1985 and introduced 1,200 technical experts, built a general factory and a test centre to improve product quality in 1986. Unfortunately, many firms still used inferior materials, renovated second-hand goods and made substandard products without business licenses. In 1988, more than 2,300 firms produced RMB 0.5 billion (USD 135 million) of industrial output in Liushi and half of them made hardware products. In 1990, seven ministries of the State Council collaborated with local working teams to clamp down on illegal manufacturers in 14 villages of Liushi for 6 months; 255 household factories and 78 firms were shut down and 965 salesrooms were closed. On the other hand, all the salesrooms were moved into a Liushi Electrical Equipment Mall to receive united management. Besides, the working teams supported the production of 28 outstanding firms, 21 series and 92 categories of selected products. In 1991, Liushi received the most production certificates in China and its economic order was finally rectified.

The third stage was the growth stage from 1992 to 2001. After 1992, with increasing awareness and persistent government regulation on product quality, Liushi's LVEE industry experienced continuous growth. Firstly, its industrial scale increased. The region of the industry spread from Liushi to nearby towns in Yueqing County. Many firms outside Liushi made components and trade materials for Liushi's LVEE production. In 2001, Yueqing had 850 shareholding firms, 3,000 private firms and 100,000 employees in the industry. Its industrial output expanded from RMB 0.1 billion (USD 20.8 million) in 1990 to RMB 16 billion (USD 1.9 billion). Its LVEE products made more than 60% of domestic market share and half of China's export value. Secondly, firm size increased greatly. In the 1990s, many household factories transformed to formal firms and some SMEs developed into large firms. A few large firms even built group firms and holding companies after 1995. By the end of 1999, there were 115 firms with output above RMB 10 million (USD 1.2 million), 23 firms above RMB 50 million (USD 6 million) and 9 firms above RMB 0.1 billion (USD 12 million) in Yueqing, and 6 firms were rated as national large firms. Thirdly, the product quality improved. From 1996 to 2000, Yueqing's firms and government agents totally invested RMB 2.4 billion (USD 48.2 million) for R&D and achieved 800 patents. According to national sample surveys in 2001, the pass rate of LVEE products in Yueqing was 94.7%, which was 20.7% higher than the national level. Moreover, 49 firms were awarded by governmental agencies as Zhejiang Famous Brands or Wenzhou Famous Brands; 4,200 firms got production certificates, 200 companies received UL and CE[6] certificates and 220 firms got ISO 9000 certificates. In 1999, Chint and Delixi got two awards as National Famous Brands in the industry. Based on their low price and good quality, Wenzhou's firms won their reputation and firmly held their competitiveness after 1998.

The fourth stage was the mature stage from 2002 to 2006. Experiencing ten-year growth, the LVEE industry became mature. Firstly, the industry spread to the whole region of Wenzhou, with its centre in Liushi. A few industrial parks were built and a series of supportive organisations took shape in Wenzhou. An ID came into being, and a great number of firms surrounding Liushi closely cooperated for LVEE production, as seen in Figure 5.1. For example, firms in Mingdong Village mainly produced electrical accessories, firms in Wengyang Town made mine accessories, companies in Hutou and Qianzhou Villages provided AC mutual inductors and enterprises in Donghuangyu Village offered electroceramics. In 2002, Liushi made RMB 11.5 billion (USD 1.4 billion) of industrial output and RMB 12,800 (USD 1,542) of income per head, becoming the strongest town in South Zhejiang. The China Machinery Industry Federation awarded Yueqing County the title of China's Capital of Electrical Equipment; 8 Wenzhou firms were listed in the Top 100 Firms of China's Electrical Equipment Industry (Xiao, 2009).

Second, many firms extended their business from the LVEE industry to the HVEE industry. In 2006, Wenzhou nurtured 1,500 firms producing EE, among which 57 firms had RMB 0.1 billion (USD 12.5 million) of output, 382 above RMB 10 million (USD 1.3 million) and 750 above RMB 5 million (USD 0.6 million). The total industrial output for the EE industry was RMB 45.8 billion

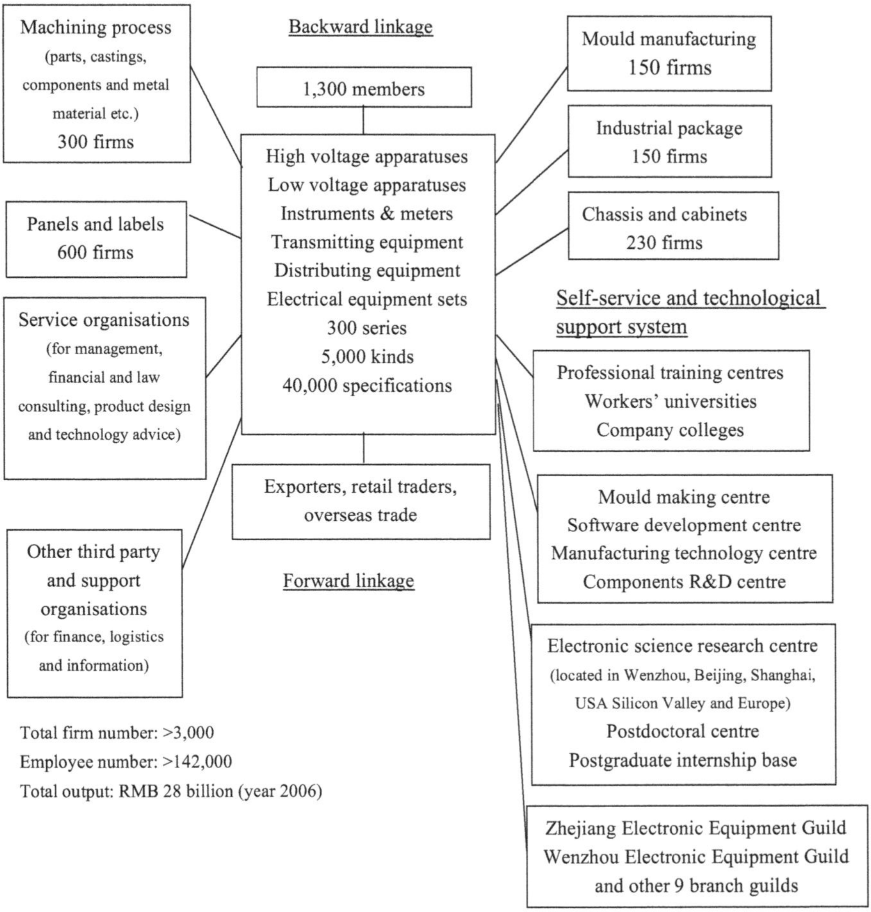

Figure 5.1 Industrial structure of Wenzhou's EE ID
Data source: Ren (2008: 54).

(USD 5.7 billion) and export reached USD 0.57 billion. Wenzhou occupied 10 Top 100 Firms in China's EE industry, 10 China's Famous Trademarks, 14 China's Famous Brands and 31 Inspection-free Products (Xiao, 2009). Wenzhou's firms could manufacture products for almost every field of the EE industry except power generation and developed their sales network throughout China and all over the world. Attracted by Wenzhou's strength, a series of foreign firms came to Wenzhou and built joint ventures. For example, Delixi and Schneider agreed to establish a Delixi Electric Company in 2006, which was the largest joint venture in China's LVEE industry.

The fifth stage was the transition stage from 2007 to present. After 2007, Wenzhou's LVEE industry stepped into a transition stage. Firstly, the competition became excessively fierce. On one hand, the market for Wenzhou's LVEE got relatively saturated, so many of Wenzhou's firms committed to price reduction to keep their customers. However, firms' costs of labour increased and profits got very thin. Firms that were not able to provide products with good performance-price rates at large scales could not survive. Moreover, the establishment of joint ventures, especially the Delixi Electric Company, accelerated firms' reshuffle in Wenzhou. Secondly, many large firms set up branch companies and developed new businesses outside Wenzhou. Due to the lack of industrial lands and R&D talents in Wenzhou, firms had to move their industries with intensive capital and technology to large cities. For example, Chint moved its HV business to Shanghai, Delixi developed its LED (large electronic display) business in Hangzhou, and the People Appliance Group conducted real estate purchases throughout China. As a result, the number of firms above the designated size in the EE and machinery industries increased from 858 in 2007 to 1,254 in 2010 and then decreased to 665 in 2012, and their employees increased from 155,087 in 2007 to 174,019 and then declined to 136,151 in 2013 (Statistics Bureau of Wenzhou Municipality, 2008, 2011–2014). The government put forward industrial policy and appealed to local firms to transform and upgrade their business.

Current situation

After five stages of development, Wenzhou's EE industry has its strength as well as predicaments at present.

On one hand, Wenzhou has the strength of a large production scale, developed ID and emerging brand influence.

Firstly, Wenzhou has a large production scale. As Table 5.7 shows, in 2014, Wenzhou produced RMB 118 billion (USD 19.3 billion) of industrial output and USD 1.65 billion of exports and hired 250,000 people in the EE industry. Yueqing County contributed RMB 103 billion (USD 16.9 billion) of industrial output and Liushi Town made RMB 51 billion (USD 8.4 billion); 60% of the output was from LVEE, 20% from HVEE and 10% from cables. Wenzhou's LVEE occupied 60% of domestic market share by output value. The products consist of 200 series, 6,000 categories and 25,000 specifications for electricity transmission, transformation and distribution, industrial control and special usage. More than 10,000 firms were involved in the industry and most of them were SMEs; 500 firms were above the designated size, 150 firms had above RMB 0.1 billion (USD 16.4 million) of output, 27 firms had above RMB 0.5 billion (USD 82.0 million), 16 firms had RMB 1 billion (USD 164 million) and 2 firms had RMB 5 billion (USD 820 million). Four firms were among the Top 500 Chinese Firms, 8 firms were among the Top 500 Chinese Private Firms, 6 were listed companies; 3 firms built national technology centres, 11 firms had Zhejiang technology centres and 67 firms were rated as high-technology companies.

Secondly, Wenzhou has a developed ID. Wenzhou's EE industry has formed a developed ID, which is the first ID with more than RMB 100 billion (USD 16.4 billion) of output in South Zhejiang. The firms in the ID are highly concentrated in the

Table 5.7 Wenzhou's EE industry, year 2014

Indices	*Data*
Output value (RMB billion)	118 (Yueqing County 103, Liushi Town 51)
Employment	250,000
Enterprise number	10,000+
Number of enterprises above designated size	500+ (150 >RMB 100 million, 27 >RMB 0.5 billion, 16 >RMB 1 billion, 2 > RMB 50 billion)
Number of high-technology enterprise	67
Number of listed enterprise	6
Number of China's Top 500 Firms	8
Certificates	Production certificate, CCC, UL, CE
National honour	China's Capital of Electrical Equipment
	China's Manufacture Base for Explosion-proof Electric Apparatus
	China's Base for Breakers
	China's Export Base for LVEE
	National Torch Plan for Intelligent Electric Apparatus
	China's Manufacture Base for Building Electric Apparatus
	National New Industrialisation Equipment Manufacture Centre
Domestic market share	>60% (LVEE)
China's Famous Brand	10
China's Famous Trademark	14
Export value (billion USD)	1.65

Data source: The author's summary.

zone of 200 km^2 near Liushi, involving 28 industrial parks, 4 production bases, 2 headquarter economic zones and 1 Chinese Electrical Equipment Mall (Wenzhou Municipal Government, 2014a). Firms communicate information, share resources and cooperate with each other regularly to reduce manufacturing costs and benefit from scale effects. In the ID, a few leading firms specialise in making key components, assembling semi-products, sales, marketing and R&D. SMEs produce components within the vertical system of large firms. Besides, there develop a great number of firms to supply materials, such as steel, copper, aluminium and various plastics, fabricated products and electronic components.

Moreover, a series of public facilities are established to promote the industry.[7] For example, six post-doctoral research institutes are founded to R&D EE products. Also, a few e-commerce websites, such as China's Industrial Electrical

Equipment Net, are set up to release product information and conduct online business. In addition, Wenzhou has an advanced transportation network of highways, railways and air and sea routes. Besides, the Wenzhou Electrical Industrial Association as well as 17 other sub-division industrial associations are nurtured. They launch forums and publish newspapers to offer firms information, protect firms' welfare and keep industrial order. They also collaborate with the government and firms to hold the Electrical Equipment Culture Exhibition every year since 2001, which helps to improve the reputation and recognition of Wenzhou's products in the country and the world. Furthermore, the industry has a broad sales network. It was reported that 75% of Wenzhou's products were sold by 20,000 distributors outside Wenzhou, 20% were sold by firms and 5% were sold via e-commerce (Wenzhou Municipal Government, 2014a).

Thirdly, Wenzhou has an emerging brand influence. With the development of the ID and firms, Wenzhou has created its influence of region brand, firm brands and product brands in the EE field. By 2014, Wenzhou had 7 national honours related to the industry, such as China's Capital of Electrical Equipment, China's Production Bases of Electronic Components and Breakers and Explosion-proof Electric Apparatus. Wenzhou also achieved 10 China's Famous Trademarks, 14 China's Famous Brands, 2 Zhejiang's Famous Brands, 45 Zhejiang's Famous Trademarks and 49 Zhejiang's Famous Products (Wenzhou Municipal Government, 2014a). In addition, Wenzhou had the most production certificates and national and international authentication certificates in China. These awards and certificates might be useful references for customers, especially domestic medium- and low-end customers. In addition, Wenzhou's large firms, such as Chint, Delixi, Tengen and the People Appliance Group created a certain degree of brand impacts on the domestic market. Furthermore, some firms specialised in producing a couple of products and made their influence on specific sub-fields. For example, Xingle is famous for cables, Huguang for transformers, Yonggu for electric metal tools and Huayi for wind power generating units. Such brand influence of the region, firms and products have contributed to the competitiveness for Wenzhou's firms in the industrial competition.

On the other hand, Wenzhou has the predicaments of disorderly firm competition, limited technology capability and insufficient public services.

Firstly, disorderly firm competition is a problem. Despite the large number of product specifications, product homogenisation is a big issue in Wenzhou. For example, an MCB product called DZ47 has been manufactured in Liushi for more than 26 years. Almost every firm produces it and its current output still reaches 4 million poles every day. Many firms share the same design map and get components and materials from the same providers. To get profits, some firms make fake products and cut down on materials. Therefore, the firms making qualified products suffer from the loss of reputation and profits. What's worse, many small firms are conducting illicit competition. Despite the large number, 70% of Wenzhou's EE firms are small and tiny. Due to their limited capability of capital and technology, some small firms often copy designs and imitate brands of outstanding firms. As a result, outstanding firms that invest in R&D can hardly get the benefit from their IPRs.

Secondly, Wenzhou has limited technology capability. Wenzhou lacks advanced technical experts. In the industry, most workers only have senior high school education. Although there are a few universities in Wenzhou, they train a very limited number of students for the EE industry. What's worse, due to Wenzhou's high living cost, very few high-end talents tend to stay in Wenzhou, where public resources for education, entertainment and living are comparatively less than large cities. Moreover, the technological spillover from large firms is weakened. With the outward migration of large firms, local SMEs can hardly get first-hand information about the latest technology. They also have difficulties in making high-end components and products because many large firms produce them by themselves or buy them outside Wenzhou.

Thirdly, Wenzhou has insufficient public services. First, the public support for R&D is not enough. Although Wenzhou has established a series of research organisations, their functions of developing key and general technology, tracing frontier technology and providing high-end technology service are weak. Second, financial service is backward. Although Wenzhou was granted the status of an experimental zone to reform the financial system, it still has very limited approaches to offer firms with funds for technology. The loan costs for firms are high and most SMEs still can hardly get financing within the formal bank system, which is big, and key barriers prevent SMEs from technical progress. Third, logistics service cannot satisfy the industrial needs. Most EE firms mainly rely on trucks to supply domestic distribution. However, there is no large-scale business freight station in Wenzhou. The operational logistics companies are small and cannot provide large-volume and high-quality transportation service. The logistics consumption of finance and time are still high for most local firms.

To take full advantage of its strength and get rid of its predicaments, Wenzhou's EE industry must commit in transformation. In the industry, large firms are the leaders within Wenzhou and the direct competitors for firms outside Wenzhou. They undertake more attention and responsibility for the upgrade and transformation. Among all the large firms in Wenzhou, Chint Group stands out due to its influence and achievements. Its ways of transformation provide important lessons and reference for firms in Wenzhou's as well as China's EE industry.

Leading firm: Chint Group

Chint Group is the largest firm in Wenzhou's EE industry. It has total assets of over RMB 30 billion (USD 4.8 billion) and 29,000 employees. Its business ranges from LVEE to power transmission and distribution equipment and services, instruments and meters, building appliances, automobile parts, industrial automation, photovoltaic power generation and equipment manufacturing. Its products are sold in more than 100 countries and its business operation spreads all over the world and within China. Compared with global giants like Siemens, it has less coverage in the international area, but has more intensive operations and a deep-rooted sales network in China. Zhejiang Chint Electrics Limited Company, a subsidiary of the Group, is the largest company in terms of production and sales volume in the LVEE industry in China. It is also the first listed company specialised in LVEE on the Shanghai Stock Exchange. It produces 406 series and 11,916 specifications of LVEE. In 2014, its operating revenue of LVEE reached RMB 12.5 billion (USD 2 billion), which accounted for more than 17% of China's LVEE industrial revenue. In 2015, Chint had more than 300 core agents and 2,000 sales points supported by a strong logistics network. It ranked 362nd among the Top 500 Chinese Firms. It collaborated with 12 of Wenzhou's private firms to establish a private bank named Myshare Bank, which specialised in providing financial service for SMEs (Zhejiang Chint Electrics Limited Company, 2015; Chint Group, 2017).

In China's LVEE industry, Chint has forged its advantages in terms of production, sales, brand and technology. Firstly, it has strong production capability. Chint can take full advantage of production scale to reduce cost. Also, located and developed in Wenzhou's EE ID, it is very convenient for Chint to build long-time partnerships with component and material suppliers to secure stable supply products with optimum price and quality. Secondly, it has sales advantages. Chint develops mature distributor networks with wide geographical coverage, which are deeply embedded in many industrial cities within China and actively interact with various potential customers, especially SMEs, and serve them with fast response and reasonable service. The distributors are usually independent from Chint Company and they procure Chint's products for sale. Chint gives distributors price discounts and utilises distributors to expand its market influence and sell products. Thirdly, it creates a good brand image within China. With more than 30 years' development, Chint has been a well-recognised local brand. It is the top LVEE brand in the list of China's 500 Most Valuable Brands in the EE industry. In the market, its products are popular and trusted by a wide range of customers in the low- and medium-end market.[8] Fourthly, it has technological advantages. Chint has built an R&D system, achieved more than 174 patents and developed more than 100 series of products with IPRs. Many of its products have an international advanced level of technical properties, and some of them, like NM8,[9] even gained national awards for engineering scientific progress (Chint Group, 2017).

Development history

Chint's growth experience reflects the development of Wenzhou's EE industry. Chint's founder and CEO is Mr Nan Cunhui, who was born in a poor family in Liushi, discontinued his study from junior high school and used to work as a cobbler to survive. In 1984, inspired by the massive development of LVEE household factories, he and his classmate Mr Hu Chengzhong with RMB 50,000 (USD 21,739) of capital founded a firm called the Yueqing Qiujing Switch Factory, which means always striving for excellence. The factory was within Mr Nan's home, hired 8 workers and sold its products to salesmen. From 1984 to 1988, like other small household factories, product quality was an issue. Fortunately, Mr Nan attached great importance to quality and made great efforts to improve technology.

With his persistency and sincerity, Mr Nan persuaded three retired engineers from the Shanghai People's Electrical Apparatus Factory to work for Chint. In 1988, the factory got a legal production certificate and was one of only four firms that firstly achieved the certificates in Liushi. With qualified products and legal license, the factory grew quickly. In 1989, its profit was RMB 100,000 (USD 26,316), and it increased to RMB 10 million (USD 2.1 million) in 1990 and RMB 20 million (USD 3.8 million) in 1991.

In 1991, due to disagreement on firm management, Mr Nan and Hu ended their cooperation. To take full advantage of national preferential policy on FIEs, Mr Nan introduced finance from his brother in-law in the USA and built up a Sino-American joint venture, the Wenzhou Chint Electrics Limited Company. He used the capital and policy to import machines and technologies for production. At the same time, he began to build Chint's domestic sales network via Wenzhou's migrant businessmen. In 1994, Mr Nan established the first group firm in Wenzhou with 53 affiliated members and registered its trademark Chint. The meaning of Chint is China's Tomorrow. Integrating capital, product and technology of local outstanding SMEs, Chint took a road to group operation and resulted in rapid expansion. In 1997, the Zhejiang Chint Electrics Limited Company was established to specialise in Chint's LVEE business. In 1999, Chint further opened its first overseas office in the Middle East, marking its first step towards internationalisation. During the process, Chint attached great importance to R&D. In 1995, its DW17–1600–2500 ACB and CJ24 AC contactor and RT15 fuse protector were awarded as national new products.[10] In 1998, the success of its N series of products indicated its capability of independent design. Moreover, Mr Nan conducted reform in stock ownership and shared stock with key technicians and managers to encourage their work. From 1997 to 2001, Chint invested RMB 10 million (USD 1.2 million) to build an automatic assemble line to produce AC contactors and MCB.

After 2003, Chint extended its business to the HVEE field. In 2004, it built a Chint Electric Limited Company in Shanghai for the projects of electricity installation and design. In the following years, it established manufacturing bases of LVEE products, instruments and meters, building appliances, power transmission and distribution equipment, industrial automation products and photovoltaic power products in Southeast China successively. Given its multiple industries, almost all of Chint's business is related to electricity. In the 2000s, it obtained over 200 Chinese and international patents and led the formulation of more than 30 standards in the industry. The Zhejiang Chint Electrics Limited Company successfully went public on the Shanghai Stock Exchange in 2010. Moreover, Chint further developed its strategy of internationalisation and set up overseas subsidiaries in America, Italy, Russia, Brazil, the United Arab Emirates and other regions. Since 2001, Chint has been continuously listed as the Top 100 Firm in China's EE industry and displayed its strong competitiveness, especially in the LVEE field. Its subsidiary company, the Zhejiang Chint Electrics Limited Company, ranked 7th among the 2015 Top 100 Firms of China's EE industry.

Peer competition

The rise of Chint has attracted great attention and it encountered fierce competition from its peers. Among all its competitors, Schneider is the most outstanding one due to its successful operation in the Chinese market and strength in the LVEE area. The competition between Chint and Schneider has influenced almost all the firms in Wenzhou's as well as China's EE industry.

Schneider was founded in 1836 in France. In the past 180 years, it has developed itself to be the global specialist in energy management. In 2014, it had more than EUR 25 billion (USD 33 billion) revenue, 170,000 employees in over 100 countries and EUR 1.1 billion (USD 1.5 billion) R&D investment; 26% of its revenue was from Western Europe, 27% from North America, 29% from the Asia-Pacific region and 18% from the rest of the world (Schneider Electric, 2015). Schneider is one of the pilot global giants entering China's market. It built the first joint venture Merlin Gerin in Tianjin in 1987 and then purchased the firm in 1992. It firstly introduced the technology of breakers and switch panels to Chinese people and made a big contribution to improved energy safety and management in China. In the past 30 years, it has succeeded in building, merging and co-funding a series of firms within the country. Currently, it has 28,000 employees, 53 agencies, 28 factories, 7 logistics centres, 1 training school, 1 energy university, 3 global R&D centres, 1,000 engineers, 1 lab and 700 distributors and a broad network throughout the country. China has been one of the most important markets, which created EUR 3.89 billion (USD 4.3 billion), accounting for more than 14.6% of Schneider's global revenue in 2015 (Schneider Electric, 2017b). With its remarkable acquisition achievements all over the world, Schneider is ambitious for the Chinese market and holds a strong position to merge large Chinese competitors. Schneider has regarded Chint as a local competitor in the Chinese market and persistently tried to beat and acquire it.

The contests between Schneider and Chint started in the 1990s and continuously enhanced in the past two decades.[11] The first visit of Schneider to Chint traces back to 1994 when Chint Group was just founded and its sales revenue was less than RMB 0.1 billion (USD 11.6 million). During the negotiation, Schneider asked for 80% of Chint's share, but Mr Nan refused its request because he did not want to lose his control on the firm. On the second day, Schneider sued Chint for violation of its appearance patents. Mr Nan had very little knowledge of IPRs then, so he was forced to compromise for compensation. Since then, he started to pay great attention to Chint's development and IPRs. In 1998, Schneider visited Chint again when it was conducting stock ownership reform. Schneider negotiated for 51% of Chint's share and promised to pay 30% more money than Chint's market value. However, Mr Nan refused its request again because he realised the purpose of Schneider's cooperation was to control Chint's development and finally beat the firm and its brand. In 2004, Schneider put forward its third negotiation plan, which wanted to buy 50% of Chint's share with RMB 10 billion (USD 1.2 billion) and agreed to hire Mr Nan as the chairman. The plan seemed to be win-win, and the local government was also happy to introduce a Global Top 500 Firm into Wenzhou. However, Mr Nan refused it finally. He thought Schneider's entry might lead to delays of making important decisions on the firm's development. Also, he was concerned that Schneider would prohibit the sale and marketing of Chint's products in foreign countries and might merge it in the future. However, Mr Nan was ambitious and determined to make Chint a global Chinese brand and global private firm. After the failure of the negotiation with Chint, Schneider turned to Delixi, the second largest EE firm in Wenzhou for acquisition.[12]

Along with the negotiation, Schneider and Chint were also opponents in the court. From 1994 to 2006, Schneider sued Chint 24 times within and outside China, claiming that Chint violated its IPRs. After 2004, Schneider filed nearly 20 patent-related lawsuits against many Chint products in Germany, Italy, France and other European countries. The purpose of Schneider was to use the IPRs as a weapon and obstruct the distribution of Chint products in Europe. Although Chint has won many cases, it lost the opportunities to introduce its products into the European market in a good time.

The successive lawsuits gave Chint great awareness of IPRs and it thereby actively conducted R&D and applied for its own IPRs. In 2006, Chint found that C65a, C65N, C65L and EA9AN[13] of Schneider's MCB products encroached its utility model patent of ZL 97248479.5. Therefore, it sued Schneider Electric Low Voltage (Tianjin) Limited Company and its retailer Yueqing Subsidiary of Star Electrical Equipment Company in the Wenzhou Intermediate Court. Latterly, the auditing department supported by the Court found that Schneider had RMB 0.88 billion (USD 115.8 million) of sales related to the products charged by Chint. Therefore, in 2007, the Court ordered Schneider to compensate Chint for RMB 0.33 billion (USD 43.4 million), which was the highest amount of compensation in China for a firm's lawsuits by then. Schneider did not accept the result and applied for the second instance to Zhejiang Superior Court. After a long-time inquisition, the Superior Court decided to keep the claim of the first instance. However, Chint and Schneider finally achieved a global compromise agreement before the Court pronounced its judgment in 2009. Schneider decided to respect Chint's IPRs and agreed to pay Chint RMB 0.15 billion (USD 22.1 million). Chint agreed to end its lawsuit on this case to contemporarily finish its long-time legal struggle with Schneider in the world. In this case, Chint did not get a formal announcement for its success and Schneider kept its global reputation at the cost of the compensation. The result of the case might implicate that Chint had achieved technical advances in certain field, but the international influence of the case was limited and Chint still has many technical battles to fight in other fields.

During the fierce peer competition, many global giants like Schneider are not able to completely defeat Chint. In contrast, Chint has been very tenacious to survive, further developed itself and gradually emerged to be an undeniable competitor in the global EE industry. It has cultivated strong IPR awareness, forged market competitiveness and strengthened the determination to upgrade and develop.

Way of transformation

Chint made great efforts to develop new products, enhance the production process, reinforce supply management, strengthen sales network and extend industrial chain.

Develop new products

Chint endeavoured to develop new products for different markets. On one hand, it upgraded its existing economical products for the low- and medium-end market. Faced with the common phenomenon of homogenous products in the market, Chint tried to explore different products, to distinguish itself and gain exclusive profits. In the late 1990s, it used to successfully release the N1[14] series of products, which had better performance and cheaper price than like products in the market at that time. However, in the following years, despite hard work, Chint could hardly promote new products that were as successful as the N1 series in sales performance. For example, in 2003, it launched its N8 series, which had better technological performance and higher price. In 2009, it promoted its fourth generation of products, the N7 series. Neither of them could replace the N1 series or meet Chint's sale targets. In 2012, Chint researched the N100 and N200 series, but they were aborted before going to the market. Although the N1 series of products were still Chint's bestsellers until now, they tended to be outdated, as the consumer needs and the LVEE technology had increased in the past decade.

When Chint was struggling for product breakthroughs, Delixi Electrics cooperating with Schneider put forward its economical products named Pilot in 2014. Based on its low-price strategy, Delixi expanded its market share quickly. For instance, its output volume of DZ47s products reached 0.3 billion poles within one year. To keep its market share, Chint accelerated its research and finally launched an NX series in January 2016. Instead of conducting a price battle, Chint paid more attention to technological improvements of the new products. It was the first time for Chint to mobilise all R&D staff in different manufacturing divisions to cooperate and develop a whole series of products, covering all specifications of ACB, MCCB, MCB, motor controllers and protectors. It was reported that the research process involved more than RMB 0.15 billion (USD 24.2 million), three years and 400 R&D staff and created more than 360 patents and experienced more than 7,860 reliability tests. This series was expected to greatly improve the product quality in Chinese LVEE field (Chint Group, 2017).

On the other hand, Chint tried to develop high-end products. It not only aimed to open its territory in the high-end market, but also to create a Chinese global brand. Chint's first trial of developing high-end products was its N8 series, but its sale performance was poor. Chint believed that the customers' stereotype that Chint was a low- and medium-end brand was the main reason of N8's failure. Thus, in 2007, it decided to create a new brand named Noark for the high-end market. Noark was an abbreviation of Noah's Ark, which aimed to build a large and reliable brand image for international customers. Based on its successful operation experience in the low- and medium-end market, Chint was optimistic to develop Noark. It built factories and regional headquarters in Shanghai, Los Angeles and Prague. In 2009, it collaborated with the SEARI to found a Shanghai Electric Science and Apparatus Technology Company to research high-end products and front-edge technology.

After a few years' efforts, based on the design of the N8 series, in 2009, Noark launched its first series of products, Ex9, with its price lower than the similar offers of global giants. In 2010, MCCB of the Ex9M[15] series won Red Dot Design Award of Germany, which was regarded as an Oscar award for the industry and Noark became the first Chinese firm in the LVEE industry to achieve the award. It also tried to improve several technological parameters of its products to an international advanced level. For example, its ACB products had the ultimate breaking capacity of 7,500 A, which was much higher than the international standard of 6,300 A. The development of Noark attracted wide attention from its global competitors and they promoted corresponding products to prevent the threat from Noark. Considering Chint's professional experience in the field and much investment in Noark, some people estimated that Noark would grow quickly and have its proper place in the high-end market soon.

Chint's development for new products showed its profound technological strengths in the industry. Firstly, it had a competent research team. Chint's R&D team consisted of skilled engineers in manufacturing divisions and professional researchers from the SEARI. The former had first-hand experience and good understanding of product production and modification, and the latter had frontier information and advanced knowledge of technological trends and ideas. The cooperation of the two forces helped Chint develop a wide range and multiple levels of products for different customer needs. Secondly, Chint laid a solid foundation for technological innovation. It had persistent and practical experience of tracing the technological trend, improving existing products and technological learning and accumulation. It did make some breakthroughs in a few products and in certain segments. Different from most other firms in Wenzhou, Chint forged good consciousness of technological exploration and started to change gradually from complete imitation to indigenous innovation. Thirdly, Chint has the broadest and most intensive sales network in China among its peers. The network makes it possible for Chint to get more access, information and feedback from customers. In this way, it can keep pace with the market trend and improve its product and technological innovation for customers.

Given the above accomplishments, it might be an overstatement that Chint is completely successful at the current stage. It tried to put forward many series of new products, but the sales results were not as good as expected. In the low- and medium-end market, Chint's development of new products is not creating an innovative product, but modifying existing popular products and providing them in the market at a lower price. However, when global giants put forward simplified products at friendlier price to the low- and medium-end customers, Chint must carefully trade off price reduction against product improvement. Although it launched the NX[16] series in a short time after Delixi's attack in its market share, the final result of the series remains to be seen. It will need some time to execute mass production and sales. During the process, there is some uncertainty of the NX series' execution, and its opponents might corrode its market share. In the high-end market, Noark's development is much slower than Chint's expectation. After eight years' growth, its revenue was RMB 294.1 million (USD 47.4 million) in 2015, which accounted for only 2.5% of Chint's revenue in the LVEE field (Zhejiang Chint Electrics Limited Company, 2016). Noark is still an unknown brand with little influence abroad to date. Given its cheaper price, the failure of Noark is related to its weaker brand influence compared with global giants, but the deeper reason is its comparatively lower product reliability. For most high-end consumers, product reliability is uncompromising to low price. Chint still needs to make up its technological gap to improve Noark's product reliability.

Among diverse technological capabilities, design capability is regarded as the most outstanding issue. Although Chint operated LVEE business for more than 30 years, its design capability is still behind global giants. This is attributed to its development history, current design process and R&D strength. First, as a late-comer, Chint's technology learning is mainly based on reverse engineering of foreign products or buying design maps from the SEARI. With its hard work, it took a shortcut to know product design structures and succeeded in producing them. Yet, Chint's large manufacture capability does not necessarily indicate its strong design ability. Chint as an external company can hardly learn various design experience and tacit knowledge of global giants through imitation. The unknown knowledge becomes technological barriers preventing Chint from further improving its product design. Chint should explore the knowledge gradually through long-time accumulation of design experience and revision of technological errors. More importantly, it should forge critical and innovative thinking to reform existing products and make technological breakthroughs. The achievement of innovation capability can hardly be gained without persistent efforts of abandoning traditional approaches, introducing fresh ideas from inside and outside, taking risks and commercialising innovations. It will be a challenge for Chint to overcome the path dependence on imitation within its company.

Second, Chint's current design process is shorter. Usually, product design is a systematic process, which needs much time and efforts from multiple parties. In global companies, the product design will normally last for a few years to ensure product reliability and maximise the possibility for commercial profits. Based on market investigation, they will make product development plans, which introduce customers' new demands on product performance and propose a proper product line arrangement. The R&D department will try to adopt new technology or designs to improve the product performance. They will use advanced design software and comprehensive stimulation technology (usually developed by themselves or with their strategic partners) to design products, conduct failure mode and effects analysis, modify technological errors and optimise product performance. In many companies, they will also involve strategic customers to provide feedback on the potential new products. In this way, the product reliability of global giants is high and they firmly hold their leading positions based on their innovative technology and designs. However, the design process in Chint is different. In most cases, there is no clear plan of product lines in advance. The motivation of product development is to produce the existing popular products in the market as soon as possible, so as to quickly grab the market share based on its cost advantage. Based on such design process, Chint is more likely to be a technological follower that is rushed for short-time market share, rather than a technological innovator grasping long-time exclusive profits.

Third, Chint's R&D strength is weaker than global giants. In terms of finance, the R&D investment of Chint is much less. For example, in 2015, its R&D expenditure was RMB 0.5 billion (USD 80.6 million), accounting for 4.15% of its operation revenue. However, the figure of Schneider was 20 times more than Chint. It reached EUR 1.3 billion (USD 1.4 billion) and accounted for 5%. Chint's R&D strength is also not competitive to FIEs. For example, in 2014, Siemens had 4,500 R&D experts and engineers in 20 R&D hubs within China, which were much larger than Chint's figures. With sufficient research expenditure, global giants can have more resources to explore frontier technology and boost their innovation. Furthermore, Chint is very cautious on long-term investment. As a private company with limited fund sources, it worries that any investment failure will lead to destructive loss. Therefore, it tends to invest the technology that can bring potentially viewable profits rather than the very frontier technology with uncertain market prospect. The cautiousness on long-run technological investment might help Chint avoid investment mistakes sometimes, but it also decelerates its technological development pace.

When it comes to human resources, Chint's R&D team is weaker. At present, the researchers from the SEARI are mainly based in Shanghai. They are more used to conducting academic and theoretical research than exploring concrete products that create direct commercial profits. In contrast, most engineers are based in Wenzhou's manufacturing divisions. They are busy in fine-tuning existing products rather than really creating new products. Given some improvements, the two groups still have difficulty in working together effectively due to the geographical separation and different education and work backgrounds. The weakness of Chint's R&D strength can only be alleviated gradually when it increases its business scale and cultivates its research team in the future.

Enhance production process

Chint enhanced its production process by implementing lean production reform, innovating management organisations, building an employee training system and automating production procedures. Firstly, it pushed for lean production reform after 2005. To maintain its cost advantage, Chint attached great importance to minimising waste within the manufacturing process. It praised highly the ideas and practices of lean production management and built partnership with experts to examine and modify its production system. In the past few years, with the experts' guidance, it conducted a series of CIP (continuous improvement process) projects,[17] strengthened 6S (sort, straighten, sweep, standardize, sustain and safety)[18] management, adopted the pull principle[19] and improved value stream mapping.[20]

The adoption of lean production benefited Chint with cost reduction and efficiency improvement. Furthermore, it actively involved workers in the lean production practices. It employed and trained some university graduates majoring in engineering as lean production managers to supervise the reform in the workshops. Also, it posted the basic knowledge and management requirements of lean production in the workshops and organised regular meetings to educate workers. Moreover, it established a reward system to encourage workers to put forward improvement suggestions.

Secondly, it innovated management organisation to improve labour productivity. In China, many private firms developed social organisations among their workers. Chint took full advantage of these organisations to facilitate its production management. Inspired by the Chairman Mao's idea of building CPC branches based on companies, Chint built its CPC branches based on workshops after 2010 and the CPC Committee of the Chint Group led all the branches.[21] It thereby organised about 300 Five United Working Groups in its production divisions. Each working group was based on one production line and actively interacted with social groups during the production process.

The working group would have five representatives from executive managers, CPC members and the members of the communist youth league, labour union and women workers. Each of them had different tasks: the executive manager was mainly responsible for the accomplishment of assigned work tasks. The CPC member played the roles of giving workers spiritual encouragement, spreading political news and collecting workers' appeals. The member of the communist youth league oversaw organising after-hour activities to facilitate the emotional communication and skill exchange among workers. The labour union member helped to solve workers' difficulties and defend their welfare. The women's representative was to provide special care for female workers. Regularly, different working groups would launch events of mutual learning and skill competition to circulate the good knowledge and practices within the company.

Thirdly, it established its employee training system. Chint made efforts to improve labour skills by providing them with a range of training programmes. In 2013, it launched its Five Eagle Training Campus to offer annual training for different employees based on their work requirements, positions, experience and interest. The five eagles referred to young eagles (new employees), flying eagles (core employees), blue eagles (division supervisors), gold eagles (managers) and strong eagles (general managers and above). For all the new employees, the training ranged from company's culture and firm regulations to the local custom. For the lower level of employees, the training involved specific skills and knowledge that they would need in daily operation. For higher levels of employees, the training mainly focused on planning, reform, innovation and leadership.

In 2015, it established a Chint Industrial Engineering College to specialise in employee training. Corresponding to Chint's organisation structure, the College was constituted by different departments, such as quality departments, lean production departments, technology departments and sales departments. It would not only involve the high level of managers in Chint, but also external experts from universities and training companies to give lectures and run workshops. The training contents would be highly related to the existing reform or production activities in Chint, so that the participants could really put what they learned into practice. After the training, the participants could not only get the diploma, but also further lead and supervise the activities they studied in the College.

Fourthly, it automated its production procedures. As Figure 5.2 illustrates, the production procedures of LVEE products could be generally divided into two parts: assembling and testing. Traditionally, these procedures were labour intensive. The former asked workers to assemble components proficiently and accurately as well as achieve good time cooperation with their forward and backward colleagues. The latter required workers to test all the products one by one and strictly obey the requirements on time and frequency. The testing process was crucial and had higher requirements on workers' skills. In the past few years, Chint successfully introduced automatic testing machines from both Chinese frontier research institutes and foreign companies for product quality examination. The machines decreased the demands on skilled workers and improved the control of product quality.

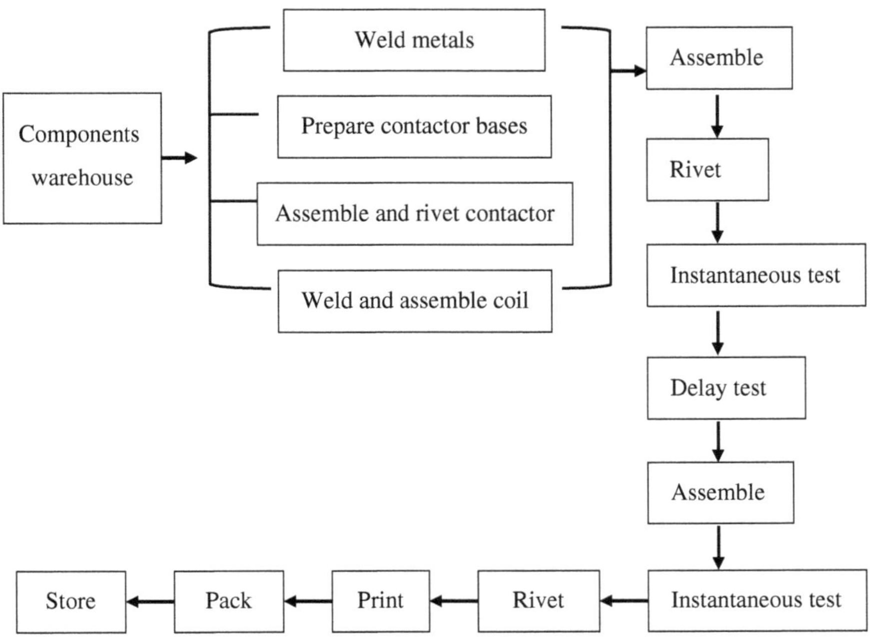

Figure 5.2 Manufacturing process of LVEE (Example of MCB)

Data source: The author's summary.

Additionally, Chint tried to innovate machines and reorganised production lines to gain automatic assembly. In 2015, it succeeded in applying for a project named *Research and Application of Digital Workshops for User-end Electrical Equipment based on Internet of Things and Energy Management* in China's Plan of Intelligent Manufacturing Project and achieving a certain degree of financial support from the Ministry of Industry and Information Technology. The project would build a digitalised workshop system for designing, production, quality control, logistics, storage and energy management. It was expected to reduce Chint's production costs, shorten the research circle, decrease the rate of unqualified products and improve the rate of energy utilisation. Currently, a couple of automatic assembly lines had taken their primary shapes and they were expected to join in the mass production soon. The success of the project would provide important reference for other manufacturing firms in the EE field.

Based on these measures, Chint made some achievements. The pass rates of finished products in the workshops increased from 2011 to 2015. In 2011, Chint was regarded as the National Model Firm for Harmonious Labour Relationship. It was a National Advanced Firm for Quality Management. In 2011 and 2012, it was awarded as a National First Class Firm for Standardised Safety Production. In 2013, it was nominated for the National Quality Prize. It was the National Experimental Firm for Corporate Social Responsibility. In 2014, it was a National Experimental Firm for Informatisation and Industrialisation.

Chint's current strength in the production process has greatly contributed to its capability of taking full use of massive labour and scale economic effects in mass production. However, the rising revolution of Industry 4.0 might corrode its advantages, and its production process will confront further challenges. With the help of advanced technology, such as IT software, big data, robots, simulation, the cloud and cyber-security, Industry 4.0 is expected to transform conventional production. Isolated and optimised cells will come together as a fully integrated, automated and optimised production flow. It will lead to greater efficiency and change traditional production relationships among suppliers, producers and customers, as well as between humans and machines. Although Chint tried to adopt a few advanced technologies, its development of Industry 4.0 is far behind global giants. There are at least three remarkable gaps.

The first gap is about digital manufacture. Take Siemens, for example. It is one of the most advanced firms in the global EE industry in digitalisation. Its core components include industrial software solutions for end-to-end processes, from development to production and services; an efficient communications infrastructure for networked data exchange; reliable security solutions to ensure protection of trade secrets in the networked and online world; and industrial services that increase its own real net output ratio by the means of digitalisation. In Siemens, the stages of product development, production planning, production engineering, production execution and services are a holistic fully integrated system instead of a chain of processes in chronological order. In each stage and in all interactions among the stages, all the relevant data will be captured, transmitted and analysed. The digital manufacture helps the firm greatly enhance production flexibility, shorten its response time to customers and reduce manufacturing costs, which are popular merits for producers and consumers, especially those in the high-end market.

However, currently, Chint's digitalisation is still at the primary stage. Although Chint tried to build a digitalised platform for its internal operation of production, sales and finance by adopting SAP/R3 (System analyses and Programme networking/Real-time data processing 3-tier) and the Product Life-Cycle Management system, the scope and depth of its digital management are limited. Its data are mainly used to know manufacturing progress and facilitate the traditional management. Chint should learn to build a united digital database to develop new products, enhance flexible production and interact with customers. The comparatively backward development of digital manufacturing weakens Chint's competitiveness in the high-end market.

The second gap is automating manufacturing. The realisation of automatic manufacturing for LVEE products is a tough mission. Firstly, it involves the reform of product design. The LVEE products are composed by various tiny components, whose diverse and irregular layouts can hardly be recognised and operated by machines to date. Chint should innovate product design and structure to adopt available machines for manufacture. Given its existing design capability, it is not easy.

Secondly, it must transform the production line. The evolution of product design might result in different production processes and orders. The success of automating manufacture highly depended on a good coordination of product design and production line design. Chint needs to research from scratch to find the optimum match for the two designs without an existing model. Also, it should calculate the input and output based on labour supply and machine costs, so that it could popularise the production line at the right time and pace.

Thirdly, it must improve the quality of supplied components. Despite intelligence technology, current machines still cannot work as smartly as human workers. In many cases, human workers are more flexible to deal with some flawed components by consciously adjusting their assembling approach. However, machines are less intelligent and any small defect might lead to the delay and failure of their work. Their work efficiency highly relies on the uniformity and quality of supplied materials. To achieve the automating manufacture, Chint must enhance its capability of components production and supply management.

Finally, Chint must forge its strength in inventing machines and software for automatic production. The introduction of automatic production needs many machines and software applications. If Chint cannot develop these hardwares and softwares, then its independence will be controlled by external firms or it will greatly increase its costs. However, developing machines and software puts forward more requirements on its R&D capabilities, which might be very different from its ability to make LVEE products.

The third gap is labour capability. With the Industry 4.0 plan, manufacturers will increasingly use robots and other advancements to assist workers. As a result, the number of physically demanding or routine jobs will decrease, while the number of jobs requiring flexible responses, problem solving and customisation will increase. Workers must combine know-how related to a specific job or process, such as techniques for working with robots or changing tools on machines, with IT competencies that range from using spread sheets and accessing interfaces to applying advanced programming and analytics skills. In addition, employees should be even more open to change, possess greater flexibility to adapt to new roles and work environments, and get accustomed to continual interdisciplinary learning. Currently, most of Chint's workers have only high school educations. Its present labour training system is far from sufficient to help them develop these capabilities. It will be a systemic project for not only Chint, but also the whole country to educate and train industrial workers for Industry 4.0.

Reinforce supplier management

Chint reinforced its supplier management by strengthening supplier selection as well as providing supplier assistance. On one hand, it increased its capability of supplier selection. Firstly, it put forward a set of supplier section standards. The standards regulated the suppliers' scale, specialty, supply price, quality and time. In principle, every supplier had to reach all the standards. Based on the standards, Chint evaluated its existing suppliers and classified them into different levels. The suppliers in the high level were given priority to get large orders, while those in the bottom level were eliminated. As a result, in the past few years, Chint reduced its supplier number and normalised its supplier management system. Secondly, it built a Procurement Centre. The Centre centralised all procurement power in the company. It was responsible for choosing proper suppliers and calculating and supplying all the demands of the whole company. Based on the large procurement volume, it increased Chint's bargaining power, reduced purchasing costs and decreased corruption risks. Thirdly, it forged its own capability of manufacturing core components. Despite a large scale of outsourcing, Chint still enhanced its own workshops to produce critical components, such as punched components, plastic components, copper wires and silver contactors. It grasped the first-hand information of manufacturing technics and production costs, so that it had a good initiative and wisdom of selecting superior suppliers and setting right purchasing prices. Also, it helped Chint master the quality of core components and then finished products.

On the other hand, Chint offered supplier assistance. At the end of 2008, it founded a Supplier Assistance and Improvement Office to facilitate suppliers to enhance technology and management. The office consisted of technician experts and quality managers from Chint's component manufacturing divisions. They gave suppliers regular training on supplier evaluation standards, quality test and control, storage management, 6S management, equipment and moulds management. At times, they were organised as teams to visit supplier firms and then examined their production. They usually selected a few important suppliers as experimental firms, conducted comprehensive diagnosis on their performance, made specific improvement plans, gave individual and customised help, examined their progress persistently, summarised case experience and finally popularised successful practices to all the suppliers step by step. In this way, Chint helped suppliers solve common technical problems and improved the whole level of supply quality.

With such a supplier management approach, Chint built a strategic partnership with its suppliers. The aim of Chint was to decrease its procurement cost as well as improve supply quality. It had the tendency to pass on the pressure to its suppliers. These goals could only be achieved when suppliers increased their efforts to improve technology and management and reduce their prices. However, suppliers were sensitive to investment costs and reluctant to reduce prices. If Chint only pushed hard on price reduction, then they might tend to cut down supply quality to keep their profits.

Chint's management approach smartly motivated suppliers to commit quality improvement as well as price reduction on their own initiatives. With the selection standards, suppliers felt peer pressure and were more likely to work harder to increase their competitiveness in the supply system. Chint's regular examination effectively avoids suppliers' race to the bottom. What's more, Chint's assistance brought suppliers benefits of technological improvement and cost reduction. Many suppliers would like to stay in Chint's supply system so that they could utilise the assistance for further development. Thus, they were more willing to improve capability and cut down price to win long-time cooperation with Chint. As a result, both Chint and suppliers achieved their goals in a beneficial cycle. When Chint got better supply, it would have more competitiveness in the market. If Chint developed better, suppliers would have more stable business and profits.

Despite the good management method, the supply quality is still an issue. Firstly, dishonest deals endanger Chint's product quality. Given strict rules, some suppliers don't have enough awareness on quality control. They sometimes consider more their own short-time profits than the potential risk for Chint's long-time development. They assume that Chint already has an unchallengeable position in the domestic market and a few low quality products might not be a big problem. In addition, due to their long-time supply partnership, they believe that Chint develops dependence on them and is less likely to expel them. Moreover, they can use personal relationships to reduce the punishment of dishonest deals. Among Chint's suppliers, most of them are from Wenzhou and many of them have personal relationships with the staff in Chint.

The effectiveness of Chint's supplier management might be reduced by the misuse of personal relationships. However, Chint can hardly eliminate the relationships, so it falls into a dilemma. The personal relationship between Chint and suppliers is a two-edged sword. It can help Chint achieve stable, various and quick supply, which greatly contributes to its fast response to the market and rapid move towards production. Additionally, the personal relationship is the foundation of the industrial relationship in Chint's manufacturing system, especially at its early stage. Nowadays, the two relationships are tightly bound to each other and it is very difficult to clearly separate. Chint tried hard to achieve harmonious supplier management as well as personal relationships, but it is not easy to make breakthroughs on the dilemma.

Secondly, the technical performance of Chint's supply is lower than global giants'. Although some global giants realised the local procurement of certain components within China, they usually import core components from developed countries to maintain product reliability. Most of Chint's suppliers are SMEs, and their capabilities of technology and management are not strong. Given Chint's assistance, their standards still can hardly meet the requirements for high-end products. To seek for higher qualified and more honest suppliers, Chint turned to the firms in Jiangsu and Shanghai for some important components and materials for high-end products. These suppliers have higher capability of technology and quality control, but their supply levels are still lower than foreign companies'. Their supply quality is highly related to primary materials, mould standards and manufacturing technics. Unfortunately, China's technological capabilities of these industries are still behind the Western countries. For example, most of China's high quality plastic materials are imported. The fineness of metal materials, such as silver and copper, is much lower than foreign countries'. China's punching technology and machines are also backward. When all the difference adds together, there will still be a big gap for final products. This gap can hardly be reduced in a short time by individual firms. It needs a comprehensive improvement of many related basic industries in the whole country.

Strengthen sales network

Chint strengthened its sales network mainly by developing direct sales and expanding international business. Firstly, it developed direct sales channels to high-end customers. In the past, Chint's sales mostly depended on distributors, but the high-end customers usually have different procurement processes than distributor's sales channels, as Table 5.8 shows. High-end customers have strict selection procedures and standards on suppliers, which could be hardly achieved by individual distributors. Thus, after 2009, Chint tried to build direct sales with the cooperation of existing distributors based on a three-partner agreement. This agreement mainly targeted at large customers in specialised markets. Under the agreement, Chint took the lead in selling and marketing products to these targeted customers. If it successfully made deals, then the customers, Chint and distributors would sign a three-partner agreement. Distributors were responsible for supplying products and providing after-sales service for the customers.

To accomplish the three-partner business, Chint founded a Large-programme Development Team. It was composed of professional members from the sales, marketing, technology, engineering and manufacturing departments. The team's job was to select large customers and try to get deals. Its sales and marketing processes were different from distributors. It would firstly introduce the target customers about their products and technology advantages, then provide them with a

Table 5.8 Different sales processes of LVEE

Distributor Sale	*Direct Sale*
Firms ↓ Core distributors ↓ (to Sub-level distributors) ↓ (directly to End users) Sub-level distributors ↓ End users	Primary contact to customers ↓ 1. Customers' primary examination on products 2. Company introduce products to customers 3. Customers examine companies' operation and ensure they meet customers' requirements ↓ Product sample examination (1 week to 6-12 months according to different industrial needs) ↓ Use a small batch of products (3-6 months) to test product quality, delivery and company response ↓ Buy large batches of products in certain projects (1-3 years) ↓ Overall and long-time cooperation

Data source: Shanghai Liangxin Electrical Limited Company (2012).

whole series of services, including building organisations, developing technology, improving technics, negotiation, testing products and setting price. Additionally, Chint launched the supporting platforms of logistics and technology to share with distributors the information of credit evaluation, market demands, final customers and professional training. The three-partnership agreement helped Chint make breakthroughs in some specialised fields, such as electricity, telecommunication, household appliance, design institutes, systematic projects and machinery. In 2015, it made 18 projects with electric power companies, built long partnerships with 158 factories for household appliance meters, explored business with 220 design institutes and participated in 12 public utility projects (Chint Group, 2017).

Secondly, it expanded international business. Chint started to export its products in the 1990s, but its scale and growth speed of international business were much lower than domestic sales. In 2009, its international sales income was RMB 3 billion (USD 441.2 million), which accounted for only 6.85% of its total sales value. Most of these sales were in developing countries for the medium- and low-end market. To change the situation, Chint reformed its international sales system in 2009. The new system covered six zones in the world, Asia-Pacific, Europe, Russian-speaking countries, North America, South America, the Middle East and Africa. Within different zones, the sales and marketing strategy could be different and various. In 2011, it introduced more than 42 distributors all over the world, developed 27 customers in specialised industries, and built logistics centres in Russia and Brazil. It also held international sales and marketing conferences in more than 65 countries and participated in more than 20 international exhibitions. In 2014, it established a new platform for international business and finance. It accelerated its pace of building regional factories in Egypt and engineering centres in Europe and North America. As a result, its international business increased quickly. It reached RMB 0.8 billion (USD 129 million), which was 10.9% of total sales revenue in 2015 (Zhejiang Chint Electrics Limited Company, 2016; Chint Group, 2017).

Chint's efforts at improving sales networks boosted its competitiveness. Firstly, direct sales made up the weakness of the traditional approach. In the traditional way, distributors could hardly achieve orders from high-end and large customers in specialised industries. This was because they did not have sufficient capacity to provide a complete series of services. The large customers might not fully know Chint's ability and could not reflect their demands directly to Chint's factories. With the help of the Large-programme Development Team, Chint nowadays can mobilise inclusive resources in the company and conduct customised service. Therefore, it can not only expand its business scope, but also increase its company recognition. Moreover, it effectively reduces the middle process of sales and increases its response towards customers. It also helps Chint grasp first-hand market information and improve its technology in a good time. Secondly, expanding international business laid a foundation for Chint's further development. The international sales would bring in more business volume, so that it could get more income and be more affordable for R&D investment and sales network construction in both domestic and international markets. Furthermore, it improves its recognition, understanding and trust from international customers and provides more chances for Chint to collaborate and learn from international high-end customers, to further forge its ability of serving international customers and upgrading technologies based on local market demands.

Despite the above promising prospects, the following problems have debilitated Chint's sales performance. The first one is the coordination between the traditional and new sales channels. In theory, direct sales is a supplement for distributor sales and tries to open new business in a different territory. However, it is difficult to make a clear boundary between the two approaches. In some cases, the products for different customers are similar. In other cases, there might be some overlapping on targeted customers between the two channels. Therefore, some distributors are worried about their business. They think if Chint further develops its direct sales, then their profit will be thinner. In the past, the distributors and Chint were interdependent on each other. The distributors were indispensable agents for Chint's sales and marketing and Chint's products were the tools for them to make profits. If the cooperation relationship were weakened, then it would be very difficult for Chint to develop before it gained a foothold with direct sales. Currently, the business proportion of direct sales is much lower than the one of distributor sales. It still takes time and effort for Chint to nurture direct sales and develop it on a good scale. Building a self-owned sales channel might bring Chint a lot of benefits, but currently it will be a difficult trade-off for it to maintain its distributors as well as expand direct sales.

The second issue is branding. On one hand, the strategy of two brands does not work effectively. Ideally, Noark is mainly for the high-end market and Chint is for the ordinary market. The two brands often compete in practice and counteract Chint Company's competitiveness. For example, in Eastern Europe, Chint has been the primary brand for distributors since the early 2000s. However, the introduction of the Noark brand makes it difficult for distributors to market the two brands at the same time, especially when the products have little difference. As a result, Noark's sales performance is weak in this area due to its more expensive price. Another instance is found in the domestic market. To get more profits, Noark put forward some economical products to cater to the ordinary market. These products might get some market shares, but they negatively affected Chint's sales. Consequently, the total sales income of Chint Company did not increase much. Chint should not only make more efforts to explore differential products for different markets, but also make a better arrangement on its branding operation.

On the other hand, its brand influence is not strong enough. In the domestic market, Chint is well known in the low- and medium-end market, but it still has some difficulty in convincing high-end customers in both domestic and abroad territories. Some high-end customers do not have much confidence in Chint or Noark's reliability, so they still prefer to buy global brands. In some cases, buying global brands instead of domestic brands even becomes a tacit strategy for procurement officers to avoid blame of potential security accidents. In the international market, neither the Chint nor Noark brand is well understood by customers. Chint needs a lot of time, investment and patience to really settle down in these regions, know the demands of local customers and gradually build its recognition and trust from international customers based on their reliable products and qualified service.

The third is about the interaction between sales and product development. Chint attaches great importance to sales. In theory, its product development is highly sales oriented. However, product development could not totally meet the needs of sales. With an approach of distributors' sales, it is a long and time-consuming process for Chint to hear customers' appeals. During the process, the information might be delayed, misunderstood or lost. Therefore, Chint's R&D staff can hardly get in-time and accurate market information and develop proper products. They could not achieve close interaction and cooperation with their customers to collaborate on R&D and product development. Furthermore, the customer service of the direct sales approach will put forward more requirements. It not only includes in-time delivery, product replacement and repairing, but also close interaction and cooperation of improving technology and innovate new products. If Chint cannot sort out the relationship between sales and R&D, then it will endanger its sustainable development of sales in the long run.

Extend industrial chain

To further upgrade its business, starting from LVEE production, Chint extended its industrial chain to HV transmission and transformation and photovoltaic power generation.

Firstly, it developed HVEE business. In 2004, Chint built Chint Electric Company in Shanghai and started to sell products for HV electricity transmission and transformation in 2007. From 2011 to 2015, the company invested more than RMB 0.1 billion (USD 16.1 million) of R&D funds, developed more than 56 new products, improved technology for 966 machines and applied for 158 patents. By now, Chint has developed a whole range of products with various specifications in the area. Its products included HV transformers, switchgears, capacitors, cables, fuse boxes, insulators and lightning protectors. These products could be used under the voltages ranging from 0.38–0.6 kV to above 500 kV. They were sold to more than 120 countries in various industries, such as petro chemistry, new energy, grids, rail transportation, metallurgical and the mining industry.

What's more, the company was competent for providing systemic solutions and building EPC projects. For example, it could provide solutions for energy and electricity distribution, wind power generation, solar power generation, smart grid and railway transportation. All over the world, more than 70 electricity utility companies purchased its products and service. Within China, more than 140 wind electric fields across 19 provinces applied its solutions. In 2009, Chint made the deal to build a 220-kV transformer substation in Pakistan. In 2011, it got the bid to establish a 132-kV transformer substation in Yemen. In 2014, it achieved cooperation with the Enel Green Power Company in Italy.

Secondly, it entered the field of photovoltaic power generation. It not only produced products, but also provided service. In 2006, it built Astronergy Company to specialise in R&D and production of solar modules. Astronergy offered monocrystalline modules, polycrystalline modules and high efficiency a-Si/μc-Si tandem junction thin film modules. In 2016, the company was listed as the top 6 solar company by Photon Consulting on its latest photovoltaic Triathlon report.[22] In 2014, Chint bought one factory in Frankfort from Germany Conergy Company, which meant that the firm owned the largest photovoltaic factory in Eastern Germany. In 2009, Chint invested in the Ideal Energy Equipment Company to research advanced equipment for the manufacturing of solar energy battery. In 2010, the company produced the first Chinese PECVD (plasma enhanced chemical vapour deposition) equipment, which helped Chint grasp the crucial equipment to manufacture photovoltaic film.

In 2009, Chint founded Chint Power to design, manufacture and supply 1-kW to 2-megawatt (MW) photovoltaic inverters and power solutions for customers. According to GreenTech Media Research's report, it ranked at number 9 among the top 10 most competitive companies in the global photovoltaic inverter market. In 2006, Chint founded a Chint New Energy Company. It not only invested in photovoltaic power generation projects, but also provided systemic solutions and built power stations with the support of loans from China Development Bank, Green Silk Road Fund, Zhejiang Private Firm Collective Investment Company and Myshare Bank of Wenzhou. Its programmes covered distributed as well as centralised power generation plants and residential and commercial rooftop systems. In 2015, it succeeded in building 2,500 MW power stations. In the following 5 years, it was expected to achieve 1,000 MW of new installed capacity. Currently, Chint is the largest private firm investing in solar power generation in China.

Based on the extended industrial chain, Chint formed an integrated advantage. It could not only provide the whole series of products in the electricity industry from power generation to distribution, but also offer the corresponding systemic service. For instance, in the solar power generation field, it could produce the products of photovoltaic panels, photovoltaic inverters, header boxes, cables, distributing boxes, ACB, MCCB and MCB. It was also capable of providing the service of designing systems, building power stations, matching products, installing equipment, energy monitoring and after-sale maintenance. Chint's comprehensive capability made it competitive in the field. On one hand, customers were more likely to trust it due to its technological and financial abilities for operating multiple industries. They were more willing to make deals with Chint to get its one-stop service. The turnkey contract with one supplier helped to ensure uniformity rather than piece-meal contracts to many suppliers.

On the other hand, Chint increased its opportunity of making profits. With systemic service, Chint could provide most equipment from its own factories and grab profits from various processes with multiply formats. For example, if it did not have profits in one sector, it could make up in another segment, so that the overall profitability of the Chint group was good. Furthermore, the whole set service was beneficial for Chint's technology improvement. It helped its subsidiary companies better understand the needs of their forward and backward manufacturing processes, so that they could develop new products and improve existing products correspondingly.

Given the attractive advantages of extended industrial chains, its further development faces many challenges. Chint's strength of systematic advantages relies on its coordination and cooperation among different industries and subsidiaries. However, at present, the cooperation among these firms is not strong and their capabilities are not even.

In terms of the HVEE field, Chint's current capability is not strong enough. Its subsidiary company Chint Electric specialising in HVEE business only ranked 36th among the 2015 Top 100 Firms of China's EE industry. First, its R&D capability is not strong. Totally different from the LVEE field, the HVEE field has more complex technology and stricter requirements on product reliability. Its R&D

process is much more time- and fund-consuming. In some cases, Chint still needs the external cooperation from universities or research institutes to develop new products. Second, it is in a disadvantaged competition environment. In the HVEE field, China has very strict regulation on the products procurement for electricity projects. SOEs and their subsidiaries monopolised most projects. As a latecomer, Chint has less chance to put its products into practical projects so that it is often deprived of the opportunity to participate in the competition in the field. Third, its systematic solution is not strong. At present, the contents of its solutions mainly refer to providing a combination of related products for customers based on its production system. However, ideally, systematic solutions should provide customised products and systemic design and also help customers save energy, improve efficiency and reduce cost. To achieve these functions, Chint still needs a lot of efforts to get the knowledge and experience of certain industries as well as energy management.

In terms of photovoltaic power generation fields, Chint's development confronts some degree of uncertainty. Firstly, price competition in manufacturing photovoltaic products is very fierce. Take the photovoltaic panel production for example. Although China is the largest manufacturer in the world, most Chinese firms only conduct manufacturing instead of technology innovation, and the competition among Chinese firms is an excessive price battle. Moreover, the technology change in this field is quick and any overnight technological breakthroughs might endanger Chint's current competitiveness. Secondly, building photovoltaic power generation stations cannot bring profits in a short time. Its investment and return cycle is very long, which highly challenges firms' capability of operating finance and dealing with private and public partnership. Additionally, any policy change from government subsidies might also negatively affect Chint's profitability.

Summary

Since the nineteenth century, the global EE industry starting from Europe and the USA has experienced a remarkable development, as electricity generation and consumption increased dramatically for industrialisation and urbanisation worldwide. EE products are capital goods sold through intermediaries to end customers. End customers are numerous, ranging from large- to small-scale business. According to their expectation on products, customers are often divided into high-, medium- and low-end users. The high-end consumers usually do not compromise technological property and reliability to low price, but the low-end users are sensitive to price and have low requirements on product technology. Medium-end users have certain requirements on product technology and prefer to buy products with good performance-price rate.

The competition in the EE industry is fierce. After massive M&A, a few global giants, mainly from developed countries, took shape, namely ABB, Schneider, GE, Siemens, Alstom, Mitsubishi and Furukawa. With advanced technology, global brands and massive finance, these giants have continuously passed down consolidation pressure to smaller players and sought for more market share throughout the world. The industrial concentration is even higher in more technology-intensive sectors. Firms in the EE industry compete in technological ability, financial strength, service capability, product quality and production cost.

China has been one of the largest producers, exporters and markets of the EE industry. In the Chinese EE industry, the LVEE field has the freest market competition for all firms regardless of their sizes and ownerships. Chinese private firms in the EE industry mainly develop their business in the LVEE sector. The LVEE industry thus provides important reference to observe the development situation of Chinese private firms in the EE industry.

Given its large scale of production and export, China's LVEE industry is not strong. Concerning products, the technological performance of Chinese products is behind foreign firms'. In the domestic market, most Chinese firms (mainly private firms) serve the low-end market, where product homogenisation and large excess capacity are common phenomena. In contrast, most high-end products are imported or made by FIEs. In recent years, based on their brand influence and innovation capabilities, foreign companies tightly hold the high-end market with their advanced products and open their low- and medium-end market with their economical products. On the other hand, most domestic firms lack competitiveness for the high-end market and their profit becomes less and less. In the international market, Chinese firms export low-end products at low prices. Most Chinese firms don't have strong sales and marketing networks to access customers and have little brand influence. In the future, China's EE industry will experience continuous growth and change: China's electric industry will increase. The rapid growth of renewable energy will extend more fields. The construction of smart grid will create new chances. The Industry 4.0 might bring revolutionary changes to the industry.

Among all Chinese firms in the EE industry, Wenzhou's firms stood out. These firms have forged large production scales, developed an ID and had emerging brand influence. However, they suffered from the predicaments of disorderly firm competition, limited technology capability and insufficient public services. The competition between Wenzhou's leading firms and global giants is shaping the future landscape of China's and even the global EE industry. Facing increasingly fierce competition, a few of Wenzhou's leading firms succeeded in expanding their scales and improving their technology. They made great efforts to hold their existing share in the medium- and low-end markets and tried hard to supply higher-end products. Chint from Wenzhou is the largest Chinese firm in the LVEE industry and it spared no efforts to transform and upgrade for its competitiveness. It tried to develop new products for different end markets, enhance the production process (implementing lean production reform, innovating management organisations, building employee training systems and automating production procedures), reinforce supplier management by stricter selection and persistent assistance, strengthen sales networks by developing direct sales and international business and extend industrial chains to the fields of HVEE and photovoltaic power generation.

Despite its hard work, Chint is currently not successful at competing with global giants. It along with other Chinese firms in the EE industry are facing many tough challenges for further development. The first challenge is technological capability. Although some Chinese firms tried hard to catch up with the advanced technology of global giants and researched four generations of products within the past three decades, there are still big technological gaps (especially in design) between Chinese firms and global giants. Most of Wenzhou's SMEs don't have the technological strength to produce high-end products, and even the leading firms like Chint are still not competent enough to succeed. The technological gaps are due to multiple factors. It is because the Chinese firms do not have sufficient tacit knowledge, design experience and R&D resources and investment. Also, an excessive focus on short-time sales records decelerates firms' paces on technological innovation. The weakness of technological capability can only be solved when firms further conduct persistent research, invest continuous finance, innovate ideas and practices and grasp market needs. It is also crucial to collaborate with customers who have strong capabilities, to learn and enhance its R&D capabilities and increase the possibility to commercialise its technology.

The second is digitalisation and automation. Firms from developed countries, especially the USA and Europe, take the lead in the Industry 4.0 revolution. They take full advantage of IT and advanced machines and closely cooperate with other giants in related industries to make digitalised manufacturing and provide customised service. Therefore, they tightly hold their competitiveness in the high-end market and build higher barriers for Chinese firms to compete in the area. Although some Chinese firms started to adopt digitalised tools, it is still far for them to achieve digitalised revolution in their production process. The automatic production forced Chinese firms to control their manufacturing costs and product quality to retain their competitiveness. It also brings firms more challenges to reform product designs, changing the production lines and building partnerships with other machinery firms.

The third is human resources. Human resources consist of researchers, engineers, managers and ordinary workers in the firms within the EE industry. They have laid the foundation for industrial competition and development. Technological innovation cannot be achieved without experienced researchers and engineers with deep understanding of professional knowledge and good visions of market demand. The automation and digitalisation put forward more requirements for employees to combine know-how related to a specific job, to be more open to change, possess greater flexibility for new roles and work environments, and get accustomed to continual interdisciplinary learning. At present, most Chinese firms cannot afford to train their employees to totally develop these capabilities.

The fourth is the supply system. The supply system is the foundation for leading firms' development and the connection between the leading firms and most SMEs. The supply system in Wenzhou's EE ID greatly involves the local social network, which was traditionally an advantage for leading firms to quickly provide products for the low-end market and for SMEs to have continuous business. However, the technological backwardness and misused personal relationships of the SMEs decrease leading firms' strength for further development and endanger the SMEs' long-run interest. Given leading firms' efforts on improving selection standards and committing in close assistance, the supply quality is still not ideal. It is not only related to firms' dilemma of trading off between social networks and economic interest, but is also due to the weaker capabilities of a series of other basic and supporting industries in China.

The fifth is sales networks. A wide and local embedded sales and marketing network is often regarded as the advantage for Chinese firms. The network helps these firms get access to low- and medium-end customers in China, but it is difficult to serve high-end customers due to their different expectations of products and service. The lack of abroad sales channels prevents Chinese firms from competing successfully in the international market. Although some leading firms tried to develop sales networks for high-end and international customers, they are not competitive to communicate with them, understand their demand and provide them with proper products. They still need to coordinate between traditional and new sales channels, nurture brand influence among customers and construct effective ways for the interactions among sales, marketing, design and production.

The sixth is developing new industries. With the shrinking profitability in the low-end LVEE field, firms tend or are forced to develop new business. Although some new industries appeared to have larger space for growth and profit, the competitions in these industries are no less fierce than the LVEE industry, in terms of R&D, finance, service, management, sales, marketing and branding. Chinese private firms still struggle for a higher niche of market under the pressure of global giants and SOEs. For all the Chinese firms, there is no way to escape from technical innovation in global competition. What matters for firms is to really forge their strong capabilities and improve their competitiveness in a few core businesses in the field where they have good technological and experience accumulation. The firms that don't devote themselves to innovation will be less likely to succeed in any industry.

To summarise, China has a large-scale EE industry and growing EE market. However, the industrial competitiveness of Chinese firms is not strong and their market shares are increasingly endangered by global giants and FIEs in international and domestic territories. Given some strength, Chinese firms, even the largest leading firms, are facing a series of challenges to deal with the global competition and catch up with foreign firms, including technological capability, digitalisation and automation, human resources, supply system, sales networks and developing new industries. The playing field for Chinese private firms in the industry is far from flat. There is no easy and simple way to solve these difficulties in a short time. Market force alone is not enough to help Chinese firms successfully compete in the field. It is necessary and urgent for the government to provide not only public goods, but also support in certain industries.

Notes

1. Circuit breakers are automatically operated electrical switches designed to protect electric circuits from damage caused by overcurrent or overload or short circuits.
2. In 1998, GEC-Alstom was renamed Alstom.
3. The author mainly referred to (Yin and Xiao, 2008) for the information of China's LVEE development history before 2008.
4. ACB, MCCB and MCB are most common circuit breakers. ACB is often used for main power distribution in large industrial plant. MCCB is used for LV distribution systems in panel boards and switchboards. MCB used to protect control circuits or small appliances that may not have sufficient interrupting capacity to use at a panel board.
5. The author mainly referred to the Zhejiang Yueqing Record Office (2001) for the information of Wenzhou's LVEE development history before 2001.
6. UL standards are the safety standards for electrical devices and components adopted in the USA. CE marking is a mandatory conformity marking for certain products sold within the European Economic Area.
7. Mazzucato (2015) argued that it is important to build a dynamic public organisation which has intelligence to envision and enact bold policies for technological innovation.
8. The market volume of Chinese low- and medium-end customers is considerable. Take industrial SMEs for example, one of the most important components of these customers. In 2015, Zhejiang Province alone had more than 38,648 SMEs and all of them are supposed to use LVEE products during their production.
9. N refers to Chint's company code, the following letter refers to product code and the number refers to series code.
10. The general rules for product names in Chint are as follows: The first letters refer to product codes, the following numbers before the en dash refer to design codes, the numbers after the en dash refer to rated currents.
11. The author mainly referred to the Economy and Law Programme (2009) for the information of the competition between Chint and Schneider.
12. After 110 rounds of long-time negotiation, Schneider and Delixi agreed to build a joint venture, Delixi Electric, for LVEE business. Both companies held 50% of the shares and the brand Delixi remained to be used within China.
13. The general rules of product names in Schneider are as follows: The letters before the numbers refer to product codes, the numbers and the following letters refer to design codes.
14. A series usually includes a range of different kinds of products, like breakers, contactors and fuses. The same series often has similar design outlook, ideas and better compatibility with each other.
15. Ex refers to product code, 9 refers to design code, M refers to MCCB.
16. N refers to company code, X refers to series code.
17. The principle of continuous improvement constitutes a self-contained part of the management philosophy. Supervised by a moderator, employees of the most different departments optimise workstations, processes and procedures in a team. The aim is to secure and enhance the standard step-by-step.
18. Cleanliness and orderliness are regarded as basic prerequisites for efficient manufacture. The 5S audit makes cleanliness and orderliness at the workstation measurable. 6S has added the additional S of safety to the original 5.
19. The pull principle constitutes a method for production control. In this method, a downstream process initiates production processes. This avoids an accumulation of orders in-between the processes, which will increase the lead-time.
20. With value stream mapping, the actual process of material and information flow is displayed graphically along the entire value creation chain, from the supplier through to the customer. Based on this actual state, the scope for improvement is shown and then concepts for increasing the value creation are developed.

21 Chint founded its CPC branch in 1993, developed it to a general party branch in 1995 and established a party committee in 1998. In 2016, there were 45 branches and 1,200 party members within the group.

22 Reports from Photon Consulting are often used as reference for major solar players for market analysis and strategic planning. The data were collected from about 30 countries around the world covering about 80% of on-grid solar plant electricity consumption.

6 Conclusion

This chapter will firstly summarise the competition situation of Chinese private manufacturing firms in globalisation. Secondly, it will conclude their current development challenges from various aspects. Thirdly, it will discuss policy implications for China's economic reform and industrial upgrade.

Competition situation

Based on the comparison and contrast of the footwear industry and the EE industry, the current competition situation for Chinese private manufacturing firms in globalisation includes increasing competition pressure, promising development prospects and rising leading firms.

Increasing competition pressure

Chinese private manufacturing firms are facing increasing competition pressure. Such pressure can be observed from their production situation and market shares. In terms of the production situation, Chinese firms are under double pressure. On one hand, they feel more and more difficult to maintain their advantages of low cost, which are fading compared with the firms in other developing countries. As shown in previous chapters, in the footwear industry, Nike, the global largest footwear brand, and Yue Yuen, the global largest footwear manufacturer, have shifted their primary destination of outsourcing from China to Vietnam. In the EE industry, firms from Mexico and the Czech Republic are challenging the position of Chinese firms. In 2015, China was the global largest exporter of LVEE products by value, Mexico ranked in the top 7 and the Czech Republic grew to the top 10. Mexican firms exported more weight and showed more attraction to low-end customers than Chinese firms. The average export value of Czech firms was slightly higher than the Chinese figure and they brought more competition to Chinese firms in the global medium- and low-end market.

On the other hand, Chinese firms are encountering the changes of production mode driven by developed counties, such as the USA, Germany and Italy. These nations put forward their re-industrialisation strategies and collaborated to implement Industry 4.0 projects. In the footwear industry, Adidas has built Speedfactories which manufacture high-performance sport shoes in a faster, greener and more intelligent way through an automated, decentralised and flexible manufacturing process. In the EE industry, Siemens has achieved digitalised manufacturing. The processes of its product development, production planning, production engineering, production execution and services are fully integrated and make full use of industrial robots, software solutions and communications infrastructure. The automated and digitalised manufacturing helps the firms from developed countries greatly enhance production flexibility, shorten their response time to customers and reduce manufacturing costs of high-end products. Such progress will bring revolutionary changes to the production modes in the industries where Chinese firms have the advantages of mass production currently. It will also build more barriers for Chinese firms to upgrade their business to high-end markets.

When it comes to market shares, Chinese firms are squeezed by foreign firms in both global and domestic market. In the global market, industrial concentration is growing pushed by global giants. The global market share of Chinese firms is small, among which most is from the Chinese domestic market. In the footwear industry, in 2015, the global top 5 athletic footwear companies had 45% of the market share, Nike ranking the first with 22.9%. The global top 5 life-style footwear companies accounted for 56.8% of the market share, Clarks ranking the first with 18.4% in 2011. The largest Chinese company, Belle, ranked 17th in the list of global top 20 brands by retail value in 2014, but its international business only accounted for 1.6% of its revenue. In contrast, Nike's overseas business reached 54% of its revenue. In addition, Chinese firms export mostly low-end products to the world at a low price of USD 4.44/pair in 2014, which was only 8.7% of the figure of Italian firms. In the EE industry, in 2011, the global market share of the top 4 firms reached more than 42%, GE 17.5%, Siemens 8.6%, Alstom 8% and Schneider 8%. In the global heavy EE sector, the top 4 firms occupied an even higher status of the market share, GE 31.9%, Alstom 19.3%, Siemens 12.8% and Mitsubishi 12.5%, reaching 76.5% in 2010. The largest Chinese firm, LVEE, Chint has limited influence outside China and the international business only accounted for 10.9% of its revenue in 2015. In contrast, Chint's global competitor, Schneider, has expanded its brand influence to the whole globe and had 74% of its revenue from outside Western Europe in 2014. Besides, Chinese firms export mainly low-end LVEE products and their average export value was only 35.9% of the figure for German firms.

In the domestic market, the market position and profits of Chinese firms are corroded by foreign firms. In both the footwear industry and the EE industry, most Chinese firms serve for the low- and medium-end markets and sit in the segments with low value added, but global giants and FIEs occupy the high-end market and gain rich profits. Although China is the largest producer of low-end products in both industries, it is the largest importer of high-end products in these industries at the same time. In the footwear industry, its average import price was USD 28.7/pair, ranking first among the global top 10 largest importers by value. In the EE industry, its average import value was USD 83.18/kg, ranking the top among the global largest importers as well. In recent years, foreign firms and Chinese firms have had the fiercest competition in the medium-end market. The market share and profits of Chinese firms become less and less. These phenomena are more notable in the EE industry. In the LVEE field, from 2004 to 2014, Schneider was the largest winner in the Chinese market. Its number of firms in the list of top 100 Chinese EE enterprises increased from five to nine and sales income increased by 422.81% to USD 2.9 billion. Its income percentage among the total income of the top 100 firms increased from 3.8% to 5.3%. On the contrary, Chinese private firms grew their sales income by 181.35% to USD 4.8 billion, but their income percentage among the top 100 firms dropped from 11.73% to 8.79%.

Promising development prospects

Given the increasing competition pressure, the development prospects for Chinese firms are promising. This can be analysed from their industrial basis and market demands. In terms of industrial basis, Chinese firms have built fair foundations. In the footwear industry, in 2014, China had more than 4,505 firms above the designated size, 3 million employees and USD 121.4 billion of industrial revenue. A few IDs took shape in eastern and inland areas and they forged their strength in different segments. China was the global largest producer (64% of the global output volume) and the global largest exporter (74.1% of the global volume and 40.5% of the global value). In the EE industry, in 2015, China had industrial revenue of USD 863 billion, 29,578 firms above the designated size and a large ID in Wenzhou. China's exports were USD 103.7 billion and it was the largest global LVEE exporter by value. Its LVEE export value was USD 13.8 billion, up to 15.1% of the global market share.

When it comes to market demands, Chinese firms face large market potential. In the footwear industry, the market demand of volume and quality will increase due to the growth of population and income standards. The growth rate of the Chinese footwear market will be much higher than the global average from 2015 to 2020. In the EE industry, with the stable growth of the electricity industry and consumption, the demands for EE products will also increase in volume and quality. The cumulative size of the EE global market is expected to increase to USD 6.8 trillion from 2016 to 2030. The market's need for medium- and high-end products will expand. The development of renewable energy and the construction of smart grid will create new chances and new fields. In China, the percentage of installed capacity of renewable energy is expected to increase from 32.1% in 2014 to 42.9% in 2020 and 60% in 2030. The Chinese government will invest USD 61 billion for smart grid construction by 2020. Therefore, if firms can forge their strength of advanced technology, good product quality, outstanding service, strong sales network and brand influence, then their development prospects will brighten in the future.

Rising leading firms

Facing increasing competition pressure and promising development prospects, some Chinese leading firms have risen. In the footwear industry and the EE industry, a few of Wenzhou's private firms stand out among their peers. These firms achieve outstanding business performance, take the lead in industrial upgrade and possess great importance to the national economy. In terms of their business performance, they gain outstanding achievements. In the footwear industry, Juyi Group has developed to be one of the largest Chinese export firms. It is a Top 500 China's Private Firm and its OEM products are widely sold in European countries via global giant retailers. Zhejiang Aokang Shoes Limited has become one of the largest Chinese private footwear firms. It is a China Genuine Leather Shoes Leader King, National Important Brand and Top 500 Chinese Private Firm. It nurtures diverse self-owned brands and Aokang is the largest domestic brand for men's shoes by retail revenue. Menglani Shoes Limited, despite its small scale, is a rising star in the R&D of footwear. It is a National High-technology Enterprise and won a IPR lawsuit over the global firm Ecco. In the EE industry, Chint has grown to be the largest domestic firm in the LVEE sector. It is a Top 500 Chinese Firm and Top 100 Chinese Private Firm. It forges brand influence in China and won IPR lawsuits over the global giant Schneider. It is regarded as a regional competitor by many global giants in its field.

About their pioneer roles, these firms explore various approaches and make great efforts at industrial upgrade. In the footwear industry, Juyi takes the lead in introducing intelligent machines into footwear production. It also builds a production base in inland China, improves supply chain management and trims its corporate operation based on buyers' appetites. Aokang takes the lead in changing the patterns of footwear retail in China. It endeavours to enhance product supply management and improve product R&D. Menglani spares no effort on R&D and forges its competitiveness in making mother lasts, improving DIP technology and producing injected shoes. In the EE industry, Chint makes great efforts to develop new products for high- and medium-end markets, enhance production processes, reinforce supplier management, strengthen sales networks and extend industrial chains to the fields of HVEE and photovoltaic power generation. All these actions help the firms improve their competitiveness in production, sales and R&D.

Concerning their importance to the national economy, these firms have become the backbone of their industries and the promising force for China's global competition. Firstly, these firms are deeply rooted in China's economic and social structure. Originating from the local economy and developing in IDs, these firms reflect the most indigenous features of Chinese history, culture, economy and social relations. Their development in globalisation not only improves Chinese industrial competitiveness, but also facilitates the interaction of Western and Eastern civilisations. Secondly, these firms have great influence on the local and national economy. Due to their large scales and deep roots, the rise and fall of these firms directly impact the business of massive SMEs and the well-being of large employment. The success and failure of these leading firms to some extent reflect the gain and loss of the country in globalisation. Thirdly, these firms have forged good character for global competition. Developing from the ground, these firms are very resilient and persistent to all kinds of difficulties, well acquainted with market mechanisms, ambitious and hardworking to carve out their niches. Compared with SOEs, they have more entrepreneurship and independence to operate their business, watching the market closely and not yielding to global pressure. With such merits, these private leading firms have much potential to be the most important force for China's global competition.

Development challenges

Under the increasing competition pressure, these rising leading firms fight hard for promising development prospects. They are currently facing multiple development challenges. These challenges not only involve the comprehensive capability of the firms, but also relate to the regulation system of the government and the development level of the nation.

The comprehensive capability of the firms determines final results of firms' competitiveness. Chinese private manufacturing firms have the insufficiency of technology strength, the shortcoming of corporate governance, the incapability of system integration, the incompetence of customer interaction and the limit of brand influence.

Insufficiency of technology strength

Technology strength increasingly becomes the key to firms' global competitiveness. In the EE industry, technology decides the reliability and security of their products. Even in the footwear industry, which is usually regarded as a low technology-intensive sector, technology is also highly relevant in the manufacturing process. Technology strength involves design experience, R&D investment, technological talents and innovation commercialisation. To achieve further competitiveness in globalisation, private firms need to change their mind-set and transform their approach from technical imitators to innovators and even to leaders. Despite their large production scale, compared with global giants, most Chinese private firms have not forged strong technology capability currently. Most SMEs have weak abilities and limited access to public resources for research activities. Large firms are cautious towards long-term investment and frontier technological projects, which decelerate their technological progress. In some cases, firms even speculate their capital in non-related businesses, such as property, coal, steel and copper, which reduce their willingness and investment in technology innovation. Compared with foreign firms, Chinese private firms have less design experience, tacit knowledge and high-end technological talents, and more difficulties in transforming technological patents to commercial profits.

Shortcomings of corporate governance

Global competition put forward higher requirements on corporate governance. Successful global firms should have global visions, global knowledge, global culture and global structure. Based on these standards, Chinese private firms have many shortcomings. Originating from grass roots, most private entrepreneurs don't have good educations. These entrepreneurs cannot match the CEOs of global firms in term of their management expertise, understanding of technological progress and visions of global strategies. Because of their limited knowledge and weak capabilities, some private entrepreneurs are reluctant to build overseas operations, which hampers the global expansion of their firms. What's worse, many firms remain family run, where the personal preference and social network of the entrepreneurs dominate the decision-making process and staff appointment. Professional managers employed from outside feel it difficult to fully ply their talents. Moreover, these firms have small numbers of foreign employees and their company management has not adapted to international languages, culture and standards. In the future, private firms must build modern management systems, reform governance mechanisms, nurture global culture and expand their international structures.

Incapability of system integration

System integration is one of the most important capabilities for competition in GVCs. Global firms need to build interactive relationships with most capable suppliers and closely collaborate with them to improve technological advantages, enhance product quality, reduce procurement cost and quicken market response. However, most Chinese private firms have weak capability to achieve system integration. On one hand, most of their suppliers are SMEs, which have fragile abilities of technology, management and finance. They can hardly provide qualified materials, machines and components for higher-end products. On the other hand, Chinese leading firms have difficulties in managing their supply system, which is deeply integrated with local social relationships. Such a supply system traditionally was at an advantage to provide low-end products at low prices in a short time. Yet, misused social relationships harm supplier management and endanger product quality. Chinese leading firms have the dilemma of trading off between social networks and firm development.

Incompetence of customer interaction

Customer interaction is essential for firms in global competition. Global firms need to get closer to their customers, better serve their needs and work together with their partners. Chinese leading firms have not forged strong competence in these aspects. Firstly, most of them are lacking financial and human resources to open international sales networks and are short of international knowledge to manage these networks. In many cases, they entrust Chinese migrants as agencies to sell products overseas, but these migrants have little professional knowledge to market their products and have limited access to high-end customers. Secondly, Chinese firms have difficulties in communicating with their customers and understanding their needs. Many firms use franchised dealers to retail products instead of direct sales, so they cannot get first-hand and in-time information about customers' specific requirements. They can hardly develop proper products to respond to their customers' demands. Thirdly, they barely work together with their partners. Collaborating with outstanding customers can help manufacturing firms improve field knowledge, innovation commercialisation, buyer satisfaction and customer loyalty. However, most Chinese firms have not built cooperative partnership because most of their customers are low-end and their own capability of developing customised products is limited.

Limit of brand influence

Brand influence is a comprehensive index to reflect firms' competitiveness. Most Chinese firms have not forged their brand influence in the world. On one hand, Most Chinese firms don't have enough finance and expertise to advertise their firms and market their products. They can hardly provide all products with good quality and outstanding features to impress customers either. Moreover, most Chinese firms are not able to portray and sell their brand values. They should improve company culture and develop deep understanding of their fields and products to create brand values. On the other hand, although some Chinese firms achieve national awards from administrative agencies, these awards don't automatically transfer to the acknowledgement of their customers, especially in the high-end and overseas markets. Some customers even stereotype Chinese products as low-end products. It will take some time for Chinese firms to win over their customers' trust by providing reliable products, sincere service and meaningful values.

The regulation system of the government has great impact on firm competition. Chinese private manufacturing firms are encountering the ineffectiveness of market supervision, inequality of resource allocation and immaturity of industrial policy.

Ineffectiveness of market supervision

The market force has expanded rapidly in China, but market supervision is not effective enough. Firstly, IPR protection is not strong enough, so the technology and products of leading firms are often copied and imitated by other firms. These leading firms cannot get reasonable payback from their R&D expenditure and suffer from bad reputations caused by under-qualified products made by the firms that infringe their rights, which dampen leading firms' enthusiasm for technology innovation. Secondly, in many non-strategic industrial fields, firms cannot get guidance to enter and exit timely based on the industrial development situation. Usually, massive private firms arrive in swarms, producing similar products and committing in similar business blindly. Excessive supply and redundant construction become common problems in many overheated industries. Thirdly, market order is not managed effectively. In the low-end market of some industrial fields, many firms rush to the bottom for price competition and some even do shoddy work and use inferior materials for survival. Such behaviours have not been prevented or punished by effective administrative actions, so that the market competition order is disturbed and the operation of leading firms is negative affected.

Inequality of resource allocation

Despite economic reform, the resource allocation in China is still unequal between SOEs, FIEs and private firms. SOEs have priorities to public resources and strategic sectors, FIEs usually enjoy preferential policy, but Chinese private firms suffer from discriminatory treatments, especially in financial support and entry opportunity. To nurture their global competitiveness, private firms must heavily invest in R&D, M&A, opening new markets, expanding company organisations, recruiting talents and branding. However, currently, private SMEs can hardly get loans from formal institutions, and large firms don't have much long-term financial support either. Moreover, private firms are not welcomed to enter many industrial fields where administrative restrictions have been reduced in appearance, but they are dominated by SOEs in reality. Much private funding can hardly find proper projects to invest in and turn to speculative business, which leads to high risk of financial crisis and slow progress of manufacturing industries.

Immaturity of industrial policy

Industrial policy is widely used in China in both central and local governments, but it appears to be immature to support firm competition in globalisation. Firstly, in many cases, industry policy focuses on high technological-intensive industries, rather than the technological-intensive segments of different industries. Such preference does not necessarily lead to leapfrog developments of high technological-intensive industries, but results in slow upgrading in lower technological-intensive industries. For example, the footwear industry is generally a low technological-intensive industry, but its design and automatic production need much technological investment. In contrast, photovoltaic power generation is viewed as a high technological-intensive industry, but the production of photovoltaic panels is labour intensive. Industry-oriented policy misleads many Chinese private firms away from traditional industries where they have rich experience and much space to upgrade, to the new industries where they have little knowledge and capabilities to make high-end products. Secondly, in most cases, industry policy tries to pick winners and nurture champions, but these ways are problematic in global competition. On one hand, many international organisations prohibit national governments from direct support on specific firms and their policy spaces get smaller and smaller. On the other hand, global firms need to compete and integrate their systems in GVCs, which means that it is not only individual leading firms, but also their systems that are important. Industry policy needs to adjust its target and approach to facilitate the system competitiveness of Chinese leading firms.

The development level of the nation lays important foundations for firms' competitiveness. Chinese private manufacturing firms are suffering from the weakness of industrial foundation and the incompetency of human resources.

Weakness of industrial foundation

Global competition is not only a battle between Chinese leading firms and foreign companies, but also a contest between their industrial foundations. Growing from China, private firms have a weaker industrial foundation than foreign firms from developed countries. Firstly, the transportation, logistics and infrastructure in many Chinese regions are less developed. They bring many barriers for Chinese firms to shift their production bases to low-cost areas and deliver their goods more widely, fast and economically. Secondly, a series of Chinese basic industries are backward compared with the ones in developed countries. To compete in global fields, Chinese firms need better materials, more advanced IT, more intelligent machines and more developed service. However, China still has some gaps with developed nations in these aspects, which makes Chinese products less competitive than advanced foreign products. What's worse, Chinese leading firms suffer from large expenditure and dependence on imported materials, software and machines for their upgrade. Thirdly, China has a large group of low-income consumers. These customers feed many Chinese firms by purchasing low-end products, but they also bring these firms much inertia to upgrade. These customers cannot afford to pay higher prices, which dampens the enthusiasm of Chinese firms to upgrade their business.

Incompetency of human resources

Human resources are vital for firm competition in globalisation. They consist of researchers, engineers, managing staff and ordinary workers. Technological advances cannot be achieved without experienced researchers and engineers who have profound expertise and good visions of market demands. International business cannot be operated without capable managerial staff who have good language skills and global knowledge. The automation and digitalisation put forward more requirements for ordinary workers to be more open to change, possess greater flexibility for new roles and work environments and get accustomed to continual interdisciplinary learning. However, compared with SOEs and FIEs, Chinese private firms are less charming to excellent human resources. Most of their ordinary workers lack proper vocational education and a professional spirit for their career. It will be a long-run task for not only leading firms, but also the whole Chinese society to value the manufacturing industry and nurture human resources by education and training.

Policy implications

Based on the current competition situation and development challenges, the study puts forward policy implications on China's economic reform and industrial upgrade.

Implications for economic reform

The government needs to promote further economic reform by advancing SOE reform, strengthening market supervision and cultivating the private sector. Firstly, the government should advance SOE reform. The government can continuously possess the ownership of public assets but allow firms with diverse ownerships to manage these assets for higher economic efficiency. In addition, it can dominate the key segments of strategic industries to control the national economy but introduce more market mechanisms in non-strategic industries and non-key segments of strategic industries. Secondly, the government should strengthen market supervision. It should provide firms with sufficient economic information and guide them to enter and exit certain industries based on the industrial development situation. Moreover, it should collaborate with industrial associations to keep good competition order and maintain brand reputations. It is also highly important to effectively implement IPR laws to encourage and protect technological innovation. Thirdly, the government should cultivate the private sector. It should acknowledge the achievement and the contribution of private firms and provide leading firms with sufficient support, especially in finance and R&D. It is also necessary to nurture a social environment that values private entrepreneurs and stimulates an entrepreneurial spirit. The government can organise regular trainings for private entrepreneurs to improve their professional expertise, management skills and global visions.

Implications for industrial upgrade

The government should facilitate industrial upgrade by enhancing high-value added segments, strengthening national innovation systems, supporting basic industries and improving vocational education. Firstly, it should enhance high-value added segments. The government should support firms, even in low technology-intensive industries, to participate in more value-added activities. Also, it can appropriately encourage capable firms to enter high technology-intensive industries based on their foundation and competitiveness. Secondly, it should strengthen national innovation systems. It is important to ensure firms' pivotal roles in the innovation system. The government should facilitate cooperation between public research institutions and private firms to tackle bottleneck technological problems and improve innovation commercialisation. Thirdly, it should support basic industries. The government should heavily invest in basic industries, such as material, machinery and IT industries, to lay solid foundations for a wider range of industrial sectors. It can also encourage firms to conduct overseas amalgamations in the fields of basic industries. Fourthly, it should improve vocational education. It is vital to cultivate a public consciousness that values the manufacturing industry and respects technical workers. The government can invest finance and human resources to build a stronger vocational education system. Also, it should support firms to provide regular and updated professional trainings for workers in different fields and at multiple levels.

Appendix

Table A.1 Yearly currency exchange rates of RMB and EUR per USD, years 1978–2016

Year	*RMB per USD*	*EUR per USD*
1978	1.7	
1979	1.6	
1980	1.5	
1984	2.3	
1985	2.9	
1986	3.5	
1987	3.7	
1988	3.7	
1989	3.8	
1990	4.8	
1991	5.3	
1992	5.5	
1994	8.6	
1995	8.4	
1999	8.3	
2000	8.3	
2001	8.3	
2002	8.3	
2003	8.3	
2004	8.3	
2005	8.2	
2006	8.0	
2007	7.6	
2008	6.9	
2009	6.8	
2010	6.8	
2011	6.5	0.72
2012	6.3	0.78
2013	6.2	0.75
2014	6.1	0.75
2015	6.2	0.90
2016	6.6	0.90

Data source: The World Bank (2017).

Table A.2 Angus Maddison's estimate on GDP per capita and GDP shares of China, major regions and the world, years 1–1950

GDP per Capita (1990 international Geary-Khamis dollars)

Year	*1*	*50*	*960*	*1000*	*1300*	*1500*	*1700*	*1820*	*1913*	*1950*
China	450	450	450	450	600	600	600	600	552	448
Western Europe	576			427		771	997	1,202	3,457	4,578
Europe	550	450	422		576		923	1,090		
USA	400			400		400	527	1,257	5,301	9,561
Japan	400			425		500	570	669	1,387	1,921
Soviet Union	400			400		499	610	688	1,488	2,841
India	450			450		550	550	533	673	619
World	467			450		566	616	667	1,526	2,113

Shares of World's GDP (%)

Year	*1*	*50*	*960*	*1000*	*1280*	*1500*	*1700*	*1820*	*1913*	*1950*
China	25.4			22.1		24.9	22.3	32.9	8.8	4.6
Western Europe	13.7			9.1		17.8	21.9	23.0	33.0	26.2
Europe							24.9	26.6		
USA	0.3			0.4		0.3	0.1	1.8	18.9	27.3
Japan	1.1			2.7		3.1	2.9	3.0	2.6	3.0
Soviet Union	1.5			2.4		3.4	4.4	5.4	8.5	9.6
India	32.0			28.1		24.4	24.4	16.0	7.5	4.2

Data source: Maddison (1998, 2007a, 2007b).

Table A.3 Paul Bairoch's estimate on the shares of world manufacturing output of China and major regions (%), years 1750–1980

Year	*1750*	*1860*	*1900*	*1953*	*1980*
China	32.8	19.7	6.2	2.3	5.0
Europe	23.2	53.2	62.0	26.1	22.9
USA	0.1	7.2	23.6	44.7	31.5
Japan	3.8	2.6	2.4	2.9	9.1
Russia (Soviet Union)	5.0	7.0	8.8	10.7	14.8
India	24.5	8.6	1.7	1.7	2.3
Developed Countries	27.0	63.4	89.0	93.5	88.0
The Third World	73.0	36.6	11.0	6.5	12.0
World absolute volume*	127.3	225.9	540.8	3,070	11,041

Data source: Bairoch (1982: 296 and 304).

Note: * On the basis: UK in 1990=100.

Table A.4 The World Bank's estimate on economic performance of China, major regions and the world, years 1960–2015

GDP (billion current USD)						
Year	*1960*	*1978*	*1992*	*2003*	*2010*	*2015*
China	59.72	149.54	426.92	1,660.29	6,100.62	11,007.72
EU	358.97	2,769.59	8,570.21	11,945.41	16,975.51	16,311.90
USA	543.30	2,356.57	6,539.30	11,510.67	14,964.37	18,036.65
Japan	44.31	966.74	3,852.79	4,445.66	5,700.10	4,383.08
Russia			460.29	430.35	1,524.92	1,331.21
India	37.68	139.71	293.26	618.36	1,656.56	2,095.40
World	1,352.93	8,438.15	25,342.93	38,875.97	65,853.16	74,152.48
Shares of World's GDP (%)						
Year	*1960*	*1978*	*1992*	*2003*	*2010*	*2015*
China	4.4	1.8	1.7	4.3	9.3	14.8
EU	26.5	32.8	33.8	30.7	25.8	22.0
USA	40.2	27.9	25.8	29.6	22.7	24.3
Japan	3.3	11.5	15.2	11.4	8.7	5.9
Russia			1.8	1.1	2.3	1.8
India	2.8	1.7	1.2	1.6	2.5	2.8
GDP per Capita, PPP (current international dollars)						
Year	*1960*	*1978*	*1992*	*2003*	*2010*	*2015*
China			1,268.3	3,961.3	9,333.1	14,450.2
EU			16,063.0	25,317.3	33,271.3	38,702.4
USA			25,493.0	39,677.2	48,374.1	56,115.7
Japan			21,052.3	28,867.9	34,996.3	40,763.4
Russia			6,854.1	9,253.6	20,497.9	24,451.4
India			1,240.0	2,361.3	4,315.4	6,100.7
World			5,768.6	8,835.1	12,853.5	15,672.8
GNI per Capita, PPP (current international dollars)						
Year	*1960*	*1978*	*1992*	*2003*	*2010*	*2015*
China			1,270	3,940	9,290	14,390
EU			16,058	25,256	33,307	38,491
USA			25,180	39,960	48,880	57,540
Japan			21,230	29,320	35,900	42,310
Russia			6,790	8,970	19,860	23,770
India			1,220	2,340	4,270	6,030
World			5,708	8,774	12,816	15,655

(*Continued*)

Table A.4 (Continued)

Shares of World's Merchandise Export Value (%)						
Year	*1960*	*1978*	*1992*	*2003*	*2010*	*2015*
China	2.1	0.8	2.2	2.7	10.3	13.8
EU	43.1	45.3	43.3	19.2	33.9	32.7
USA	16.6	11.5	11.7	4.4	8.4	9.1
Japan	3.3	7.7	8.9	2.9	5.0	3.8
Russia				0.8	2.6	2.1
India	1.1	0.5	0.5	1.6	1.5	1.6
World absolute	124.45	1,272.12	3,830.44	16,482	15,301	16,482

Data source: The World Bank (2017).

Note: The author calculated the shares of world's merchandise export value.

Table A.5 UNIDO's estimate on the shares of world manufacturing value added of China and major regions (%), years 1992–2015

Year	*1992*	*2003*	*2010*	*2015*
China	4.5	10.8	18.7	23.8
EU	32.0	27.6	22.7	20.9
USA	19.1	20.7	17.8	16.5
Japan	15.0	11.1	10.4	8.9
Russia	2.9	2.1	1.9	1.8
India	1.1	1.6	2.4	2.4
World absolute volume (billion constant 2010 USD)	5,599	7,949	10,300	11,907

Data source: UNIDO (2016).

Bibliography

ABB Group (2017a) *ABB* [online]. Available from: www.abb.com/ (Accessed 29 March 2017).

ABB Group (2017b) *Annual Report 2016 Committed to Unlocking Value*. Zurich: ABB Group.

Adidas Group (2016) *Annual Report 2015 How We Create Value*. Herzogenaurach: Adidas Group.

Amighini, A. and Rabellotti, R. (2006) How Do Italian Footwear Industrial Districts Face Globalization? *European Planning Studies*, 14(4), 485–502.

Amsden, A. H. (1989) *Asia's Next Giant: South Korea and Late Industrialization*. Oxford: Oxford University Press.

APICCAPS (Portuguese Footwear Components and Leather Goods Manufacturers' Association) (2014) *Footwear Consumer 2030: Incorporating Global Trends to Foresight Footwear Market*. Porto: APICCAPS.

APICCAPS (2015) *World Footwear Yearbook 2015*. Porto: APICCAPS.

Aronsson, C. (2014) *In the Same Footsteps?* Stockholm: Fair Trade Center.

Bai, J. (2002) Zengqiang Qiye Hexin Jingzhengli Fazhan Juyou Guoji Jingzhengli de Daqiye [Enhancing Firms' Core Competitiveness and Developing Global Competitive Firms]. *Expanding Horizons*, 4, 26–29.

Bai, O. (2004) Guoji Jiancai Jutou Zhongquan Chuji Zhongguo Shichang [Global Construction Material Giants Struck Out Chinese Market]. *Building Materials Industry Information*, 2, 15.

Bairoch, P. (1982) International Industrialization Levels From 1750 to 1980. *Journal of European Economic History*, 11(2), 269–333.

Bazan, L. and Navas-Alemán, L. (2004) The Underground Revolution in the Sinos Valley: A Comparison of Upgrading in Global and National Value Chains. In Hubert Schmitz (ed.), *Local Enterprises in the Global Economy: Issues of Governance and Upgrading*. Cheltenham: Edward Elgar, pp. 110–139.

Becattini, G. (1992) The Marshallian Industrial Distirct as a Socioeconomic Notion. In Frank Pyke et al. (eds.), *Industrial Districts and Inter-firm Co-operation in Italy*, 2nd edition. Geneva: International Institute for Labour Studies, pp. 37–51.

Becattini, G. et al. (2009) *A Handbook of Industrial Districts*. Cheltenham: Edward Elgar.

Belle International (2014) *Baili Xieye (Suzhou) Youxian Gongsi Longzhong Kaigong* [*Belle Footwear (Suzhou) Limited Company Went to Production Grandly*] [online]. Available from: http://belleintl.com/index.php?c=channel&molds=jt&id=164 (Accessed 30 May 2017).

Belle International (2015–2016) *Annual Report*. Hong Kong: Belle International.

Best, M. H. (1990) *The New Competition: Institutions of Industrial Restructuring*. Cambridge: Polity Press.

Brandt, L. and Thun, E. (2015) Competition and Upgrading in Chinese Industry. In Barry Naughton and Kellee S. Tsai (eds.), *State Capitalism, Institutional Adaptation, and the Chinese Miracle*. New York: Cambridge University Press, pp. 154–198.

C&J Clark International (2016) *Clarks* [online]. Available from: www.clarks.com/ (Accessed 25 May 2017).

Cai, J. (2010) *Shehui Ziben Shijiao Xia de Wenzhou Moshi yu Fazhan Zhuanxing* [*The Wenzhou Model and Its Development Transformation From the Perspective of Social Capital*]. Shanghai: Shanghai Academy of Social Science.

Cainelli, G. et al. (2012) Production and Financial Linkages in Inter-Firm Networks: Structural Variety, Risk-sharing and Resilience. *Journal of Evolutionary Economics*, 22(4), 711–734.

Carbonara, N. (2002) New Models of Inter-firm Networks Within Industrial Districts. *Entrepreneurship & Regional Development*, 14, 229–246.

Cawthorne, P. M. (1995) Of Networks and Markets: The Rise and Rise of a South Indian Town, the Example of Tiruppur's Cotton Knitwear Industry. *World Development*, 23(1), 43–56.

Chandler, A. D. (1990) *Scale and Scope: Dynamics of Industrial Capitalism*. London: The Belknap Press of Harvard Univeristy Press.

Chandler, A. D. et al. (1997) *Big Business and the Wealth of Nations*. Cambridge: Cambridge University Press.

Chang, J.-H. et al. (2016) *ASEAN in Transformation: How Techonology Is Changing Jobs and Enterprises*. Geneva: International Labour Organization.

Chen, K. (2008) *12 Ming Wenzhou Daibiao Weiyuan zhong You 5 Ming Qiyejia* [*There Are 5 Entrepreneurs Among 12 Wenzhou's Representative Committee Members*] [online]. Available from: http://news.66wz.com/system/2008/03/04/100506835.shtml (Accessed 13 March 2017).

Chen, L. (2005) *Wenzhou Rendi Guanxi Yanjiu 960–1840* [*A Study on Wenzhou Man-Nature Relationships: 960–1840*]. Hangzhou: Zhejiang University.

Chen, M. (2008) *Wenzhou Jinrong Gaige Sanshinian* [*Three Decades of Wenzhou's Financial Reform*]. Hangzhou: Zhejiang People's Publishing House.

Chen, Y. (2004) *Zhongguo Minying Qiye 500 Qiang Paixu Jiexiao* [*The Rank of China's Top 500 Private Firms Released*] [online]. Available from: www.people.com.cn/GB/jingji/1037/2740837.html (Accessed 16 March 2017).

Chiarvesio, M. et al. (2013) Sourcing From Northern and Southern Countries: The Global Value Chain Approach Applied to Italian SMEs. *Transition Studies Review*, 20(3), 389–404.

China Electrical Equipment Industry Association (2016) Dianqi Gongye Shisanwu Fazhan Zhidao Yijian [The Guide for Electricial Equipment Industry in the Thirteenth Five Year Development Plan]. *Dianqi Gongye*, 5, 49–59.

China Energy Research Society (ed.) (2015) *Zhongguo Nengyuan Zhanwang 2030* [*China Energy Outlook 2030*]. Beijing: Economy Management Publishing House.

China Leather Industry Association (2016) Duochong Yali Youzai, Jiegou Zhubu Youhua, Jingzheng Youshi Chongsu [Multiple Pressure Still Exists, Structure Gradaully Improve, Competitive Advantages Rebuild]. *West Leather*, 38(9), 4–7.

Chint Group (2017) *Chint* [online]. Available from: http://en.chint.com/ (Accessed 30 May 2017).

Corò, G. and Grandinetti, R. (1999) Evolutionary Patterns of Italian Industrial Districts. *Human System Management*, 18, 117–129.

Corò, G. and Grandinetti, R. (2001) Industrial District Responses to the Network Economy: Vertical Integration Versus Pluralist Global Exploration. *Human Systems Management*, 20, 189–199.

Crestanello, P. (1996) The Industrial Districts in Veneto: Changes and Tendencies. In Francesco Cossentino et al. (eds.), *Local and Regional Response to Global Pressure: The Case of Italy and Its Industrial Districts*. Geneva: International Institute for Labour Studies, pp. 67–96.

Datamonitor (2011) *Global Heavy Electrical Equipment Industry Profile*. New York: Datamonitor.

Dawson, R. S. (1964) *The Legacy of China*. Oxford: Clarendon Press.

Deichmann (2017) *Our Growth* [online]. Available from: http://corpsite.deichmann.com/gben/our-business/our-growth/ (Accessed 30 May 2017).

Dei Ottati, G. (1996a) Economic Changes in the District of Prato in the 1980s: Towards a More Conscious and Organized Industrial District. *European Planning Studies*, 4(1), 35–52.

Dei Ottati, G. (1996b) The Remarkable Resilience of the Industrial Districts of Tuscany. Francesco Cossentino et al. (eds.), *Local and Regional Response to Global Pressure: The Case of Italy and Its Industrial Districts*. Geneva: International Institute for Labour Studies, pp. 37–66.

Department of Industry Statistics National Bureau of Statistics of China (ed.) (2016) *China Industry Statistical Yearbook*. Beijing: China Statistics Press.

Dianlaohu (2016) *Zhongguo Dianqi 100 Qiang Shinian Bianqian* [*A Decade Change of China's Top 100 Electrical Equipment Firms*] [online]. Available from: www.7895.com/a/dlhzx/2605_2.html (Accessed 30 May 2017).

Dicken, P. (2015) *Global Shift: Mapping the Changing Contours of the World Economy*, 7th edition. London: SAGE.

Di Maria, E. and Webster, P. (2012) *Shoe Intelligentce News and Analysis of the International Market*. Bry-sur-Marne: EDM Publications.

Ecco Sko A/S (2016) *Annual Report 2015*. Bredebro: Ecco Sko A/S.

Economy and Law Programme (2009) *Jiaoliang* [*Competition*]. Beijing: China Central Television Channel 2.

Editing Group of the Book Three Decades' Development of Wenzhou's Private Economy (2008) *Wenzhou Minying Jingji Fazhan Sanshinian: Fazhan Zongshu Juan* [*Three Decades' Development of Wenzhou's Private Economy: Development Review*]. Hangzhou: Zhejiang People's Publishing House.

The Editorial Office of Southern Weekly (2011) Wenzhou Huozhun Jingwai Zhijie Touzi [Wenzhou Was Approved for Individual Outward Direct Investment]. *Southern Weekly*, 11 January.

Elms, D. K. and Low, P. (2013) *Global Value Chains in a Changing World*. Geneva: WTO Publications.

Euromonitor (2017) *Euromonitor International* [online]. Available from: www.euromonitor.com/ (Accessed 29 May 2017).

Feenstra, R. C. (1998) Integration of Trade and Disintegration of Production in the Global Economy. *The Journal of Economic Perspectives*, 12(4), 31–50.

Financial Times (2010) *Chinese Firms in FT 500 2010* [online]. Available from: www.ftchinese.com/interactive/180 (Accessed 13 March 2017).

Fortune (2011) *Chinese Firms in Fortune 500 2011* [online]. Available from: www.fortunechina.com/fortune500/c/2011-07/07/content_62516.htm (Accessed 13 March 2017).

Fortune (2017) *Global 500* [online]. Available from: http://fortune.com/global500/list/filtered?hqcountry=China (Accessed 18 May 2017).

Gadiesh, O. et al. (2007) Market the Battle for China's Good-Enough Market. *Harvard Business Review*, September, 80–89.

Gao, B. and Zhang, J. (eds.) (2002) *Wenzhou: Zhongguo Xiedu* [*Wenzhou: China's Capital of Shoes*]. Beijing: China Light Industry Press.

General Electric (2016) *Annual Report 2015 Digital Industrial*. Fairfield: General Electric.

General Electric (2017a) *Annual Report 2016 Leading a Digital Industrial Era*. Fairfield: General Electric.

General Electric (2017b) *GE* [online]. Available from: www.ge.com/ (Accessed 30 May 2017).

Geox S.p.A. (2016) *Geox* [online]. Available from: www.geox.com/ (Accessed 20 April 2017).

Gereffi, G. (1994) The Organization of Buyer-driven Global Commodity Chains: How U.S. Retailers Shape Overseas Production Networks. In Gary Gereffi and Miguel Korzeniewicz *Commodity Chains and Global Capitalism*. London: Praeger, pp. 95–122.

Gereffi, G. (1999a) A Commodity Chains Framework for Analyzing Global Industries. *Institute of Development Studies*, 8(12), 1–9.

Gereffi, G. (1999b) International Trade and Industrial Upgrading in the Apparel Commodity Chain. *Journal of International Economics*, 48(1), 37–70.

Gereffi, G. et al. (2005) The Governance of Global Value Chains. *Review of International Political Economy*, 12(1), 78–104.

Gereffi, G. and Korzeniewicz, M. (1994) *Commodity Chains and Global Capitalism*. London: Praeger.

Gerschenkron, A. (1962) *Economic Backwardness in Historical Perspective: A Book of Essays*. Cambridge: Harvard University Press.

Ghemawat, P. and Hout, T. (2008) Tomorrow's Global Giants Not the Usual Suspects. *Harvard Business Review*, November, 80–89.

Giuliani, E. et al. (2005) Upgrading in Global Value Chains: Lessons From Latin American Clusters. *World Development*, 33(4), 549–573.

Giuliani, E. and Rabellotti, R. (2005) Clusters Facing Competition: Some Concluding Remarks. In Elisa Giuliani et al. (eds.), *Clusters Facing Competition: The Importance of External Linkages*. Aldershot: Ashgate, pp. 291–294.

Guan, Y. (2012) *Waihuan Neiyou zhi xia, Zhongguo Pixie Ruhe Zuowen Shijie Diyi* [*How Chinese Leather Footwear Can Maintain Global Top 1 Under Interal and External Challenges*] [online]. Available from: www.qianzhan.com/analyst/detail/220/20120425-74947ca1f549fb7c.html (Accessed 30 May 2017).

Guyol, N. B. (1969) *The World Electric Power Industry*. Berkeley: University of California Press.

Hanemann, T. and Rosen, D. (2012) *China Invests in Europe*. New York: Rhodium Group.

He, M. and Li, Z. (2010) Zhongguo Daqiye Guoji Jingzhengli Chaju yu Zhengce Jianyi [The Gaps for Chinese Large Firms in Global Competitivenss and Policy Suggestions]. *Intertrade*, 11, 12–16.

He, R. (1989) *Wenzhou Minjian Shichang Kaocha* [*Investigation on Wenzhou's Private Market*]. Beijing: People's Publishing House.

Hirschman, A. O. (1958) *The Strategy of Economic Development*. New Haven: Yale University Press.

Hobday, M. et al. (2005) Systems Integration: A Core Capability of the Modern Corporation. *Industrial and Corporate Change*, 14(6), 1109–1143.

Huang, M. (2004) *Zhongguo Minying Jingji Fazhan Baogao No.1 (2003)* [*China's Private Economy Development Report No. 1 (2003)*]. Beijing: China Social Science Press.

Huang, M. (2011) *Zhongguo Minying Jingji Fazhan Baogao No.8 (2010–2011)* [*China's Private Economy Development Report No. 8 (2010–2011)*]. Beijing: China Social Science Press.

Huang, M. and Hu, D. (2006) *Zhongguo Minying Jingji Fazhan Baogao No.3 (2005–2006)* [*China's Private Economy Development Report No. 3 (2005–2006)*]. Beijing: China Social Science Press.

Huang, Z. et al. (2008) The Role of Clustering in Rural Industrialization: A Case Study of the Footwear Industry in Wenzhou. *China Economic Review*, 19(3), 409–420.

Humphrey, J. and Schmitz, H. (2002) *Developing Country Firms in the World Economy: Governance and Upgrading in Global Value Chains*. Brighton: IDS-INEF Project.

IBISWorld (2017) *Footwear Manufacturing in China*. Los Angeles: IBISWorld.

IEA (International Energy Agency) (2009) *World Energy Outlook 2009*. Paris: IEA.

IEA (2013) *World Energy Outlook 2013*. Paris: IEA.

IEA (2015) *2015 Key World Energy Statistics*. Paris: IEA.

ILO (International Labour Organization) (2017) *International Labour Organization* [online]. Available from: www.ilo.org/global/lang – en/index.htm (Accessed 30 May 2017).

Industry and Transportation Division of National Bureau of Statistics (2000) *Zhongguo Gongye Jiaotong Nengyuan 50 Nian Tongji Ziliao Huibian* [*The Collection of 50 Years' Data on China's Industry, Transportation and Energy*]. Beijing: China Statistics Press.

Industry Statistics Division of National Bureau of Statistics (2012) *China Industry Economy Statistical Yearbook*. Beijing: China Statistics Press.

Ingstrup, M. B. (2014) When Firms Take the Lead in Facilitating Clusters. *European Planning Studies*, 22(9), 1–17.

International Federation of Robotics (2016) *World Robotics Report 2016*. Frankfurt: International Federation of Robotics.

Intrepid Investment Bankers (2015) *Apparel, Retail and Lifestyle Brands M&A Report*. Los Angeles: Intrepid Investment Bankers.

IRI-Economics of Industrial Research and Innovation (2015) *The 2015 EU Industrial R&D Investment Scoreboard* [online]. Available from: http://iri.jrc.ec.europa.eu/scoreboard15.html (Accessed 17 March 2017).

IRI-Economics of Industrial Research and Innovation (2016) *The 2016 EU Industrial R&D Investment Scoreboard* [online]. Available from: http://iri.jrc.ec.europa.eu/scoreboard16.html (Accessed 30 May 2017).

ITC (International Trade Centre) (2017) *International Trade Statistics 2001–2017* [online]. Available from: www.intracen.org/itc/market-info-tools/trade-statistics/ (Accessed 25 June 2017).

Jiang, H. and Yu, J. (2011) Unofficial Chamber's Participating in Local Governance: A Case Study of Wenzhou. *Yinshan Academic Journal*, 24(3), 12–17, 29.

Jin, B. (2009) Zhongguo Gongye Biange Zhenxing 60 Nian [Chinese Industry's 60 Years of Change and Revitalization]. *China Industrial Economics*, 6, 5–16.

Johnson, C. (1982) *MITI and the Japanese Miracle: The Growth of Industrial Policy, 1925–1975*. Stanford: Stanford University Press.

Juyi Group (2017) *Juyi Group* [online]. Available from: www.juyi.cn (Accessed 30 May 2017).

Kaplinsky, R. (2000) *Spreading the Gains From Globalisation: What Can Be Learned From Value Chain Analysis?* Brighton: Institute of Development Studies.

Kaplinsky, R. and Morris, M. (2002) *A Handbook for Value Chain Research.* Brighton: Institute of Development Studies.

Knorringa, P. (1999) Agra: An Old Cluster Facing the New Competition. *World Development*, 27(9), 1587–1604.

Krugman, P. R. (1991) *Geography and Trade*. London: MIT Press.

Lardy, N. R. (2014) *Markets Over Mao: The Rise of Private Business in China.* Washington, DC: Peterson Institute for International Economics.

Lazerson, M. H. and Lorenzoni, G. (1999) The Firms that Feed Industrial Districts: A Return to the Italian Source. *Industrial and Corporate Change*, 8(2), 235–266.

Leavy, P. (2014) *The Oxford Handbook of Qualitative Research.* Oxford: Oxford University Press.

Li, B. (1991) Jianlun Jiangnan Diqu de Jieding [Brief Discussion on the Scope of Jiangnan Region]. *The Journal of Chinese Social and Economic History*, 1, 100–105, 107.

Li, B. (1998) *Agricultural Development in Jiangnan, 1620–1850.* Basingstoke: Macmillan.

Li, B. (2000) *Jiangnan de Zaoqi Gongyehua* [*Jiangnan's Early Industrialisation*]. Beijing: Social Sciences Academic Press.

Li, X. (2003) Guoji Liang Jutou Jueli Zhongguo Shichang [Two Global Giants Fought for Chinese Market]. *Distance Education in China*, 22, 21–22.

Li, X. (2010) *30 Wenqi Shangbang Zhongguo Minying 500 Qiang, Zhengtai Ju Wenqi zhi Shou* [*30 Wenzhou's Firms Were Listed on China's Top 500 Private Firms, Chint Ranked the First Among Wenzhou's Firms*] [online]. Available from: http://news.66wz.com/system/2010/09/01/102054460.shtml (Accessed 16 March 2017).

Li, Z. and Zhuang, J. (2015) *2015 Zhongguo Minying Qiye 500 Qiang Bangdan Chulu Wenzhou 9 Jia Qiye Shangbang* [*Wenzhou Had 9 Firms Listed on the 2015 China's Top 500 Private Firms*] [online]. Available from: http://news.66wz.com/system/2015/08/26/104553600.shtml (Accessed 16 March 2017).

Liu, A. P. L. (1992) The "Wenzhou Model" of Development and China's Modernisation. *Asian Survey*, 32(8), 696–711.

Liu, Z. and Zhang, J. (2007) Quanqiu Daigong Tixi Xia Fazhanzhong Guojia Fuhuoxing Wangluo de Xingcheng Tupo yu Duice [Forming, Breakthroughs and Strategies of Captive Network in Developing Countries at Global Outsourcing System]. *China Industrial Economy*, 5, 39–47.

Local Annals Office of Wenzhou Municipal Government (2002, 2005, 2011) *Wenzhou Yearbook.* Beijing: Zhonghua Book Company.

Local Annals Office of Wenzhou Municipal Government (2015) *Lighter Industry* [online]. Available from: www.wenzhou.gov.cn/art/2016/1/11/art_1214512_1374152.html (Accessed 16 March 2017).

Lu, H. (2014) Quanqiu Jiazhilian Zhili Xia Difang Chanye Jiqun Shengji Yanjiu [Upgrading Local Clusters in GVCs]. *Productivity Research*, 2, 65–69, 154.

Maddison, A. (1998) *Chinese Economic Performance in the Long Run.* Paris: Development Centre of the OECD (Organisation for Economic Co-operation and Development).

Maddison, A. (2007a) *Chinese Economic Performance in the Long Run.* Paris: Development Centre of the OECD.

Maddison, A. (2007b) *Contours of the World Economy 1–2030 AD*. Oxford: Oxford University Press.

MarketLine (2012) *Global Electrical Equipment Industry Profile*. London: MarketLine.

MarketLine (2014a) *Global Electrical Components & Equipment Industry Profile*. London: MarketLine.
MarketLine (2014b) *Global Electrical Equipment Industry Profile*. London: MarketLine.
MarketLine (2016a) *Footwear in China Industry Profile*. London: MarketLine.
MarketLine (2016b) *Global Footwear Industry Profile*. London: MarketLine.
Markusen, A. (1996) Sticky Places in Slippery Space: A Typology of Industrial Districts. *Economic Geography*, 72(3), 293–313.
Marsh, P. (2011) *China Became the Global Largest Manufacturer* [online]. Available from: www.ftchinese.com/story/001037460 (Accessed 11 March 2017).
Marshall, A. (1920) *Principles of Economics: An Introductory Volume*. London: Macmillan.
Marx, K. (1976) *Capital*, Volume 1. London: Penguin Books.
Mazzucato, M. (2015) *The Entrepreneurial State: Debunking Public vs. Private Sector Myths*. London: Anthem Press.
Merriam, S. B. (2009) *Qualitative Research: A Guide to Design and Implementation*. San Francisco: Jossey-Bass.
Ministry of Commerce of People's Republic of China (2009–2016) *Statistical Bulletin of China's Outward Foreign Direct Investment*. Beijing: Ministry of Commerce of People's Republic of China.
Mintel Group (2017) *Mintel* [online]. Available from: www.mintel.com/ (Accessed 20 May 2017).
Nadvi, K. and Schmitz, H. (1994) *Industrial Clusters in Less Developed Countries: Review of Experiences and Research Agenda*. Brighton: Institute of Development Studies.
National Bureau of Statistics of China (1981–2016) *China Statistical Yearbook*. Beijing: China Statistics Press.
National Renewable Energy Centre (2015) *Zhongguo Kezaisheng Nengyuan Fazhan Baogao* [*The Renewable Energy Industry Development Report*]. Beijing: China Economic Publishing House.
Navas-Alemán, L. (2011) The Impact of Operating in Multiple Value Chains for Upgrading: The Case of the Brazilian Furniture and Footwear Industries. *World Development*, 398, 1386–1397.
Needham, J. (2004) *Science and Civilisation in China Volume VII: 2*. Kenneth Girdwood Robinson (ed.). Cambridge: Cambridge University Press.
Nike Inc. (2009, 2015, 2016) *Nike Form 10-K*. Oregon: Nike Inc.
Nolan, P. (1999) *Coca-Cola and the Global Business Revolution: A Study With Special Reference to the EU*. Cambridge: Judge Institute of Management.
Nolan, P. (2001) *China and the Global Business Revolution*. Basingstoke: Palgrave.
Nolan, P. (2007) *Integrating China: Transition Into Global Economy*. London: Anthem Press.
Nolan, P. (2014) *Chinese Firms, Global Firms: Industrial Policy in the Age of Globalization*. New York: Routledge.
Nolan, P. et al. (2007) *The Global Business Revolution and the Cascade Effect: Systems Integration in the Global Aerospace, Beverage and Retail Industries*. Basingstoke: Palgrave Macmillan.
Nolan, P. and Dong, F. (1990) *Market Forces in China: Competition and Small Business – The Wenzhou Debate*. London: Zed Books.
Pan, X. and Weng, Q. (2013) *2013 Shijie Wenzhouren Dahui Bimu* [*2013 World Wenzhou People's Conference Closed*] [online]. Available from: http://news.66wz.com/system/2013/02/17/103539028.shtml (Accessed 14 March 2017).
Peng, S. (ed.) (2003) *Zhongguo Jingji Tizhi Gaige Nianjian* [*China Economic Systems Reform Yearbook*]. Beijing: China's Reform Publishing House.

Penrose, E. (2009) *The Theory of The Growth of the Firm*, 4th edition. Oxford: Oxford University Press.

Pietrobelli, C. and Rabellotti, R. (2005) Upgrading in Global Value Chains: Lesson Form Latin American Clusters. In Elisa Giuliani et al. (eds.), *Clusters Facing Competition: The Importance of External Linkages*. Aldershot: Ashgate Publishing Limited, pp. 13–38.

Piore, M. J. and Sable, C. F. (1984) *The Second Industrial Divide: Possibilities for Prosperity*. New York: Basic Books.

Porter, M. E. (1990) *The Competitive Advantage of Nations*. London: Macmillan.

Porter, M. E. (1998) *On Competition*. Boston: Harvard Business School Press.

Pyke, F. and Sengenberger, W. (1992) *Industrial Districts and Local Economic Regeneration*. Geneva: International Institute for Labour Studies.

Qin, S. (2011) Zhongguo Qiye Chuangxin he Chanye Shengji Mianlin de Xin Tiaozhan: Mokuaihua Quanqiu Jiazhilian [Chinese Firms' Innovation and Industrial Upgrading Are Facing New Challenges From Modularity Global Value Chains]. *China Business and Market*, 8, 52–56.

Qing, H. (2009) Guoji Cheqi Zhuanwei Zhongguo Shichang Gaitou Huanmian [Global Automobile Firms Made Changes Especially for Chinese Market]. *China Market*, 47, 70.

Rabellotti, R. (1999) Recovery of a Mexican Cluster: Devaluation Bonanza or Collective Efficiency? *World Development*, 27(9), 1571–1585.

Rabellotti, R. et al. (2009) Italian Industrial Districts on the Move: Where Are They Going? *European Planning Studies*, 17(1), 19–41.

Ramazzotti, P. (2010) Industrial Districts, Social Cohesion and Economic Decline in Italy. *Cambridge Journal of Economics*, 34(6), 955–974.

Rawski, T. G. (1989) *Economic Growth in Prewar China*. Berkeley: University of California Press.

Ren, X. (2008) Yuanshengshi Neishengxing Chanye Jiqun de Xingcheng Jiqi Yanbian [The Formation and Evolution of Original Industrial Clusters]. *Social Science Research*, 5, 52–58.

The Research Group of China's Global Value Chains (2014) *Quanqiu Jiazhilian yu Zhongguo Maoyi Zengjiazhi Hesuan* [*Global Value Chains and China's Trade Value Added Accounting Report*] [online]. Available from: http://images.mofcom.gov.cn/www/201412/20141226182657100.pdf (Accessed 31 May 2017).

Rhodium Group (2017) *China Investment Monitor* [online]. Available from: http://rhg.com/interactive/china-investment-monitor (Accessed 11 March 2017).

Rinaldi, A. (2007) The Emilian Model Revisited: Twenty Years After. *Business History*, 47(2), 244–266.

Sa, S. (2016) *Sa Sha Tan Jiefangjun de Laoyou: Buneng Bushuo de Jiefang Xie* [*Sa Sha Talk About the Old Friend of Liberation Army: Must Mention Xiefang Shoes*] [online]. Available from: http://news.qq.com/a/20160419/047025.htm (Accessed 31 May 2017).

Schmitz, H. (1999) Global Competition and Local Cooperation: Success and Failure in the Sinos Valley, Brazil. *World Development*, 27(9), 1627–1650.

Schmitz, H. (2004) *Local Enterprises in the Global Economy: Issues of Governance and Upgrading*. Cheltenham: Edward Elgar.

Schmitz, H. (2006a) Learning and Earning in Global Garment and Footwear Chains. *The European Journal of Development Research*, 18(4), 546–571.

Schmitz, H. (2006b) *Reducing Complexity in the Industrial Policy Debate*. Brighton: Institute of Development Studies.

Schneider Electric (2015–2017a) *Financial and Sustainable Development Annual Report*. Rueil-Malmaison: Schneider Electric.

Schneider Electric (2017b) *Schneider Electric* [online]. Available from: www.schneider-electric.com/ww/en/ (Accessed 30 May 2017).

Schneider-Levy, B. (2015) *Adidas Group Sells Rockport to Berkshire Partners and New Balance Holding* [online]. Available from: http://footwearnews.com/2015/business/athletic-outdoor/adidas-sells-rockport-new-balance-berkshire-9170/ (Accessed 29 May 2017).

Shang, C. (2006) Guoji Nengyuan Jutou Zhengduo Zhongguo Shichang [Global Energy Giants Fought for Chinese Market]. *Guancha yu Sikao*, 2, 48–49.

Shanghai Liangxin Electrical Limited Company (2012) *Shanghai Liangxin Electrical Limited Company Prospectus*. Shanghai: Shanghai Liangxin Electrical Limited Company.

Shao, X. (2006) Wenzhou Jingji yu Wenzhouren Jingji [Wenzhou Economy and Wenzhou People's Economy]. *Zhejiang Economy*, 4, 56–57.

Sheng, S. (2004) Cong Chanye Jiqun Shijiao Kan Wenzhou Moshi [View the Wenzhou Model From the Perspective of Industrial Clusters]. *Zhejiang Social Sciences*, 3(2), 1–5.

Sheng, S. and Zheng, Y. (2004) *"Zhejiang Xianxiang": Chanye Jiqun yu Quyu Jingji Fazhan ["The Zhejiang Phenomonon": Industrial Clusters and Regional Economic Development]*. Beijing: Tsinghua University Press.

Shi, S. (2013) *Zhuanjia Zonglun Wenzhou Duiwai Zhitou [Experts Discuss Wenzhou's Outward Direct Investment]* [online]. Available from: http://news.66wz.com/system/2013/03/08/103561221.shtml (Accessed 14 March 2017).

Siemens AG (2017a) *Annual Report 2016*. Munich: Siemens AG.

Siemens AG (2017b) *Siemens* [online]. Available from: www.siemens.com/global/en/home.html (Accessed 30 May 2017).

Sina News (2016) *2016 Zhongguo Zhizaoye Qiye 500 Qiang Fabu, Menkan Xiajiang 3.95% [The List of 2016 China's Top 500 Manufacturing Firms Was Released and the Entrance Level Reduced by 3.95%]* [online]. Available from: http://finance.sina.com.cn/meeting/2016-08-27/doc-ifxvixeq0574453.shtml (Accessed 17 May 2017).

Sirkin, H. et al. (2014) *The Shifting Economics of Global Manufacturing: How Cost Competitiveness Is Changing Worldwide*. Boston: Boston Consulting Group.

The State Council (2013) *Guowuyuan Guanyu Huajie Channeng Yanzhong Guosheng Maodun de Zhidao Yijian [The State Council's Guide on Solving the Problem of Excessive Over Production]* [online]. Available from: www.gov.cn/zwgk/2013-10/15/content_2507143.htm (Accessed 17 March 2017).

The State Council (2015) *Made in China 2025* [online]. Available from: www.gov.cn/zhengce/content/2015-05/19/content_9784.htm (Accessed 17 May 2017).

State Grid Hubei Electric Power Company (2013) *2020 Nian Zhineng Dianbiao Shichang Rongliang Chao Qianyi [The Market Capacity of Intelligent Electrical Meters Will Reach 100 Billion in 2020]* [online]. Available from: www.hb.sgcc.com.cn/html/main/col12/201301/18/20130118111840366862286_1.html (Accessed 30 May 2017).

Statista (2017) *Athletic Footwear Market Share Worldwide by Company in 2015* [online]. Available from: www.statista.com/statistics/246501/athletic-apparel-companies-ranked-by-global-market-share-in-footwear-sales/ (Accessed 29 May 2017).

Statistics Bureau of Anhui Province (2014) *Anhui Statistical Yearbook*. Beijing: China Statistics Press.

Statistics Bureau of Fujian Province (2014, 2015) *Fujian Statistical Yearbook*. Beijing: China Statistics Press.

Statistics Bureau of Guangdong Province (2006–2016) *Guangdong Statistical Yearbook*. Beijing: China Statistics Press.

Statistics Bureau of Jiangsu Province (2016) *Jiangsu Statistical Yearbook*. Beijing: China Statistics Press.

Statistics Bureau of Jiangxi Province (2014, 2016) *Jiangxi Statistical Yearbook*. Beijing: China Statistics Press.

Statistics Bureau of Shanghai Municipality (2016) *Shanghai Statistical Yearbook*. Beijing: China Statistics Press.

Statistics Bureau of Sichuan Province (2004–2015) *Sichuan Statistical Yearbook*. Beijing: China Statistics Press.

Statistics Bureau of Wenzhou Municipality (1990a) *Wenzhou Shi 1990 Nian Disanci Quanguo Renkou Pucha Zhuyao Shuju Gongbao* [*Main Data Communiqué of Wenzhou's the Fourth National Census in 1990*] [online]. Available from: http://wztjj.wenzhou.gov.cn/art/2004/5/20/art_1243861_5868346.html (Accessed 17 March 2017).

Statistics Bureau of Wenzhou Municipality (1990b–2016) *Wenzhou Statistical Yearbook*. Beijing: China Statistics Press.

Statistics Bureau of Zhejiang Province (2014–2016) *Zhejiang Statistical Yearbook*. Beijing: China Statistics Press.

Sun, Q. (2015) 2014 Nian Diya Dianqi Hangye Jingji Yunxing Tongji Fenxi Baogao [2014 Statistical Report of Low Voltage Electrical Equipment]. *Dianqi Gongye*, 8, 14–21.

Sutherland, D. (2001) Policies to Build National Champions: China's Naiontal Team of Enterprise Groups. In Peter Nolan (ed.), *China and the Global Business Revolution*. Basingstoke: Palgrave, pp. 67–140.

Tang, X. (2015) *2015 Shijie 500 Qiang Qiye Mingdan 88 Jia Guoqi 6 Jia Minying Qiye Shangbang* [*2015 Global Top 500 Firms, 88 SOEs and 6 Private Firms Were Listed*] [online]. Available from: www.qianzhan.com/indynews/detail/242/15072627e4847e.html (Accessed 25 May 2017).

Technology Bureau of Wenzhou Municiplity (2013) *Zhixieye Lianbang Zhusu Gongyi Zhuanli Jishu Fenxi Baogao* [*Patent Report of Footwear Direct Injected Production Technology*]. Wenzhou: Technology Bureau of Wenzhou Municiplity.

Teng, Y. (2013) Wenzhougang Maoyi de Lishi Bianqian [The Historical Changes of Trade in Wenzhou Port]. *Journal of Wenzhou Vocational & Technical College*, 13(4), 22–28.

Tsai, K. S. (2002) *Back-alley Banking: Private Entrepreneurs in China*. Ithaca: Cornell University Press.

UN (United Nations) Comtrade (2017) *UN Comtrade Database* [online]. Available from: https://comtrade.un.org/ (Accessed 31 May 2017).

UNCTAD (United Nations Conference on Trade and Development) (2002) *Trade and Development Report*. Geneva: UNCTAD.

UNCTAD (2005, 2011, 2016) *World Investment Report*. Geneva: UNCTAD.

UNESCO (United Nations Educational Scientific and Cultural Organization) (2017) *UNESCO* [online]. Available from: http://en.unesco.org/ (Accessed 30 May 2017).

UNIDO (United Nations Industrial Development Organization) (2016) *MVA Manufacturing Value Added Database*. Vienna [online]. Available from: http://stat.unido.org/ (Accessed 7 March 2017).

Vista (2016) Lingdaoren Chufang Shenmeyang de Qiyejia Neng Peiban Zaice [When Leaders Visited Foreign Countries, What Kind of Entrepreneurs Can Accompany Them?]. *Lingdao Wencui*, 1, 78–81.

Wade, R. (1990) *Governing the Market: Economic Theory and the Role of Government in East Asian Industrialization*. Princeton: Princeton University Press.

Wagner, D. B. (1997) *The Traditional Chinese Iron Industry and Its Modern Fate*. Surrey: Curzon.

Wan, R. (2011) Guoji Qiaokeli Pinpai Zhengzhan Zhongguo Shichang [Globbal Chocolate Brands Fought for Chinese Market]. *China Brand & Anti-Counterfeiting*, 7, 36–39.

Wang, J. (2001) *Chuangxin de Kongjian: Qiye Jiqun yu Quyu Fazhan* [*Innovative Spaces: Enterprise Clusters and Regional Development*]. Beijing: Peking University Press.

Wang, J. and Mei, L. (2009) Trajectories and Prospects of Industrial Districts in China. In Giacomo Becattini et al. (eds.), *A Handbook of Industrial Districts*. Cheltenham: Edward Elgar, pp. 598–612.

Wang, P. and Zhang, Y. (2008) Minqi Guojihua: Wenzhou 'Zouchuqu' de Qishi [The Globalisation of Private Firms: Wenzhou's Experience of Going Out]. *International Business Daily*, 18 December.

Wang, X. (2012) Economic Prosperity and the Shift of the Economic Center of Gravity to the South. In Xingpei Yuan et al. (eds.), *The History of Chinese Civilization Volume III Sui and Tang to Mid-Ming Dynasties (518–1525)*. Cambridge: Cambridge University Press, pp. 143–212.

Wang, Y. and Ye, Z. (2002) *14 Nian Zouguo Bainian Lu, Zongwei Bieren Zuo Jiayi, Zoujin Wenzhou Dahuoji* [*Wenzhou's Ligher Industry Used 14 Years to Beat the Result That Others Used a Hundred Years to Achieve, But It Did Not Benefit Much*] [online]. Available from: http://news.xinhuanet.com/fortune/2002-06/05/content_425393.htm (Accessed 18 March 2017).

Wang, Z. (2010) *Zhongguo 500 Qiang Qiye Fazhan Baogao 2010* [*The Development Report on Top 500 Enterprises of China 2010*]. Beijing: Enterprise Management Publishing House.

Wenzhou Government's Official Web Portal (2011) *Renhang Wenzhoushi Zhongxin Zhihang Fabu Wenzhou Minjian Jiedai Shichang Baogao* [*The Wenzhou Branch of Bank of China Released a Report About Wenzhou Private Borrowing and Lending Market*] [online]. Available from: www.wenzhou.gov.cn/art/2011/8/12/art_3906_175835.html (Accessed 30 May 2017).

Wenzhou Municipal Government (2014a) *Wenzhoushi Dianqi Chanye Tisheng Fazhan Guihua (2014–2020)* [*The Development Plan to Enhance Wenzhou's Electrical Equipment Industry (2014–2020)*]. Wenzhou: Wenzhou Municipal Government.

Wenzhou Municipal Government (2014b) *Wenzhoushi Xieye Chanye Tisheng Fazhan Guihua (2014–2020)* [*The Development Plan to Enhance Wenzhou's Footwear Industry (2014–2020)*]. Wenzhou: Wenzhou Municipal Government.

Whitford, J. (2001) The Decline of a Model? Challenge and Response in the Italian Industrial Districts. *Economy and Society*, 30(1), 38–65.

Whittaker, D. H. et al. (2010) Compressed Development. *Studies in Comparative International Development*, 45(4), 439–467.

The World Bank (1993) *The East Asian Miracle: Economic Growth and Public Policy*, Volume 1. Oxford: Oxford University Press.

The World Bank (2001) *China Overcoming Rural Poverty*. Washington, DC: The World Bank.

The World Bank (2017) *World Bank Open Data* [online]. Available from: http://data.worldbank.org/ (Accessed 30 May 2017).

The World Bank & Development Research Centre of the State Council, the People's Republic of China (2013) *China 2030: Building a Modern, Harmonious, and Creative Society*. Washington, DC: The World Bank.

WPP (2016) *Most Valuable Gloabl Brands 2015*. London: WPP.

Wu, Q. (2006) *The Rise of the Wenzhou Model and Its Influence on China's Development Strategy*. Cambridge: University of Cambridge.

Wu, X. (2013) *2013 Shijie Wenzhouren Dahui Zhaokai* [*2013 World Wenzhou People's Conferences Opened*] [online]. Available from: http://news.66wz.com/system/2013/02/16/103537912.shtml (Accessed 14 March 2017).

Xiao, J. (2009) Zhongguo Dianqi zhi Du Liushi de Lishi Tiaozhan zhi Lu [The Historical Challenges for Liushi China's Capital of Electrical Equipment]. *Dianqi Shidai*, 4, 46–56.

Xinmin Evening News (2007) *Cong Zhongguo Zhizao Zouxiang Zhongguo Chuangzao, Zhongguo Xie Bulv Zhashi* [*From Made in China to Created in China, Chinese Shoes Made Solid Progress*] [online]. Available from: http://shoes.chinaleather.org/Pages/News/20071003/120668.shtml (Accessed 30 May 2017).

Xu, D. and Wu, C. (eds.) (2000) *Chinese Capitalism, 1522–1840*. Basingstoke: Macmillan.

Xu, S. (1957) *Song Huiyao Jigao VI* [*Song Dynasty Manuscript Compendium VI*]. Beijing: Zhonghua Book Company.

Yang, W. (2009) You Qiye Waiqian Yinqi de dui "Wenzhou Moshi" de Fansi [Introspection on the "Wenzhou Model" Based on Firms' Outward Migration]. *Northern Economy*, 5, 81–83.

Yin, C. and Xiao, J. (2008) Diya Dianqi 30 Nian Jixing [Recording for the 30-year Development of Low Voltage Electrical Equipment]. *Dianqi Shidai*, 8, 50–56.

Yin, R. K. (2009) *Case Study Research: Design and Methods*. London: SAGE.

Yu, Y. (2015) *2015 Zhongguo Qiye 500 Qiang Bangdan Xianshi Zhuanxing Jian Chengxiao, Tisheng You Kongjian* [*2015 China's Top 500 Firm List Showed That Transformation Gain Achievement and There Was Space for Improvement*] [online]. Available from: www.gov.cn/zhengce/2015-08/23/content_2917905.htm (Accessed 17 March 2017).

Yue Yuen Industrial (Holdings) Limited (2016) *Annual Report 2015*. Hong Kong: Yue Yuen Industrial (Holdings) Limited.

Zeng, D. Z. (2010) *Building Engines for Growth and Competitiveness in China: Experience With Special Economic Zones and Industrial Clusters*. Washington, DC: The World Bank.

Zeng, M. and Williamson, P. J. (2007) *Dragons at Your Door: How Chinese Cost Innovation Is Disrupting Global Competition*. Boston: Harvard Busienss School Press.

Zhang, R. and Li, H. (1990) *Wenzhou Moshi Yanjiu* [*Research on the Wenzhou Model*]. Beijing: China Social Science Press.

Zhang, Y. and Sun, S. (2005) *Zhongguo Qiye Fazhan Baogao 2005* [*A Report on the Development of Chinese Enterprises 2005*]. Beijing: Enterprise Management Publishing House.

Zhao, H. and Peng, Y. (2011) Houweiji Shidai Quanqiu Jiazhilian Shijiao Xia Woguo Zhongxiao Qiye Chanye Jiqun Shengji Yanjiu [Upgrading SMEs Clusters in GVCs After the Financial Crisis]. *Enterprise Strategy*, 12, 28–30.

Zhao, Ji. (2016) *Zhongguo Lianxu 21 Nian Chengwei Quanqiu Zaoyu Fanqingxiao Zuiduo Guojia* [*China Had Been the Country Encountered the Most Anti-dumping Investigations in the World for Successive 21 Years*] [online]. Available from: http://finance.qq.com/a/20160726/006991.htm (Accessed 14 March 2017).

Zhao, W. (2007) Minying Qiye Guojihua Jige Jichu er Xianshi de Lunti [Some Basic and Real Issues of the Globalisation of Privately-run Firms]. *Study and Practice*, 3, 43–50.

Zhejiang Aokang Shoes Limited Company (2012a) *Zhejiang Aokang Shoes Limited Company Prospectus*. Wenzhou: Zhejiang Aokang Shoes Limited Company.

Zhejiang Aokang Shoes Limited Company (2012b–2016) *Annual Report*. Wenzhou: Zhejiang Aokang Shoes Limited Company.

Zhejiang Aokang Shoes Limited Company (2017) *Aokang International* [online]. Available from: www.aokang.com/ (Accessed 30 March 2017).

Zhejiang Chint Electrics Limited Company (2015–2016) *Annual Report*. Wenzhou: Zhejiang Chint Electrics Limited Company.

Zhejiang Yueqing Record Office (2001) *The Capital of China's Low Voltage Electrical Equipment*. Wenzhou: Zhejiang Yueqing Record Office Press.

Zhong, J. (2013) *Lingdaoren Waijiao Zhenrong Minqi Chengfen Zengduo* [*More Private Entrepreneurs in Leaders' Diplomatic Group*] [online]. Available from: www.51fenghuang.com/news/shehui/1947.html (Accessed 14 March 2017).

Zhong, S. (2003) Guoji Jichuang Jutou Qiangtan Zhongguo Shichang [Global Machine Tool Giants Fought for Chinese Market]. *Machinery & Electrical New Products Guide*, 6, 32–34.

Zhou, H. (ed.) (1990) *Wenzhougang Shi* [*The History of Wenzhou Port*]. Beijing: China Communications Press.

Zhou, M. (2005) *Ye Shi yu Yongjia Xuepai* [*Ye Shi and the Yongjia School*]. Hangzhou: Zhejiang Ancient Books Publishing House.

Zhuo, Y. and Zhang, M. (2008) Quanqiu Jiazhilian Zhong de Shouyi Fenpei yu Beican Zengzhang – Jiyu Zhongguo Fangzhi Fuzhuangye de Fenxi [On Distribution of Gains in GVCs and Immiserizing Growth – An Analysis Based on China's Apparel Industry]. *China Industrial Economy*, 7, 131–140.

Index

Note: Page numbers in italic indicate a figure and page numbers in bold indicate a table on the corresponding page.

www.ingramcontent.com/pod-product-compliance
Ingram Content Group UK Ltd.
Pitfield, Milton Keynes, MK11 3LW, UK
UKHW011015180926
475701UK00004B/755

* 9 7 8 0 3 6 7 4 3 8 5 5 5 *